DRIVE HIM WILD

A Hands-on Guide to Pleasuring Your Man in Bed

by

Graham Masterton

A SIGNET BOOK

SIGNET
Published by New American Library, a division of
Penguin Putnam Inc., 375 Hudson Street,
New York, New York 10014, U.S.A.
Penguin Books Ltd, 27 Wrights Lane,
London W8 5TZ, England
Penguin Books Australia Ltd, Ringwood,
Victoria, Australia
Penguin Books Canada Ltd, 10 Alcorn Avenue,
Toronto, Ontario, Canada M4V 3B2
Penguin Books (N.Z.) Ltd, 182–190 Wairau Road,
Auckland 10, New Zealand

Penguin Books Ltd, Registered Offices:
Harmondsworth, Middlesex, England

First published by Signet, an imprint of New American Library,
a division of Penguin Putnam Inc.

First Printing, September 1991
20 19 18 17 16 15 14 13 12

Contents

1

Can You Still Go Wild in Bed?

These days—in spite of the fact that we live in a sexually outspoken society—we are more confused and anxious about sex than ever before.

Our greatest worry, of course, is the fear of contracting AIDS. And this fear has affected almost everybody's sexual behavior in one way or another—from sexually awakening teenagers to solid married couples of many years' standing.

Clear and sensible information about AIDS is widely available—from magazines, from educational leaflets, from TV documentaries—right the way back to the historic thirty-six-page report on AIDS produced in 1986 by the surgeon general, Dr. C. Everett Koop.

But AIDS is still surrounded by superstition, myth, moral prejudice, and misunderstanding. Can you catch it from kissing, from door handles, from toilet seats? Can you catch it by sharing the same coffee spoon?

The specter of AIDS has had the tragic effect of making us afraid of sex and afraid of sexual pleasure. And, most of all, afraid of *wild* sexual pleasure.

Understandably, many religious and moral leaders have interpreted AIDS as a punishment for the wanton sexual behavior of the swinging sixties and the swapping seventies. They see it as God's way of obliging us to return to abstinence, monogamy, and "normal" lovemaking.

They oppose the education of young people about safe sex, and in particular the distribution and advertising of condoms, because they regard them as a license to practice promiscuity, unnatural sexual acts, and homosexuality. Dr. Koop was labeled "Dr. Condom" and derided by conservatives as an advocate of "safe sodomy."

A book on sexual excitement isn't the place for a discussion of the religious or moral implications of AIDS. But these days, people of all ages and all backgrounds have a greater interest in sex and sexual satisfaction. And they have a right to know just how much erotic pleasure they can *safely* enjoy.

- Adolescents have greater freedom and privacy than ever before, and access to much more sexual education and sexual stimulation—such as magazines and videos.
- Women understand that they have as much right to erotic pleasure as men—and erotic satisfaction, too. Twenty-five years ago, women used to write and ask me what an orgasm actually was. These days, more and more women ask me "how can I make my orgasms even more intense?" (And, yes, I'll tell you, a little later on.)
- Men have learned much more about sex from magazines and movies, and realize that they have a responsibility to be skillful lovers and to satisfy the women in their lives. (And, yes, I have plenty of new and arousing ideas about *that*.)

Curiosity about sex is going through a tremendous resurgence. Sexually active men and women want to know what they can safely do to satisfy their natural erotic urges. The intensity of their curiosity is clearly indicated by the number of new sex manuals on the market and the release of scores of educational and not-so-educational videos.

I have personally received more letters during the past eighteen months than at any time in my quarter century of sex counseling, and (in different ways) all of those letters have asked me the same question: you've always advocated total sexual excitement. But is it still possible to have a really wild time in bed?

Here's Tracey, a thirty-three-year-old accountant from Denver, Colorado: Dear Graham . . . I first read about oral sex in your book *How to Drive Your Man Wild in*

Bed. I was very shy in those days, and although I knew about oral sex, I was not at all confident about how to do it. However after reading your book I learned to suck my husband's cock and became really good at it. Not only that, I enjoyed it, too . . . so much that I used to do it to him two or three times a week, every week. Because of other reasons (not sex) my husband and I have now broken up, and I'm dying to put my mouth around another man's cock. The problem is, I'm really worried about AIDS. I used to love swallowing my husband's come, but what if I swallow a man's come and he's HIV-positive? Is that a risk, and if so, what precautions can I take, or do I have to stop swallowing altogether?

Here's John, a twenty-six-year-old architect from Tucson, Arizona: Dear Mr. Masterton . . . sorry to be so formal . . . I've formed a relationship with the woman who lives next door. I've been living with my parents ever since my last serious relationship broke up. . . . The woman next door is married and eleven years older than me, but she's very sexy with a full figure and a wonderful sense of humor. Her husband is away for weeks at a time on business and we've been making love pretty much every day while he's been away. Of course I've been using a condom, but I've been scared to give her oral sex in case of AIDS. She keeps trying to coax me into going down on her . . . and I'd love to . . . but what are the risks?

Here's Angela, a twenty-nine-year-old auto rental clerk from Cincinnati, Ohio: Dear Graham Masterton . . . your book *More Ways to Drive Your Man Wild in Bed* really opened my eyes to exciting lovemaking. I tried out several of your techniques on my boyfriend, and he went crazy for them. The trouble is, I've fallen for another man who works for the same airline as me. I think he's fantastically attractive, but he has a reputation for being a "ladies man," and I'm concerned in case sleeping with him might expose me to the risk of AIDS. How do I make sure that he's HIV-negative without upsetting him and killing the whole relationship stone dead before it even starts?

"I discovered a vibrator"

Here's Karen, a twenty-seven-year-old interior designer from Boston, Massachusetts: Dear Graham . . . I'm very frightened and I don't know where to turn for help, because my problem is a very personal and embarrassing one, too. About a month ago a girlfriend of mine allowed me to use her vacation home for a long weekend break. While I was looking for an alarm clock I discovered a vibrator in her nightstand, a really huge one in the shape of a man's penis. During the night, I took it out and masturbated with it, rubbing it around my vaginal lips and also inserting it right into my vagina. When I next met my girlfriend she told me that she had been diagnosed HIV-positive. Now of course I'm terrified that I've contracted AIDS from her vibrator, but I daren't tell anybody because I'm too ashamed to admit what I did.

Here's Jake, a thirty-two-year-old computer operator from Houston, Texas: Dear Graham Masterton . . . I'm kind of footloose when it comes to girls, and I probably date three or four different girls a year, and sleep with them whenever I get the chance. I always use a rubber because you never know what you might pick up . . . even if it isn't AIDS it could be clap or some other kind of venereal disease. Lately I've been dating a terrific girl called Sue who says she loves me madly and wants us to make love without a rubber. She says she's on the pill so there's no chance of her getting pregnant, but I'm worried. My friends say she's slept around quite a bit. I don't want to lose her because she's something else . . . one of the sexiest girls I've ever known. Do you think I should risk it, and make love to her without a rubber, or what?

Here's Mary-Jane, a twenty-one-year-old waitress from Seattle, Washington: Dear Graham . . . my fiancé Paul introduced me to anal lovemaking and I have to say that for the first few times I found it very exciting and wanted to do it all the time. I just adore sitting on his lap with his big stiff cock right up my ass as far as it will go. But yesterday evening my friend told me that you get AIDS from anal lovemaking. I'm real frightened that I might have caught it already because Paul and I have had anal intercourse so many times. What can I do? I'm afraid to go to my doctor because he's a member of our church congregation and I know that he would think that Paul and me had been real wicked.

Here's Bill, a forty-one-year-old sales executive from Portland, Oregon: Dear Mr. Masterton . . . during last year's company sales conference I was foolish enough to pick up a girl in the hotel bar and invite her back to my room for sex. I didn't think of using a condom, although I wish to God that I had. Now I find myself suffering from constant colds and headaches and dizziness, and I dread seeking medical advice in case I discover that my worst fears are true. I'm also terrified that I might have passed my sickness on to my wife.

It's the same story in letter after letter. Anxiety, fear, and superstition. I've been asked if it's possible to contract AIDS from sharing the same sandwich, from using the same telephone as an AIDS sufferer, from kissing, from washing with the same soap, from breathing the same air.

As far as sexual fulfillment is concerned, the tragedy of AIDS is a double tragedy. It is a potentially fatal disease which is transmitted by the exchange of bodily fluids—saliva, semen, vaginal lubricants, and especially blood. Because of this, we have been stricken with an unholy terror of casual sexual contacts, and for young people all over the world the idea of making love with a new partner without wearing a condom has become unthinkable. As for spontaneous oral sex—well, forget it.

And as for spontaneous anal sex—forget it *totally*.

The risk of contracting AIDS from normal sexual penetration, provided neither partner has any ulcers or abrasions in the genital area, is probably not much more than one in a hundred. But the risk of contracting AIDS from oral sex may be as much as ten times greater, and the risk of contracting it from anal sex may be twenty times greater. I have to say "may" because accurate and comprehensive statistics on the risks of catching AIDS are not yet available, and probably never will be. This is because a high proportion of victims simply do not know where and how they might have contracted AIDS—and because an even greater proportion are reluctant to admit to homosexual or bisexual practices, or the use of intravenous drugs.

But the fear of AIDS doesn't have to affect your sexual satisfaction or your sexual pleasure. You *can* live in the age of AIDS and enjoy an enormous number of thrilling and erotic activities without any fear at all. Just so long as you're sane and sensible, and just so long as you never allow your sexual urges to override your self-control.

Many of the pleasures in this book *do* involve the use of condoms . . . but only where they can enhance your sexual pleasure—or, at the very least, not interfere with it. You have to accept the use of condoms as part and parcel of today's sexual pleasure, and the best way to treat them is as a sexual stimulant, rather than a clinical necessity.

To quote one inventive example sent to me by a young wife from London, England: "My husband and I are both shaving devotees. I hadn't shaved for almost a month, so I was good and hairy down there. After Bill shaved my pubes off and went through to the bathroom to fetch the sponge, I did something really wicked. I took a pinch of bristles and popped them into his condom, which was on the bedside table ready for action. He rinsed my pussy, patted it dry with a towel and then peeled the rubber on to his dick. Only when he was up me did I tell him what I had done, and do you know what? The sensation of my bristles tickling his knob drove him crazy. He made love to me in so many positions I lost count, and even though he came pretty quickly, he kept his cock up me and it didn't soften in the slightest."

Or, from a twenty-one-year-old legal assistant from St. Louis, Missouri: "Condoms are a fact of life when you're having sex with a man these days. There's no point in being squeamish about them. I like taking my boyfriends' condoms off after we've been making love, and letting all the come pour out of them while it's still warm. Sometimes I let it drip onto my nipples, and then I rub it all over my breasts. Other times I take a handful and smear it between the guy's legs, all over his balls, and everywhere. It's amazing how quickly that makes them go hard again."

Fruit-Flavored Condoms

Or, from a nineteen-year-old student from San Francisco, California: "I *love* condoms . . . you can get them in so many different colors and shapes and stuff. You can even get them in fruit flavors. I like condoms with ribs and bumps; they're always a turn-on. But the real fun is putting them on. Most guys are used to putting their own condoms on, but when a girl does it for them, that always blows their mind, especially if she does it really well, and massages their cocks while she's doing it, which I always do. I believe in safe sex, for sure . . . but I don't see why safe sex has to stop you from having a good time."

Some lovers have taken safe sex to limits which I consider to be closer to self-defeating. Some women, for instance, wear "safe sex" panties, which have a latex crotch, and wouldn't consider intercourse or oral sex without them. Some men won't think of licking a woman's vulva without the protection of a dental dam.

But you and your partner can have a wild time in bed and still be safe. This book has been specifically researched and written to tell you how. There are dozens and dozens of highly exciting things that you can do to give yourself and your partner the kind of sexual satisfaction that most people only dream about.

Yes—you will need to be much more sexually creative. Yes—you will have to think about your lovemaking in ways in which you have never thought about it before. You will have to be prepared to be bold, startling, and sexually adventurous. But then that's you all over, isn't it?

Drive Him Wild: A Hands-on Guide to Pleasuring Your Man in Bed is a guide for those lovers who don't want to be tyrannized by the need for safe sexual practices, but who want to use them positively in order to enhance their sex lives. It's a guide for lovers who want to look *forward,* not back—lovers who realize that sexual responsibility can actually spice up their relationships and challenge their erotic imaginations.

There are several ways in which you can substantially lower the risk of contracting AIDS.

In a clinically ideal world, of course, every potential lover would have regular AIDS antibody tests and carry a notarized letter around with them stating they were HIV-negative. Sexual encounters wouldn't start with a kiss, but with a mutual exchange of health documents.

But this isn't a clinically ideal world, and I don't think that very many of us want it to be. There has to come a time when we trust each other—otherwise life would have no excitement, no romance, and sex would become about as arousing as flossing your gums.

It's only fair to yourself and your own lovers if you take all the reasonable precautions you can to avoid contracting or transmitting AIDS. For instance, if you have the slightest doubt that you may have exposed yourself sexually to an HIV carrier, you should immediately seek a blood test and medical advice. And until you're sure that you *haven't* contracted the AIDS virus, you should avoid all sexual contact.

But there should be little or no risk if you observe the simplest of sexual rules.

• Use discretion when choosing your sexual partners. A partner who is obviously bisexual or who shows clear signs of intravenous drug abuse is obviously going to be a higher risk than a partner who isn't. Likewise, take care when considering sex with hookers, rent-boys, or anyone whom you suspect to be promiscuous. In spite of all the publicity about AIDS, many hookers still have a very casual attitude toward safe sex. Recently, I took some investigative walks along Lexington Avenue in New York, Hollywood Boulevard in Los Angeles, and the King's Cross area of London, England. I discovered that without any difficulty at all, it is still possible to bargain for very high-risk sexual activities—regular sex without a condom, oral sex with sperm swallowing guaranteed, anal sex without a condom, and "golden rain"—urination with copious drinking of urine by either or both participants.

None of these sexual acts, when carried out by two perfectly healthy people, is at all dangerous (yes, even urine is sterile, and scores of lovers have written to me about their "water sports"). But if you have any suspicions about your partner's sexual fidelity . . . acts like that have to be a total unconditional no-no.

- Except with a partner you *know* to be HIV-negative (such as your husband or wife or long-term lover) heed the words of Dr. Ruth and always use a condom. It's much less intimate, whatever the manufacturers try to tell you about "extra thin" or "sheer" or "naturally penis-shaped." Even with years of practice, it can be messy and it can also be very frustrating. After all, the natural drive behind all acts of sexual intercourse is the eventual ejaculation into the female vagina of the male semen, with the object of making more of us. But in this case we have to put up with a little frustration in order to protect our very lives.
- Avoid oral sex and in particular the swallowing of sperm or sexual juices.
- Avoid anal sex without a condom. In spite of its intense pleasures, anal sex is one of the riskiest activities as far as the risk of contracting AIDS is concerned. This is because the tightness of the rectum and the sensitivity of its lining make it very susceptible to minor tears during intercourse—directly opening your bloodstream to the risk of infection by HIV-carrying semen.

A New York doctor told me that one of his women patients—once she had discovered that anal intercourse carried such a high AIDS risk—had started to insist that her lovers always use a condom during sex, but that she had often allowed them to lubricate the condom with their own saliva—not as risky as taking a naked penis up her bottom—but riskier than using a sterile proprietary lubricant such as KY or nonoxynol-9. Incidentally, those

who dislike the latex odor of condoms or who regularly
enjoy anal intercourse can buy lubricants that are fra-
granced with cinnamon or fruit.

- Never use a hypodermic syringe that has previously
  been used by somebody else. Reduce the risk of infection when you travel abroad by carrying your own
  "AIDS kit" of surgical needles, scalpels, and scis-
  sors. You can buy them extremely cheaply at most
  drugstores.
- Since AIDS is a blood disease, take sensible precautions to avoid situations in which you could be open
  to infection. Make sure your dental surgeon always
  wears new latex gloves. Make sure that any doctor
  who examines you intimately is wearing new latex
  gloves. Never let a stranger suck blood from a cut
  finger: it sounds petty, but I've seen it happen more
  than once, and it does carry a small risk.

Remember, though: taking sensible precautions means
taking *sensible* precautions. You can't catch AIDS from
doorknobs, holding hands, eating food prepared by an
AIDS sufferer, or even from sitting on a warm toilet
seat.

Remember—even today—sex is still exciting. Sex is
still arousing. Sex can still be really wild. And with the
help of dozens of real lovers, I've prepared this book to
show you how.

AIDS has obliged lovers to be even more inventive
than ever—not only to find sexual satisfaction without
exposing themselves to the risk of infection—but to find
greater sexual excitement with the same (or with far
fewer) partners.

Here's Lydia, a twenty-six-year-old beautician from
Oakland, California: "I have to admit that I had dozens
and dozens of boyfriends and that I slept with most of
them. I can't tell you how many men I've slept with but
it's probably forty or fifty. It used to turn me on, sleeping
with a new man. It gave me a feeling of excitement that
I'd managed to arouse him . . . and also, men are all
completely different, mentally and physically, and they
all make love in different ways. Some men are hairy,

some men hardly have any hair at all. Some men are muscular, some of them are really slender. And you'd be amazed how different their cocks are. You get short, fat ones, you get long, skinny ones. You get circumcized cocks and uncircumcized cocks. You get some huge ones that you can hardly get into your mouth without choking. You get some really small ones that go in and out of you like a rabbit jumping in and out of a rabbit hole.

"I worked harder at sex"

"I was experienced, in the sense that I'd slept with a whole lot of men. But in actual fact I wasn't very creative in bed. I didn't have to be. I got my kicks out of making love with somebody new. The fact that he was different and that he made love in a different way, that was enough to turn me on. It's incredible how differently different men make love.

"But of course when AIDS started to be a real threat, I had to sit down and do some serious thinking about my sex life; and I had to say to myself, 'Lydia, you're going to have to change. One day you're going to take a guy home to bed and that guy is going to be HIV-positive and he's going to kill you. No two ways about it.'

"So instead of sleeping around so much, I began to work harder at the relationships that I already had. I was dating a photographer called Peter when I first made up my mind to cool things off. I liked Peter a lot, and I knew that he liked me, but I hadn't been treating him too good. You know, I hadn't been returning his phone calls, stuff like that. But that weekend I called him and asked him if he wanted to spend the weekend.

"That was the beginning of my first really long-term relationship. Some friends of my parents have a house on the Silverado Trail in Napa Valley, and Peter and I stayed there from Thursday night through Monday morning. It was great. For the first time in my life I began to relax, and not to think, 'Who am I going to date *next* week?' And for the first time in my life I began to think about making love to the same guy night after night, week after week, month after month.

"I read some magazine articles on sex and a couple of books, too, and I was amazed how much I didn't know about sex. I didn't know anything about my own physical responses. I didn't know anything about *men's* physical responses . . . apart from the fact that their cocks get hard and then they climax.

"One of the most interesting things I learned was the 'squeeze technique,' when you squeeze your lover's cock to stop him from climaxing too soon. Peter had always had kind of a hair trigger when it came to climaxing— which was one of the reasons I'd been thinking of ditching him and finding somebody new. But I used the squeeze technique, right, and really worked on it, and in the end he could make love to me for twenty minutes without climaxing, sometimes longer.

"That was when I truly realized that having a long-term sexual relationship with one man can actually be wilder and more exciting than having dozens of different partners. Peter and I stayed together for nearly two years before we split up. We're still friends, and I see him from time to time. Now I'm living with Ralph; he's an engineer. He's very handsome, very physical. And, believe me, my experience with Peter really makes me appreciate him all the more. I can tell you for nothing, there isn't *anything* we haven't tried. And it just gets better all the time.

"Sometimes Ralph has to work Saturdays, and we've developed this kind of a game. He calls me up from time to time during the day, and I talk really dirty to him, telling him all the sexy things I'm doing, and all the sexy things I'm going to do to him when he gets home. Like, I'm wearing nothing but panties, and I'm massaging my breasts and rubbing my nipples, and I can't think about anything but working my hand into the front of his pants and feeling that big warm hard cock in his shorts.

"Then I'm sliding my hand into my own panties, and running the tip of my finger up and down my pussy, until it starts to get all wet and slippery, and I feel like dipping my middle finger into my hole.

"Then I hang up and I won't answer the phone for at least an hour, which really builds up the tension. When he does ring back, I'll tell him that I'm naked now, and that I'm lying back on the couch with my legs slightly open, and that I'm gently playing with my clitoris, touching it and teasing it, and that I'm dipping my finger into my pussy from time to time, to make it all juicy, and then I'm massaging my nipples with pussy juice, until they're really stiff.

"Sometimes I rub the phone up against my pussy so that he can hear it squishing. The first time I did that, he actually climaxed in his shorts. But just when he's getting real excited, I hang up again, and let him wait some more. Then I call him up, and tell him that I'm down on all fours on the rug, and that I'm slowly sliding this huge cucumber up into my pussy. I mean, I'm actually doing it, and I hold the phone real close so that he can hear it sliding in and out.

"I keep calling him all day, so that by the time he comes home he's really hot. About two weeks ago, when he came home, I laid out all the cutlery and linen on the dining table, and then I climbed up onto the table wearing nothing but a black garter belt, black stockings, and high-heeled shoes. When I heard him come in through the door, I called out 'Dinner's ready!' and he came through to the dining room and saw me. Let me tell you, he was all ready to jump on the table right on top of me. But I told him to sit down properly. This was dinner. Then I spread my legs wide and slid myself right up to him, so that he could eat my pussy.

"He loved it. I pulled open my pussy and he licked me right inside, and I had feelings like you wouldn't believe. This wasn't like any of those one night stands . . . he knows just where to touch me, just where to lick me. Then, while he was licking me, he took hold of his dinner knife and pushed the round stainless-steel handle up my bottom, so that when I looked down between my legs, all I could see was my pussy, all licked and wet, and this metal knife blade sticking out of my bottom.

"He kept on licking me, and he stirred the knife around, and it didn't take more than three or four times and I climaxed, and the knife blade scratched the table.

The other day, when my mother came to visit, she said, 'That's a nasty scratch on that table,' but all *I* could say was, 'I think it's a great scratch.'

"I don't worry about AIDS anymore, because I've put myself in a position where my sexual relationships are stable and safe. Ralph feels the same way about sleeping around: in fact, most guys are really, really careful these days . . . so he's not about to go off and sleep with some HIV-positive girl and bring AIDS back to me.

"I really miss the days of complete sexual freedom. But there's no point in trying to pretend that AIDS doesn't exist, or that we can all go back to one night stands and orgies and swinging—we can't. All we can do is enjoy what we've got—and, boy, we've got quite a lot, when you think about it.

"Staying in a long-term relationship, my whole attitude toward sex has changed completely . . . not because I've been converted to the idea of traditional one-to-one sex, or marriage or anything . . . but because a long-term relationship gives you the chance to explore your partner's sexuality in real depth . . . and it's amazing what you can find out about people, if you live with them long enough. For instance, I didn't realize to begin with that Ralph was so heavily into oral sex . . . but he just loves to eat my pussy . . . it's his favorite thing, and don't think for a moment that *I'm* complaining. But he was pretty reserved about doing it at first . . . and it took a whole lot of lovemaking before he felt relaxed enough to do it the way he really wanted to do it . . . kissing and sucking my pussy lips and getting his tongue right up there, and smothering my pussy juice all over his face. He loves it, and I love it, too—but if it had been a one night stand, I never would have found out about it.

"It's incredible that couples can live together for *years* and still keep so much of their sexual personalities hidden from each other. I could have been like that. I could have lived my whole life and never known what it was like to be totally satisfied. You know something? I scarcely ever had orgasms, when I was having sex with a different man every week. I was *excited*, for sure . . . but very rarely satisfied. Now, I'm almost *always* satisfied.

"I'm not so selfish, sexually speaking. I'm very much

happier. I'm not risking my life. And I'm having a wild time.

"I recommend it."

I've quoted my talk with Lydia at some length because it epitomizes so many of the interviews and letters and conversations that I've had with both men and women over the past two years. Most of them have come to terms with the threat of AIDS, but more than that, most of them have discovered that there is far more sexual excitement to be had in their existing relationships than they ever considered possible.

Chapter 2

Same Lover—
Thrilling New Love

There was a time when many men and women thought
that the instant solution to a dull, run-of-the-mill sex life
was to find a new lover. Either that, or try a few dangerous games, like swinging, or swapping, or one night
stands.

But these days, we're all worried about the possible
risks of having sex with people we don't know too well.
And that means that it makes much more sense to pep
up your existing sexual relationship than to go out looking for casual excitement with strangers.

Personally, I've always been the number one advocate
of improving the sexual relationship you already have,
rather than immediately giving up on it and looking for
somebody new. To work at improving your existing relationship takes thought, compromises, and great sexual
maturity. It takes imagination. It takes bravado. It takes
real sexiness, not just the kind of selfish instant gratifica-
tion that so many couples, sadly, think of as sex.

Emotionally, far too many couples are doing very little
more than masturbating with each other. They're always
holding themselves back, when they should be opening
up. They never tell each other what they really want.
They never really get to *share* each other, body and soul.

And it's not only the shy, reticent lovers who fail to
communicate. Sometimes the most athletic of couples
need just as much advice as those who always turn out
the light and wouldn't dream of trying anything wilder
than man-on-top-woman-underneath.

Here's Tina, nineteen, a student from Houston, Texas:
"Greg and I do everything in bed. We fuck this way, we
fuck that way. He rubs his cock on my breasts. He goes

down on me. He fucks my ass. Once he even fucked my ass with a champagne bottle. He shook it up, and when he took it out, champagne came fizzing out of my ass. But do you know something, it's *boring*. It's so mechanical. He never kisses me. He never holds me in his arms and tells me he adores me. I love the sex, it turns me on. But it would turn me on so much more if he was romantic, too."

Here's an excerpt from conversations with a fifty-five-year-old restaurant owner from Boston, Massachusetts: "My wife and I had stopped making love six or seven years ago, I don't know why. Maybe we just got out of the habit. We still loved each other, we were quite confident about that. I still found Maria attractive. But both of us had come from straitlaced families, and I guess our lovemaking was what you might call conventional. Nothing 'kinky,' nothing out of the ordinary.

"We'd had three beautiful children who were beginning to grow into young adults, and—I don't know—somehow we seemed to have lost the sexual urge.

"Then, about three months ago, a new couple moved in next door to us, Doreen and Ted. They were both about the same age as we were, maybe a little older. But I couldn't help noticing how much they *sparkled*—and how close to each other they always seemed to be. My wife remarked on it, too.

"Not long after Doreen and Tom moved in, Maria invited Doreen around for coffee, and although I wasn't there at the time, Maria told me all about it afterward. Apparently, Maria mentioned Doreen's brightness and pretty looks, and Doreen said, 'Well, it's a happy marriage that does it,' and Maria asked her what she thought the secret of a happy marriage was. Doreen said, 'Why, sex, of course.'

"Maria was a little shocked, but then as I said she was brought up pretty straitlaced, like me. But Doreen went on to tell her that she and Ted made love three or four or more times a week, that they watched sexy videos together, and that she did everything she could to turn him on. She invited Maria back to her house and showed her what she meant. She had a whole closet full of sexy underwear, like G-strings and peephole bras.

"Maria said she was kind of frightened by all of this sexy stuff at first. It made her feel threatened. But Doreen told her that it was all for fun and all for love. I guess it was about then that Maria told her that we never made love, or hardly ever. She told me that Doreen was genuinely shocked, and for the first time in her life she felt guilty about sex. About *not* having sex, is what I mean.

"About a week later, Doreen and Ted invited us both around for supper. We had a good meal, linguine, and a good light wine, and the atmosphere was pretty convivial. We all got along together real well. And by that I mean *real* well. At about eleven o'clock, when Maria and I were ready to leave, Doreen said that she had to show us the latest outfit that Ted had bought her . . . she'd give us a fashion show. Ted poured us some more wine while Doreen got herself ready, and kept saying, 'You wait until you see this. You'll go weak at the knees.'

"Anyway, the living room door opened, and in she came. And, believe me, I did go weak at the knees. She was wearing nothing at all except this black leather bikini and black patent stiletto shoes. And you could hardly call it a bikini. It was nothing more than two circular straps around her bare breasts, linked together by a chain, and a studded leather G-string with a completely open crotch, except for a chain which went from front to back, right between the lips of her sex.

"Doreen's fifty-two or fifty-three years old, but she's still a natural ash blonde, and she has an incredible figure. Her breasts are very big but very firm for her age, and she has a trim waist, slightly rounded stomach, but on her that looks natural and attractive. When she came in that night she walked in full of confidence and pride in her body. Her nipples were sticking up like I've never seen a woman's nipples stick up. Her eyes were alight. I had the biggest hard-on I'd ever had in my life, when Doreen walked in. I almost shot my load there and then, right in my shorts.

"Maria glanced at me and I could tell what she was asking me, even though she didn't speak. She was asking me, 'Do you think we ought to leave?' But I wanted to stay. I was very turned on, and I wanted to see what would happen next. Besides, I had the feeling that Doreen and Ted were doing this on purpose, to show us what it was that made their marriage so hot.

"Doreen laughed and did a twirl and a kind of a dance for us. She said, 'What do you think?' and we said, 'Pretty damned sexy,' both of us in unison. I felt real hot and I was short of breath. I understood what Maria had told me about feeling threatened, but I had the feeling that this particular sexual situation was going to turn out okay. Doreen and Ted weren't leaning on us. They weren't trying to involve us in any swinging or wife-swapping or whatever. They were simply showing off; that was all.

"Anyway, Doreen went up to Ted, who was sitting cross-legged by the fire, and she did this really erotic dance for him, grinding her hips around and massaging her breasts and cupping the cheeks of her bottom in her hands. Then she knelt down and unbuttoned his shirt, kissing him and pressing her breasts up against him. She stripped off his shirt and then she unbuckled his pants and pushed him back onto the cushions so that she could drag his pants right off him. He was wearing these really tight blue shorts, and you could easily see the outline of his hard cock. Maria reached over and squeezed my hand, and that was the first time I realized that *she* was really turned on, too.

"Doreen climbed over Ted and kissed him and swung her breasts from side to side so that her nipples brushed against his chest. Then she pressed her breasts against his face and pushed her nipples into his mouth so that he could suck them and lick them. He caught one of her nipples gently between his teeth so that when she tried to sit up, it really stretched out.

"Both Maria and I sat on our cushions holding hands and watching all this like we were hypnotized. It was very sexy to watch, but there was still no feeling that Doreen and Ted were trying to pressure us in any way, and I was real glad of that.

"Doreen crawled further down on the cushion and took hold of Ted's cock through his shorts. She stroked it and rubbed it and then she gradually eased his shorts off. His cock stood up swollen and incredibly hard, with

all the veins showing. His balls were tight like coconuts.
He was completely shaved, he had no pubic hair at all,
and his cock looked like some kind of marble column.
The tip was already glistening and wet, and Doreen stuck
out her tongue and licked all the juice from out of his
hole. Then she took the whole head of his cock into her
mouth and sucked it, slow and rhythmic, taking it further
and further into her mouth with every stroke.

"She licked all the way down the side of his cock, and
then she lay with her head resting on his thigh and gently
took his balls into her mouth and ran her tongue all
around them. I heard Maria make a kind of sighing
noise, and she edged up closer to me, and the next thing
I knew her hand was in my lap, cautiously stroking my
hard-on through my pants.

"They built up sexual tension"

"What really impressed me about the way in which
Doreen and Ted made love was that they took their time
. . . they relished every moment. If they enjoyed something they didn't rush over it. The built up the sexual
tension little by little, and let me tell you there was some
sexual tension in that room that night.

"Doreen spread Ted's thighs with her hands and then
lifted the cheeks of his ass so that his asshole was completely exposed. She continued to kiss and lick his cock,
but at the same time she dipped her finger between her
own legs, to lubricate it, and then she gradually pushed
her finger into his anus, right up to the hilt. She twisted it
around and around, and Ted was gasping with pleasure,
literally gasping.

"Then Ted took hold of Doreen and lifted her up and
turned her over. He kissed her lips, he kissed her breasts,
he kissed all the way down her stomach. He slid his
tongue into the open front of her leather G-string and
flickered the chain against her sex. Then he reached
around her and unbuckled the G-string and took it off.

"Doreen was completely shaved, too. Her sex looked
like some kind of a plump, ripe fruit. Ted took the whole

of her bare sex into his mouth, and I could see his tongue sliding into her vagina and her juice dripping down his chin. Then he started very gently to chew at her sex-lips, pulling them wide open with his fingers, so that we could see right up inside her vagina. He licked and sucked deep between her legs, and then he spread her bottom and pushed the index and middle finger of *both* hands into her anus, four fingers in all, then stretching her anus open.

"Both Maria and I were dumbfounded by now. We couldn't really believe what we were watching. And to think that I had hardly ever touched Maria *down there* with my fingers, and never during intercourse, as if love-making was some kind of tightrope-walking act that you could only do with your cock. I guess our backgrounds were partly to blame: the way I was brought up, sex was for having children, and if you touched your partner with your fingers or your tongue . . . well, that was nothing to do with having children, that was for amusement purposes only, and that wasn't allowed. As for anal stimulation, I had heard about it, but it had never occurred to me that a guy's wife might actually enjoy having four fingers pushed up her ass . . . or that a guy might enjoy it himself. Pushing fingers up your ass, that was what gays did. Normal guys wouldn't enjoy that.

"Ted lay next to Doreen and lifted her leg, and then he opened up her sex and we watched him slide his cock right up inside her. Doreen looked across at us and smiled and said, 'Come on, come and join in, come and feel what it's like.' Of course I hesitated for a moment, but the sight of Ted's hard red cock sliding in and out of Doreen's sex, while at the same time she was just lying back smiling at me, I have to admit that sight turned me on too much for me to be able to say no.

"I went over and knelt beside Doreen, and Doreen took hold of my hands and pressed them against her breasts. I rolled and tugged at her nipples, and the feeling of her soft flesh was irresistible. At the same time, Maria came over and started running her hands down Ted's back and around his shoulders.

"Doreen took hold of Maria's hand and guided it down between Ted's legs so that Maria could fondle Ted's

balls. Then she took hold of *my* hand and guided it down
to her clitoris. She held her sex apart with her own fingers so that I could gently flick at her clitoris while Ted
thrust in and out of her. It was incredible to fondle another woman's sex while another man made love to her.
I could actually feel where Ted's cock was sliding into
her, and I could feel Maria's hand around him, gently
squeezing his balls and stroking the base of his cock.

"Doreen suddenly climaxed, silently shaking. Then
Ted climaxed, too. There was a couple of seconds' pause,
and then sperm came welling out of Doreen and all over
Maria's fingers. She continued to massage his balls, and
massage his cock; while I slid a couple of fingers up Doreen's vagina and then another finger up her ass.

"When it was all over, Ted said, 'There . . . you can
see what you're missing?' and Doreen said, 'We're not
asking you to have regular sex sessions with us. If you
like, we can just be good neighbors and leave it at that.
But you're a good-looking couple, you're still young, you
should make the most of your marriage.'

"Doreen and Ted put on wraps, and we finished off
the wine. Then Maria and I went home. We didn't have
to speak to each other. There was nothing to say. I undressed Maria in the bedroom and we couldn't stop kissing each other. I took off her bra and fondled her
breasts, and you don't know how sexy her breasts felt. I
tugged and squeezed her nipples the same way I'd tugged
and squeezed Doreen's nipples, and she closed her eyes
and let out a sigh like you wouldn't believe, as if she'd
been waiting for this for years.

"I tugged down the zipper of her skirt and it dropped
to the floor. Underneath, she was wearing panties and
pantyhose, and they were both soaked through. I slid my
hand inside her pantyhose. Her sex was so juicy you
would have thought that she had wet herself. She opened
my pants and took out my cock, and before I knew it
she was kneeling down and she had her mouth around
it, which was something that she had never ever done,
not in thirty years of marriage.

"She was cautious, she was shy, but that was under-
standable. But to look down and see my Maria with my
cock in her mouth, that was the most beautiful thing I'd

seen in years, and it felt like it, too, and I was in heaven, you can believe me.

"I was so fired up, I could have had intercourse with her there and then. But I thought of the way in which Doreen and Ted had been doing it, and I kissed her and told her I loved her and that whatever had happened at Doreen and Ted's, she was the most exciting woman ever. She said, 'Well, if Doreen can do it, then so can I. And Doreen's so bright and young-looking!'

"She suddenly climaxed"

"We lay on the bed and we made love that night like we'd never made love in all of those years of courtship and marriage and rearing children. We loved each other, we admired each other, and for the first time ever we actually showed ourselves off to each other, the way that Doreen and Ted had shown themselves off to us. That night, I had seen right up inside Doreen's vagina—how was Maria going to refuse to show me hers? That evening, Ted had sucked Doreen's sex and given her the kind of climax that rates way, way up on the Richter scale. How could I refuse to do the same?

"That night, Maria lay back on the bed and opened her legs wide and I held my cock in my fist and massaged it all around her sex. We made love like there was no tomorrow—kissing, sucking, licking, just enjoying each other's bodies. Maria climaxed first. I'd been fondling her clitoris and she suddenly came, just like that, no warning. I started to thrust into her harder and harder, and I could feel the sperm rising up inside me. But she said, 'No!' and she took my cock out of her, and slid down on that satin comforter, right between my legs. She kissed and rubbed and sucked at my cock, until I couldn't hold it back any longer. I closed my eyes for a second, and when I opened them again I was pumping thick white sperm all over Maria's face—her mouth, her cheeks, her nose, her eyelashes, her hair, I couldn't stop pumping out sperm—and she was massaging it over her face like it was some kind of high-priced face cream, and licking her lips, and sucking the last drops out of my cock. Even when my cock was soft she held it in her mouth and wouldn't let me go.

"She waited until it was real soft, kissing it and licking it, and then she opened her mouth wide and took my whole cock and most of my balls into her mouth, too, as if she wanted to eat me up. Afterwards we couldn't stop touching and kissing and fondling each other, and I felt like I was reborn, I can tell you.

"These days, we make love all the time, four or five times a week, sometimes more. Maria's lost a whole lot of weight and looks really sparkling and happy, the way that Doreen does, and I feel fit as a goddamned fiddle. Ten years younger.

"We don't have any inhibitions anymore. We try everything . . . although Maria isn't too keen on my shaving my cock, the way that Ted does. She prefers the beast to be hairy. We've discovered our own sexual preferences, our own way of driving ourselves wild in bed, to quote the title of your book. Maria loves oral sex, loves sucking my cock, sometimes I wake up in the night and she's lying down the bed a ways with my cock in her mouth. Just licking, just sucking, just gently nibbling. And of course that usually leads to us making it, whatever time of the night it happens to be.

"I like to get one or two fingers up her asshole when we're making love, and two or three times we've had full anal sex, with my cock right up her ass, but I enjoy that more than she does, and she has to feel very relaxed and in the mood, although she likes it when I climax up her ass, she likes the feeling of that, the way the sperm leaks out of her ass all night.

"It's oral sex that Maria goes for, and she still loves me climaxing in her face, she loves it, or right in her mouth, even when I'd rather climax inside her. Or in her hair, she loves that, too. Do you know how relaxed and loving we are about sex these days? We were watching a video of *Field of Dreams* about two weeks ago and Maria had her head resting in my lap. She reached around and opened my zipper and slowly masturbated me while we were watching the movie. I mean, she never would have touched me before. And when I came, she wrapped my cock in her hair so that I was pumping sperm all over her hair and it was running down her cheek.

"You could say that almost every night between us is like a porno movie, except that it isn't a porno movie, it's two middle-aged people who love each other and don't care what they do to show it. If I could give one word of sexual advice to anybody my age—or maybe *any* age—I'd say, trust your partner, show your partner everything, tell your partner everything, both of you, and if you want to lick each other or suck each other or come in each other's hair, then do it. There's no harm; there's only happiness.

"That night with Ted and Doreen was never repeated. We never got sexually involved with them again, although they became very close friends. Maria and Doreen go to aerobic classes together and Ted and I have been fishing quite a few times. I only talked to Ted once about what happened. I said that it was exciting, and that it had changed our sex life. But I did admit that I was shocked, initially. Ted said that Maria and I had shocked him. He couldn't understand how a couple like us could have no real sex life, to speak of. He said that he could always tell when a couple weren't having sex too often: the men looked prematurely old and the women always looked dull and jaded and never did their hair.

"Ted said that sex was the elixir of youth and I have to agree with him. Not only that, he gave me the name of the mail-order company that sells those leather bras and G-strings with the chain in the middle of the pussy, and I'm looking forward to that. And that's an understatement.

"I'm proud of myself and I'm proud of Maria. She's proved that a woman in her fifties can let go of her sexual inhibitions and be a dirty-minded, passionate, and exciting lover. I wouldn't trade her for all the *Playboy* center-folds ever. Maria tells me that some middle-aged women are frightened to let themselves go, sexually, because they're afraid that their husbands won't respect them. They don't realize that their husbands have been having secret fantasies for years about having their cocks sucked or about going down on their wives or maybe seeing their wives in some sexy underwear. Let me tell you, I respect Maria much more these days than I ever did before. I worship the ground she walks on."

It's notable that Ted and Doreen, while they encouraged their neighbors to join them in an extremely intimate and provocative sexual act, at no time did anything that would have exposed any of them to the risk of AIDS. Presumably, neither Ted nor Doreen was HIV-positive, so their act of intercourse together was quite safe, and their contact with John and Maria was exclusively manual—even though Maria massaged Ted's genitals with his own semen. It would have been inadvisable for Maria to do this, however, if she had any open cuts on her hands and she should have washed her hands immediately after.

While the risk of AIDS is very much lower in the heterosexual community than it is among bisexuals, homosexuals, and users of intravenous narcotics, it is still better to be safe than very sorry. (And I would like to add that I am not being judgmental about bisexuals, homosexuals, and users of intravenous narcotics. The simple fact is that, in purely epidemiological terms, their lifestyle renders them more vulnerable to the AIDS virus than heterosexuals are.)

Sexual education is very much more open and comprehensive than it used to be. A young girl can pick up a magazine these days and read about masturbation, orgasms, oral sex, lovemaking during menstruation, how to cope with sexual harassment at work, and you name it. But there is still a critical gap in most women's sexual understanding—and that gap is simply that they cannot believe that the men in their lives have such stark and pornographic sexual fantasies.

As part of my reply, I sent out three questionnaires to all of those couples who had written to me with sexual difficulties. One questionnaire was to be filled out by both partners together. The other two were to be filled out separately and in confidence, and sent back to me *without the other partner seeing it*. Most of the questions dealt with sexual preferences, sexual desires, and sexual fantasies, especially those fantasies which lovers had always kept secret from their partner.

It was remarkable how few men would admit to the real nature of their sexual fantasies in front of their partners . . . and how few women realized what the men in their lives would really like to do in bed (not to mention *out* of bed, and in the shower, and in the car, and even— in one case—on a flat roof, in the pouring rain.)

- In the *secret* questionnaire for men, 71 percent of respondents said that they would like more oral stimulation from their partners.
- In the *joint* questionnaire, only 19 percent of men said they would like more oral stimulation from their partners, while 5 percent of women said that they thought their partners desired more oral stimulation.
- In the *secret* questionnaire, 9 percent of women said that they thought their partners desired more oral stimulation—while 3 percent said they would be prepared actually to give their partners what they wanted.

And so it went on—characterizing an enormous gap between what men want, what women *think* they want, and what women are prepared to do for them if they *do* know what they want.

This book is based on the results of these questionnaires, as well as the personal experiences of scores of real-life lovers. It shows you how you—as a woman—can learn what really turns your partner on, and how you can use that newly learned knowledge and *dramatically* improve your sex life.

Many "how-to" books make promises they can't keep. They promise to make you slim; they promise to turn you into an indoor-plant expert; they promise to tell your future; they promise to make you rich.

But the promise that I am making now is a cast-iron promise. I promise you that—if you follow the sexual suggestions in this book—you will turn your sex life around, almost overnight, and your relationships with it. If you're young, you'll develop new skills and discover new pleasures. If you're not-so-young, you'll be able to revive a sex life that may have been running out of steam. Even if you're living alone right now, and you don't have a sexual partner, I'll show you how you can stimulate yourself more excitingly, so that when you *do* meet the man or woman of your bedtime dreams, you'll be a much better lover.

I'm not afraid to make a promise like this because my counseling has been proven time and time again with *real* people who want *real* sexual excitement. All that I will ask of you is that—while you read this book—you will understand that it recounts the sexual pleasures of lovers who are just the same as you and me, ordinary people with ordinary bodies and ordinary looks, and that their desires and needs are perfectly natural and normal.

In other words, I'm asking you not to be shocked and not to turn up your nose and say "You'd never catch *me* doing anything like that!" It's precisely that kind of attitude that leads to so many sexual relationships ending up in boredom, frustration, and failure.

Sex is one of the greatest pleasures that you will ever enjoy. It is an expression of your whole personality and your love for the man in your life. It can bring you physical satisfaction, mental fulfillment, and enormous joy. It's no accident that one of the best-selling sex books of all time is called *The Joy of Sex*. It's also no accident that another of the best-selling sex books of all time is called *How to Drive Your Man Wild in Bed*.

My questionnaires showed that 84 percent of men would like their women to wear erotic underwear—while only 27 percent were prepared openly to admit it. They showed that 68 percent of men would like to make love with their women on top—while only 12 percent were prepared openly to admit it.

They showed that 73 percent of men would like to give their women cunnilingus—oral sex—while only 18 percent were prepared openly to admit it.

Sixty-four percent wanted the women in their lives to trim or shave off all of their pubic hair. Only 9 percent would openly admit it.

And so it goes on—wider and wider. The huge gap between what men secretly want and what they're brave enough to *admit* that they want. The huge gap between what women perceive as men's desires, and what men's desires really are.

This book will tell you a hundred different ways in which you can bridge those gaps. A hundred different ways in which you can show your man that you understand him, that you know what he wants, and that you're more than happy to give it to him.

A hundred different ways in which you can show your lover that you're a lover in a million.

None of these techniques is mandatory. Everybody has different sexual tastes, and that includes you. Many sexually inexperienced women balk at oral sex, for example—particularly taking their lover's penis right into their mouth. But you are not *obliged* to kiss or suck your lover's penis; and for his part he should show you both understanding and consideration.

A large proportion of the girls and women who have written to me about oral sex have been put off it by lovers or boyfriends who have been aggressive or clumsy in their demands for fellatio (which is the fancy Latin name for a woman stimulating a man's penis with her mouth). Their stories have all been very similar. Either a lover has said nothing, but has positioned himself in such a way that he has made it blatantly obvious that he expects oral sex (i.e., with his erect penis almost touching her mouth). Or he has physically taken hold of her head and forced her down onto his erection. Or he has demanded oral sex by emotional blackmail. ("You can't love me if you won't suck my cock.")

Oral sex is an integral part of skilled sexual technique, and if they have been introduced to it with care and affection, most women discover that they enjoy it almost as much as intercourse.

"I used to hate it," said Sandy, a twenty-two-year-old fashion designer from St. Louis, Missouri. "Mainly because my first lover always seemed to expect it, and also because I wasn't at all sexually experienced and I simply didn't know what to do. I didn't mind kissing his cock and I didn't mind taking it into my mouth. In fact, I loved the feeling of that big hard cockhead filling my mouth up, and licking the little hole in it. But I didn't know whether I was supposed to suck or blow or chew or what. My lover used to get very frustrated and we'd

always end up arguing, which used to spoil everything
. . . and put me off oral sex for a long, long time.

"It was only when I met my current boyfriend Mike
that I learned how to give good head. I was kissing his
cock one evening and he said that he really liked it. I
took it in my mouth and he actually *told* me what he
wanted. He said, 'If you lick it around and around, and
if you gently suck at it, and if you rub it up and down
with your hand while you're sucking it . . .' You know,
kind of explaining what to do as I went along.

"Also, he gave me the chance to take his cock out of
my mouth before he climaxed. He said, 'I'm coming, but
you don't have to swallow it.' But I didn't want to take
him out. I had a sudden urge to find out what it felt like,
to have a man climax inside your mouth. He suddenly
squirted all this salty warm stuff all over my tongue. I
could actually feel it jetting out of the hole in his cock.
That really turned me on, so much that I almost climaxed
myself. I swallowed some of it. The rest of it just dripped
down my chin. I can't say I like it as much as cookie
crunch ice-cream, but it was the actual sperm of the man
I'm in love with, and it was me who teased it out of him,
and that's why I enjoyed it.

"Some nights I feel like swallowing"

"Afterwards, he went down on me and licked my cunt
and my clitoris and it was only a few moments before I
climaxed, too. That was partly what made it all so exciting and satisfying, you know? I'd satisfied him and—in
return—he'd wanted to satisfy me. I didn't feel so much
like a concubine, the same way I had with my first
lover."

Countless women complain to me that they enjoy oral
sex but that they don't always like to swallow their lover's
ejaculate. As one thirty-three-year-old homemaker from
Fort Worth, Texas, told me: "Some nights I feel like it,
some nights I don't. But John insists on it all the time.
He has this habit of clutching my head close to his crotch
when he's coming, so that I can't take his cock out of

my mouth. It turns him on to think he's shooting his sperm directly down my throat, without even giving me the chance to decide whether I'm going to swallow it or not. It used to turn me on, too, I'll admit it. But I have choices, too, and I'm tired of being half-choked and I find any excuse not to go down on him anymore."

It seems to me that your enjoyment of oral sex depends not only on your readiness to do it (and your confidence that you can do it well) but on the skill and sensitivity of your lover. Taking your lover's penis into your mouth is one of the most explicit demonstrations of your love and trust and desire to please him; and in return he should be considerate, responsive, and highly alert to your needs and desires.

In lovemaking, it is practically impossible to draw up hard-and-fast rules about the degree of tenderness or aggression that either partner should be showing. A woman may complain about the forceful way in which her lover is thrusting his penis into her, but at the very same time she may find his forcefulness exciting. On some nights, she may genuinely not want to give him oral sex, but on other nights she may be aroused if her lover overcomes her objections and *insists* that she suck his penis. A man may not feel like making love, but his lover may kiss him and stimulate him and *demand* that he satisfy her. Or she may thrust a finger into his anus while he is making love to her, causing him pain, but at the same time giving him an extra *frisson* of sexual excitement, too.

Sexual excitement is all about aggression and surrender; domination and submission; stimulation and soothing. It is one of the most complex of all the acts that we perform while we live on this planet, and it involves more of our psychological and physical faculties than anything else we do.

For a lover to be sexually brilliant, however, she doesn't need to understand all of the complexities of sex. In previous books I have explained in detail all of the internal workings of the human body as it becomes sexually stimulated and moves toward climax. This detailed information is useful because it enables lovers to understand what is happening to themselves and their partners at any given moment during lovemaking. It helps to reas-

sure women who are worried—for instance—because
their vaginas become so wet and lubricated when they
kiss their lovers. It helps to reassure men—for instance—
who are concerned about the size of their penis, and
whether they're producing enough sperm with each
ejaculation.

You can find all of this kind of information in *How to
Drive Your Man Wild in Bed* and *How to Make Love
Six Nights a Week* and other titles. In this book, however,
I have directed my attention to giving you all the knowl-
edge and skills that you will need to drive your lover (or
lovers) to the absolute peaks of erotic pleasure.

And, of course, how to do it safely.

Some women have asked me if there isn't something
a little demeaning about learning to turn on their men.
"After all, I'm his lover, not his whore."

Certainly, some of the sexual skills which you will acquire may seem like the skills of a hooker or a geisha.
But I have chosen or modified all of them to turn *you*
on, too. Whatever excitement and satisfaction you can
give *him,* you're entitled to expect just as much excitement and satisfaction in return.

The more skillful you become at pleasing *him,* the
more your own sexual pleasure will increase. For instance, in an adaptation of the Thai body-body massage,
you can caress him all over with your vulva—an experience which will not only blow his mind, but which will
give *you* a high degree of stimulation, too—stimulation
which *you* can control to suit your own sexual sensitivity.

And you will find that your partner's responsiveness in
itself will turn you on.

This is Joy, a twenty-three-year-old dental assistant,
whose thirty-one-year-old lover Peter had lost his job in
the print business, and who had been suffering from
stress and anxiety for more than three months. The most
frustrating effect on his stress had been to render him
temporarily incapable of sustaining an erection.

"We hadn't made love properly in almost eight weeks.
I know that Peter wanted to make love, but every time
he had an erection it died away as soon as he tried to
put it in me. He could have cried with frustration. In fact
he *did* cry a couple of times. But of course the more

often he failed to keep his erection, the worse he felt about it, and the more difficult it was for him to keep his erection the next time. His doctor wasn't very helpful. He gave Peter some beta-blockers to relieve the stress, and they helped some. But they didn't give him his sexual confidence back. It got so bad that for a while I believed it was *me* that was causing all the problems—that he didn't really love me anymore. Then I read in one of your books about restoring a man's virility. I thought why not give it a try, I don't have anything to lose.

"When Peter came home that night, I had his favorite Cajun chicken casserole waiting for him, and a bottle of good red wine, and I acted real calm and laid-back. He asked me what was going on, and I told him that I'd been just as tense as him and I was determined to relax and get my head back together. We had dinner and talked about what we'd been doing during the day. Peter had been for more interviews, but it still didn't look like he'd found a job yet.

"After dinner I ran a bath for him and undressed him. I kissed him and I fondled his cock and he began to get half a hard-on, but all I did was rub it up and down a little and fondle his balls and then tell him to get into the bath.

"Once he was in the tub, I went through to the bedroom and undressed, except for my white stockings and my white garter belt and my little white cotton panties. Then I came back into the bathroom and climbed into the tub with him. I told him I'd come to scrub his back, and his front, too. I straddled him, and kissed him, and he was really turned on. But I remembered what you said in your book, take it slow, take it easy, and not to let Peter feel like I was expecting anything. After all, from what you wrote, I knew that I may not *get* anything, not at first, and I wasn't supposed to let Peter feel that I was disappointed.

"He loved me being in the tub with my stockings and panties on. As soon as my panties were soaked, you could see right through them, all my dark pubic hair, so they didn't hide very much.

"I sat behind Peter and soaped my breasts all over.

Then I rubbed them against his back. It was quite a turn-on for me, too. My nipples were sticking up through the foam, and I began to feel distinctly sexy.

"Next I reached around him and soaped his chest, and then I reached between his legs and massaged his cock and soaped his balls and his ass. He began to grow stiff again, but I could feel that he was still very tense, and that he was trying too hard to get an erection. His whole body was tight, like he was *willing* himself to get stiff.

"I climbed out of the bath and gave him a towel, then I took off my stockings and my panties and dried myself, too. We kissed for a very long time, just standing in the bathroom. What you said about live-in lovers forgetting to kiss each other is totally true. They make love, but they forget to have those real steamy necking sessions that always used to turn them on so much when they were first dating.

"We kissed like that: like new lovers. All tongues and teeth. I could feel Peter growing harder underneath his towel, but I knew that I shouldn't rush anything.

"We went through to the bedroom. I spread a big dry towel on the bed and told Peter to lie facedown on it. He asked me what I had in mind and I told him that this was a new relaxing technique. The only condition was: he wasn't allowed to touch me until I said so.

"He grinned and said okay and lay back on the bed.

"I climbed naked onto the bed and sat astride the small of his back. I pressed my pussy against him and rotated my hips. I said, 'Can you feel how *wet* you've made me?' Then I reached for the bottle of massage oil and poured some into my hand.

"It wasn't a strong-perfumed oil. Not sandalwood, or anything like that. It just had a light, woody kind of fragrance. I circled and smoothed it into his shoulders, and of course that relaxes *anybody*. Peter sighed and I could feel his muscles easing and all that knotted-up tension beginning to loosen.

"I smeared massage oil onto the insides of my thighs and especially between my legs. That meant I could massage his shoulders with my hands and massage his sides and his back by gripping him and squeezing him between my slippery legs—and all the time I rotated my hips around and around so that I was pressing my pussy up against him.

"After I could feel that he was much more relaxed, I rolled him over onto his back. I sat astride his stomach and massaged his shoulders and his chest. I kissed him quite a few times, too. Then I turned around and massaged his thighs, gradually working closer to his cock.

"He was fully hard by now, but I only gave him a few glancing touches with my hands. At last I made him lift his knees a little, so that he was lying with his legs well apart, and I massaged deep in the cleft of his bottom, and all around his balls, and at last started to massage his cock, gripping it quite tight and rubbing it up and down, with my thumb pressing just below the head of it, the way you wrote about it.

"At the same time I gradually lifted my bottom so that he would be able to look directly into my pussy. I reached around behind me and parted my pussy lips with my fingers so that he would be able to see right up inside me, but I kept on rubbing his cock up and down, faster and faster.

"He touched my leg, but I said, 'No . . . the rules are, you mustn't touch.'

"He said, 'I want to fuck you. I'm dying to fuck you.' But I said, 'No . . . there's plenty of time for that.'

"I rubbed him quicker and quicker, and I could see his balls tightening, and his thigh muscles tensing up. The head of his cock was dark crimson and slippery with massage oil. I rubbed harder and harder and I was totally enjoying myself, too. Sometimes it's a turn-on, being in charge.

"I spread my pussy-lips wider and wider, and pushed three fingers deep inside myself. I was just wondering how much this would turn Peter on when he shouted out, and a huge fountain of white sperm came shooting out of his cock, then another, then another. I'd never seen so much of it, and so thick. It dribbled down my hand and slid down my wrist.

"I turned around and kissed Peter and held him close.

I felt very turned-on, and more than a little frustrated, but I knew that this was all for the best.

"We had two more massage sessions. Halfway through the second session, Peter got up and turned me onto my back and slid his cock up inside me. It was the best thing I'd felt for weeks. He made love slowly and beautifully, and his cock didn't soften at all. He hasn't had any more problems since then. The beauty of it is, he knows that if he *does* lose confidence in himself, we can always go back to the massage sessions, no problem."

This massage session was based in part on the highly successful "pleasuring" technique which was prescribed by Drs. Masters and Johnson back in the 1970s for the treatment of male impotence. One of the most distinctive added ingredients is the woman's open display of her sex during the massage. It is done in such a way that the man can look as closely and as intently at his partner's vagina as he wants to, without being embarrassed or shy because she can see him doing it.

As Nicholas Bornoff points out in *Pink Samurai,* his excellent review of sex in Japan: "Sigmund Freud once outraged the prim turn-of-the-century West by stating what has always been obvious to the East: the human male is excited by the sight of the female genitals. Nowhere is this biological fact more taken for granted than in Japan. Many erotic *shunga* woodblock prints (were) explicitly detailed closeups of the vagina." At a live sex show in modern Tokyo "Miss Emi prances around in front of the men in the audience. At intervals she squats or lies down inches away from them and spreads her thighs to the utmost. As a beam of light homes in to make Miss Emi's privates public, she draws them apart with her fingers. The men peer intently at the brilliantly illuminated holy of holies; its rosy glow is reflected in their glasses."

So many wives and lovers fail to understand how fascinated men are by the sight of naked women; or else they find this fascination to be degrading or even disgusting. Unlike women, men can look at pornographic magazines full of naked women they don't even know and be aroused almost to the point of climax. Men can look at a photograph or a drawing of a completely disembodied vagina and find it exciting. But there is nothing perverted or unusual in this response, and except in some extreme cases (such as heavily sadomasochistic magazines) it does nothing to degrade women. Quite the opposite: it shows that men find women stimulating and exciting just for themselves, regardless of who they are. Often the models in porno magazines are not especially beautiful, neither do they have spectacular bodies. They arouse men simply because they are women displaying their femininity.

More importantly—you can use this irresistible male response to excite your lover in ways that he never thought possible. Not nearly enough women realize that the answer to transforming their love lives overnight is right in front of them, right in front of their noses, day after day. The answer is in the pages of *Playboy* and *Penthouse* and *Hustler* and all the rest of those "magazines for men." The answer is in chorus lines and strip shows and sexy videos.

The answer is that men are turned on by *looking,* and if you give them something really wild to look at, you'll drive them wild.

You don't have to act as blatantly as a stripper or a centerfold girl. You can seriously arouse the man in your life while still being serene and dignified. No matter how extreme some of the sexual suggestions in this book may be, all of them are designed to enhance your femininity and your sex appeal without compromising your self-respect.

As Mandy, twenty-seven, a jewelry designer from Dallas, Texas, told me, "I suddenly opened my eyes and caught sight of myself in the closet mirror. I was kneeling on the rug in front of my husband with his erect penis held in my hand. His penis was shining because I'd been sucking it. Was I embarrassed? Of course not. Did I feel degraded? Of course not. How can you be embarrassed or degraded by arousing the man you love and who loves you in return? I looked and I felt like a queen. My eyes were bright, my cheeks were pink, my hair shone, I was full of sparkle. I loved myself, when I saw myself in the closet mirror, I really loved myself, and I loved my husband, too; and I thanked God for making human beings as loving and as beautiful as they are."

Let's start by seeing how you can use your look-appeal to drive your man wild—not next month, not next week, not tomorrow—but *tonight*.

Chapter 3

The Sexiest Show-and-Tell

When it comes to sexual attraction, that hoary old adage, "You can't tell a book by its cover," just doesn't apply. A woman who wants to arouse the man in her life—a woman who enjoys sex and isn't ashamed to display her sexuality—is a woman who shows what she has in mind by the way she looks and the way she acts.

Looking sexy isn't all down to makeup and lipstick. Of course your hair should always be clean and shining and your nails should always be well-manicured, but these are essentials of basic hygiene which you should expect from the man in your life, too. Most men prefer a carefree, "natural" look when it comes to makeup, and are attracted by the lighter perfumes rather than the muskier variety.

"I like a girl who looks like she's just come back from a long morning ride," said thirty-two-year-old Lorne, from Springfield, Massachusetts. "Hair blown wild, rosy cheeks, tight, tight jeans, and a plain old plaid shirt."

Whereas Lorne's girlfriend Gina, twenty-eight, told me: "I feel my sexiest when I'm wearing my black sequin matador coat, my short black skirt, and sheer black pantyhose, and high heels. And all my black silk lingerie underneath."

The look that men find arousing and the look that women *think* is arousing are often dramatically different.

On the whole, women seem to think that elegance and vampishness is sexually stimulating. They feel at their sexiest in fine fabrics, well-cut gowns, and anything which they feel effectively conceals their "bad points."

Sherri, twenty-three, from Tucson, Arizona, doesn't like her legs. "I think I have thick ankles." Because of

these, she always feels more attractive in long skirts and
boots and loose-fitting slacks. Janie, nineteen, from Albany, New York, is worried about the size of her breasts.
"I always wear big sweaters that hide how large they are,
or coats, or blouses that have ruffles on the front to
distract people's attention from my bosom."

Again and again, with very few exceptions, women
have said that the key to sexy dressing is to be "groomed,
elegant, and a little bit mysterious."

It's true that men do respond to a woman who is very
well-groomed and very well-dressed. But that's not what
really stirs them up when it comes to dressing seduc-
tively. I have talked to literally hundreds of men about
what they find sexy in the way that a woman dresses,
and it's clear that the key to arousing the man in your
life is what I call *invitational dressing*.

A woman can be dressed invitingly even if she is wearing a thick fisherman's sweater. She can be dressed invitingly in the plainest of business suits. It takes only the
slightest hint that she is interested in attracting a man to
turn the least obvious of outfits into something that really
sizzles.

Your invitation can be heightened by the way you wear
your makeup and the way you do your hair. If you leaf
through the pages of *Playboy* and *Penthouse* looking at
the girls' *hairstyles* rather than their bodies, you will notice a remarkable consistency. They all have clean, fresh,
well-brushed hair, but even if it's occasionally tied with
a ribbon, it's invariably tousled, as though the girls have
been driving in an open-topped sports car or romping in
bed.

I gave a detailed questionnaire on women's sexual appearance to over a hundred men from a wide variety of
socio-economic backgrounds, and over ninety of them
thought that "long, tousled hair" was the sexiest, although many also expressed a strong attraction to women
with extremely short urchin styles. Their least favourite
coiffure was hair tightly combed back and braided. They
thought that this gave the impression of emotional inhibi-
tion—like a spinsterish school marm or a woman who was
too meticulously dressed to want to jump immediately
into bed. (The only exception to this rule was Bo Derek,

as she appeared in *10*, but then she was bare-breasted, which rather outweighed the schoolmarmish effect.)

It was a similar story with cosmetics. Men are attracted by vivid eye makeup. Many of them still think that false eyelashes are sexy. They like highlights on a girl's cheeks. But they very much *dislike* thick foundation and overdone lipstick. Again, they say they feel that a woman who puts on too much makeup appears to putting on a remote face—a mask, almost—which distances her and makes her appear less sexually available. I found it interesting that one of the most popular of recent books of erotic photographs is called *Explicit Luxury Girls*. Its advertising announces: "You've seen them. The ultimate in femininity—dressed in expensive clothes. You've seen them on planes and in shiny Porsches, Mercedes, Jaguars and Rolls-Royces. So proud, so haughty, so stunningly beautiful—yet untouchable. These are the luxury girls—the jet class girls. The girls who move in expensive circles with their sheer silk stockings and expensive underwear. How would you like to see these girls take off all their clothes and lay their most intimate treasures open before you for your enjoyment?"

Almost all of the girls in the photographs would normally look aloof and unapproachable. They have elaborately styled hair, heavy make-up and formal jewelry—all of the grooming that makes *women* feel attractive, yet which men find formidable. I talked to a wealthy businessman in San Diego who makes sure that his wife always dresses in the most expensive of couture clothes and the most spectacular jewelry, and that she has her hair fixed by a stylist whenever they go out on social occasions. "If you want to know the truth, she's a very attractive woman. I want her to look terrific, but at the same time I also want to make sure that other men feel that she's out of their reach."

In *Explicit Luxury Girls* the attraction, of course, is that all of these "aloof" girls are exposing their bare vulvas to the camera, some of them pulling their vaginal lips wide apart with their fingers, which is hardly an aloof thing for a woman to do. Dressing and grooming yourself elegantly but leaving off your skirt and panties is some-

thing you can do for your man in the privacy of your
own home, but hardly practicable in public.

Invitational dressing means giving a man small but obvious clues that he attracts you and that you would like
him to take you up on your invitation. There are times
when you may inadvertently give a man invitational signals when you don't find him attractive and the very last
thing in the world you want is for him to take your
clothes off . . . so it's worth being aware of those details
of dress which men find stimulating.

When it comes to casual wear, men find girls in blouses
or oversized masculine shirts attractive. In the 1960s, one
of the most successful advertising campaigns of all time
(eventually killed off by feminist protests) showed a
blond girl wearing nothing but a man's white shirt. The
catchline: "Looks even better on a man." The girl, incidentally, had tousled, devil-may-care hair.

An invitational signal is for the blouse to be unbuttoned just one button lower, revealing cleavage or even
bra. Of course one of the most obvious invitational signals is for you to go braless, so that the movement of
your bare breasts is apparent underneath your shirt or
blouse, and any stiffening of your nipples is visible, but
men *don't* particularly like the look of bras that are visible under translucent blouses, and they can be quite
scared off by a woman whose bare breasts can be easily
seen through muslin or any other diaphanous fabric.

Should You Put Your Nipples on Display?

Remember: you should be *invitational* rather than sexually aggressive. If your nipples are virtually an open
show, you will be putting your man into an impossible
position. Does he stare at them? Does he pretend that
he can't see them? Does he assume that you're coming
on to him, or does he try to be blasé and treat you just
as if you were wearing a double knit sweater?

Regardless of what feminists may say about women's
and men's nipples being equal, you and I know darn well

that they're not. He finds your nipples about a hundred times sexier than you find his, and by showing your nipples you will have made such an obvious and provocative sexual statement that you will almost certainly make him feel rushed and uncomfortable. All successful seductions depend on timing . . . and on allowing your man to think that *he's* making the play. It increases his sense of power and control, and this increases his feeling of virility. Men derive erotic pleasure out of winning, out of conquering. That's why I place such a strong emphasis on being sexually invitational rather than sexually up-front. As one thirty-two-year-old musician put it to me: "The two least sexy words that any girl can say to you are 'Let's fuck.' "

Being invitational also means having confidence in your own sexuality and your own body. You must believe first of all that the man in your life *wants* to undress you, *wants* to make love to you. When it comes to confidence in their own bodies, women are their own worst enemies. I worked for nearly a decade as an editorial director of men's magazines, and I still keep in close touch with the world of centerfold girls and strippers and pornographic models even today, since we can often learn so much about our own everyday sexuality from their experiences at the leading edge of sex.

I have known literally hundreds of nude models, some of whom were exceptionally beautiful. They included Julie Ege, several Miss World winners, and Shakira Baksh (now Mrs. Michael Caine). Yet it was amazing how many of these stunning girls were dissatisfied with their bodies. The large-breasted girls almost invariably said that they wanted breast reductions and the small-breasted girls sighed and dreamed of silicone implants. Hardly any of them liked their own faces, they *all* criticized their own bottoms ("too flat" "too wide" "too droopy"). Above all, they were really merciless about their legs. You would have thought from their descriptions of their legs that they were talking about heavy nineteenth-century furniture.

Quite a sizeable proportion of women don't like the look of their own vulvas. "I have very prominent vaginal lips," wrote twenty-four-year-old Susan, from Minneapolis, Minnesota. "They hang down and I don't like my boyfriend to see me naked. He keeps wanting to have oral sex but I squeeze my thighs together and I won't let him."

Kathleen, a twenty-eight-year-old bookstore assistant from Oakland, California, said, "My vulva is very darkly colored, kind of browny-crimson, and I think it looks awful. Now my husband wants me to shave off my pubic hair, but I don't want to because my vulva is such a dark color."

It's very hard to be reassuring about somebody's looks when you haven't met them face to face, but I want you to know that most men are very much less critical about a woman's looks than women themselves believe them to be.

Most men have a surprisingly narrow range of taste when it comes to the women who turn them on. They respond to a particular face, a particular look, a particular complexion, and a particular personality. Some men are excited by dark Latin-looking women with abundant black hair. Some men go for blonde Nordic types with ice-green eyes. Some men are crazy for very small woman; some men like Amazons with wide shoulders.

If a woman has that particular air about her that attracts a man he will never be picky about the size of her breasts or the flatness of her bottom or the thickness of her ankles. If nit-picking physical details were so important, then 75 percent of the women on Earth would be loverless, which they're not.

Every society has a collective vision of an ideal woman. In the Western world, it's usually a large-breasted blonde with wide blue eyes and endless legs. She doesn't sag, she doesn't have cellulite, her nipples are wide and prominent and her vaginal lips are unpigmented. But men are fully aware that this ideal woman is a fantasy. They may masturbate over images of women like this. But when it comes down to everyday sexual relationships, they prefer their women real and approachable. If women understood how undemanding most men really are when it comes to choosing a partner, they would put their hair dryers to their heads and pull the trigger.

When I say "undemanding," I don't mean that they

don't like their women to be well-groomed or well-dressed. I mean undemanding in the sense that they prefer women to be relaxed, casual, friendly, nonaggressive and—here's that word again—*invitational*.

Of course, every woman's attitude toward men is different. Every woman's expectations are different. And every man she meets and wants to attract is different. You have to judge each potential sexual encounter on its own merits. Play it as it lays, so to speak.

Many men and women find that their immediate response to meeting someone who attracts them sexually is to be hostile. This is quite usual and natural. It's a way of concealing our true feelings; of protecting ourselves. Go to a dinner party and listen to the conversation around you. The man and the woman who are attacking each other the most ferociously will be the man and the woman who secretly attract each other the most. They're fascinated with each other, but they both consider it a weakness to show it. So, they scrap. But you just try to chip into their argument. They won't have it. Their attention is riveted solely on each other.

The other most common reaction is extravagant (and often embarrassing) flirtatiousness. The kind of over-the-top breathy-seductive behavior that has everybody else coughing in disbelief behind their hands.

Both of these reactions—while they're perfectly normal—are not the best way of being sexually invitational. If you want to seduce a man and *be sure that he's the kind of guy you'll be glad you seduced,* then you have to try your best to be calm and controlled. Be still, my heart!

Even when you're flirting with your long-term lover or your husband, you'll have a much more fulfilling response if you understand what he finds exciting in women in general and you in particular. So many women complain about their sex lives ("he's never romantic" "he rolls over and goes to sleep and ignores me" "he seems to be more interested in beer and football these days") yet they fail to exploit whatever it was that attracted their men in the first place.

Think: did he like the way you laughed, the way you used to be so funny and relaxed? Did he like your hair, the way it used to be? Did he like the way you dressed?

Did he like your figure? Or was it just those particular looks of yours—your pretty eyes, your good clear skin, your lips, your face?

In a long-term relationship, it's very easy to settle into a sexual rut . . . to forget that your lover or husband still needs seducing, every now and then, that your love life occasionally needs a little refreshment. That's where the look of love comes into it.

First of all, remember that you're sexually attractive to the man in your life. However much you may criticize yourself (don't like your breasts, tummy's too protuberant, thighs are too heavy) the man in your life doesn't see your body in the same way. He sees the woman he's won, and he's proud of you. I always cringe when I hear a woman criticizing herself to her lover or her husband—he says "You look beautiful tonight" and she says "Oh, don't be stupid, I'm not beautiful." I know that many women are embarrassed by compliments and find them difficult to accept, but when they tell their lovers that they're *not* beautiful, they're criticizing not just themselves but their lover's taste in women and his achievement in having won their affections.

What to Say If He Praises Your Breasts

If you want to please the man in your life—*please* accept his compliments glowingly and gracefully. You might think your breasts are far too big and far too droopy. But if he says that he loves your breasts, be flattered, take his compliment and smile and be pleased. Most men like big breasts, and most men are fully aware that as a woman gets a little older, big breasts obey the command of gravity. They might look pop-eyed at eighteen-year-olds in girlie magazines whose just-sprouted breasts seem to be self-supporting, but that doesn't mean they find *your* breasts any the less arousing.

And if you happen to have teeny tiny breasts, and your lover says he loves them . . . take his word for it. Bask in his praise. You may worry that your body isn't perfect, but then nobody's body is perfect. Brigitte Neilsen (the former Mrs. Stallone) has had spectacular silicone breast implants, but to my mind she looked very much prettier before, with small breasts.

An essential part of driving your man wild in bed is making him feel manly and virile . . . and by being proud of yourself and pleased with the praise that he gives you, you will be going a very long way to achieving that goal.

Here's Lyle, twenty-seven, an auto mechanic from Austin, Texas: "I first met Hanna at a barbecue. She's a big girl, no doubt about it. Not tall. Five feet four inches, or thereabouts. But she's got big breasts, big hips. But what a pretty face, and what a dynamite personality. I fell in love with her in about five minutes flat. That first night I saw her looking at me and she was just sitting on the porch and her blouse was just unbuttoned enough to show the curve of her breast, and I sat next to her and asked her if she wanted a drink.

"She was so damned nice, that was what I liked about her. So natural. She could talk about anything without being sarcastic or scornful, which a whole lot of women are. I'm an auto mechanic, right, so I talk about automobiles too much, but Hanna just kind of accepted that, and showed some interest, and made me explain what I meant when I said anything too technical.

"She was overweight. You couldn't fail to notice that she was overweight. But she was so direct and so goddamned natural that overweight wasn't negative, if you know what I mean. I looked down her blouse, I admit it, and I admit that I lusted after her, okay? We were dancing and I asked her back to my place and she thought about it and then she nodded and said, 'Okay. Sure.'

"I'd never been with a fat girl before. But, you know, when she took off her clothes, she wasn't ashamed of herself, that was *her,* what did she have to be ashamed about? And I'm not ashamed to say that she was fat, because she was fat, if you're talking average standards. She was terrific. She had brunette shoulder-length hair, curly and soft, so much beautiful hair, and a beautiful, beautiful face, with lovely brown eyes. Her breasts were truly enormous, there was no use in pretending that they weren't, but they were so beautiful. The first thing I did was hold her breasts in my hand and feel how soft and warm and heavy they were, and they were incredible, so feminine, beautiful. She had wide, wide nipples, a beautiful pale pink. I think I could have loved her for her nipples and nothing else.

"Her tummy was fat, and her hips were quite fat, but she had lovely legs and beautiful ankles. She had shaved off all of her pubic hair because she didn't like pubic hair, and her cunt was so pretty you couldn't describe it. Plump lips, lovely, like some kind of flower, you know? We stood in my bedroom and kissed, both of us naked, and I had this huge boner that pressed into her stomach, and there was juice coming out of my cock already. She rubbed my cock with her hand and then massaged my juice all over her stomach, and if we hadn't made love I swear I would have climaxed anyway, she turned me on so much.

"We climbed onto the bed and kissed and fondled. She was a terrific lover—very enthusiastic, very passionate. I mean she was *hot*. I was crazy about her breasts. I kissed and twisted her nipples between my fingers, and then I sat astride her and I rubbed my cock all around them. She squeezed her breasts tight together, and I fucked her breasts, pushing my cock right into her cleavage.

"I was almost on the point of climaxing over her breasts, but I very much wanted to fuck her. I opened her thighs, and there amongst the folds of flesh was her totally bare cunt, with beautiful pink lips, and it was literally shining with cunt-juice. She reached down with both hands and held herself wide open, stretching those bare cunt-lips as far as they would go. She was showing me everything, you know, so that I could see it the way that a man wants to see it. I could see her clitoris and her pee-hole and her vagina and her asshole; and I bent down and I ran the tip of my tongue around her clitoris, and pushed the tip of my tongue into her pee-hole, and then curled my tongue up and slid it into her vagina.

"She shivered and she moaned, and I sat up again and pushed my cock right up to her cunt, so her cunt-lips kind of half-enclosed it. Then I slid right into her, right up to the balls, and she shivered again.

"She wasn't shy and she wasn't ashamed. She knew she was fatter than most girls, but she was a brilliant lover. She was warm and giving and she knew just what it was that turned a man on. Our first fuck didn't last long because I was too excited and I climaxed too quickly, but she didn't mind about that. She rolled me over onto my back and gave me the longest, slowest, most incredible blowjob that I've ever had. She took the whole of my cock into her mouth and gently sucked at it until it started to stiffen up again. She took both of my balls into her mouth and at the same time massaged her cheeks with my cock.

"With Hanna, sex was *visual*. Watching yourself fucking made it ten times more exciting. That night, we made love twice more; and toward daylight she turned her back on me and reached around and guided my cock toward her asshole. I knew what she wanted, so I rolled on another condom and then massaged the head of my cock around her cunt so that it was good and slippery, and then pushed it up her asshole. She had huge fa´ bottom cheeks, and there it was, right in front of me, my cock sliding in and out of her ass, her bright red asshole clinging to my cock, her cheeks shivering with every stroke. She was panting and clutching the pillow. It hurt her but she liked it. She was so tight I could hardly ram my cock into her. I mean her asshole clutched at my cock like Hulk Hogan's fist. But I pushed, and I pushed, with my balls bouncing against her wet cunt with every push, and in the end I climaxed deep inside her ass, and she held me inside her for as long as she could, until she finally flexed her ass muscles and squeezed me out. I'll never forget the sound it made. *Schlupp.*

"I saw Hanna two or three times more; then we didn't connect any more. I don't know why. She was a sweet girl, a really terrific girl, but sometimes I think that the pressures of being a fat person in a thin society were a little too much for her. She was sexy, she was passionate, but she was afraid of committing herself, in case she got hurt. But she understood how to attract a man more than any other girl I've ever met. Even though she was fat, she didn't play the clown. She was natural, and open; and by the way she dressed and the way she looked, she was attractive without being threatening, if you understand what I'm trying to say.

"I'm an ordinary guy, a very ordinary guy. I love women, and of course I like to go out with a looker. But I guess you could say that I'm kind of defensive when it comes to women who dress too smart. I always have the feeling that at some stage of the proceedings they're going to put me down.

"I took Hanna out three or four times, and I was never ashamed of being seen out with her. Why should I? She was terrific, and if I met her again I'd ask her out without any hesitation at all.

"She always managed to look *inviting,* do you know what I mean, without looking cheap or whorish or anything like that. Sometimes she wore a half-open blouse that showed off her cleavage; sometimes she wore good-fitting pants that showed off her ass. And she was always fresh and bright and smelling of perfume."

Dressing to suit your own personality and your own appearance and your own lifestyle is critical if you want to look sexually attractive to the man in your life. It will make you feel confident and relaxed, and your confidence and sense of relaxation will put your man at ease, too. There is nothing more irritating and off-putting for a man than a woman who is constantly fretting that she doesn't look good—a woman who is constantly readjusting her jacket or tugging at her hem or checking herself in the mirror to make sure that she doesn't look quite as bad as she feels.

When you dress for a date with a man that you really want to go to bed with, always dress a little way down. Not too much. You don't want to turn up in a jogging suit when he's wearing a tuxedo. But have enough confidence in your looks not to overembellish yourself. Men like natural. Men like approachable. Men like *invitational.*

Here's Mandy, twenty-five, a computer analyst from Chicago, Illinois, who found herself attracted to the forty-one-year-old vice-president of a major construction corporation. "I went to ten or eleven meetings and social functions where Dean was present, and even though we talked a few times and I had the feeling that he liked me, we never managed to click. Each time I knew I was going to meet him, I dressed up in my very smartest business suits and spent *hours* on my hair, but it didn't seem to make any difference. I knew he was divorced, and as far as I could find out he didn't have a steady girlfriend, but he always seemed to draw the line at asking me out.

"Then one Saturday morning my boss phoned me and asked me to take round a whole bunch of papers to Dean's apartment at Marina Towers. He said they were urgent and that Dean was expecting them in twenty minutes. Well, of course I didn't have time to change or fix my hair or anything. So I thought what the hell. I was wearing tight white pedal pushers and a big yellow angora sweater and that was about it. I hadn't had time to make up my face, and my hair looked like I'd been walking through Hurricane Freddie backwards.

"I looked at myself in the mirror before I left and I thought, oh well, what difference does it make? He hasn't made a pass at you yet. You could be wearing some exclusive gown from Marshall Field and he still wouldn't make a pass at you. He's not interested, whatever you think.

"You could see my breasts bouncing"

"But the only thing I *did* do (and I'm really not sure why I did this) was to take off my bra, and to take off my panties, too. I'm quite big-breasted, so you could see my breasts bouncing under my sweater. I mean you could tell that I wasn't wearing a bra, even though you couldn't see anything. And my white pedal-pushers were pretty revealing, too, once I'd taken off my panties. You could see the outline of my pussy quite clearly; but my sweater was really long so it was covered up.

"I gave my hair a quick brush and that was it: I was ready. I felt sexy but I felt relaxed, and to tell you the truth I'd flirted with Dean so many times without any success that I didn't really care whether he found me attractive or not. I took a taxi to Marina Towers and he let me in. Beautiful apartment, let me tell you, and what a view!

"He asked me to wait while he went through the paperwork. He asked me if it was too early for a glass of champagne, but I said, sure, why not? It's not every Saturday morning you get to visit Marina Towers and drink champagne. He was looking through the papers but I couldn't help noticing that he kept glancing at me. It was then that I knew that he found me attractive. And I was wearing my scruffiest clothes and my hair was an absolute mess!

"After a while, he threw the papers aside, and he said, 'I have a confession to make. I'd rather sit down and finish this bottle of champagne with you than go through these papers.' And so I said, 'Sure, I don't mind.'

We sat on the floor in the sunshine overlooking the river and drank champagne and played Verdi opera and talked. It was so relaxing, it was fabulous. I mean there was plenty of sexual tension between us, but that was all, and it wasn't aggressive or competitive or upsetting or anything like that. Sometimes men seem to think that the only way they can show you how much you turn them on is by bringing you down, by making you look really small. The number of times men have done that to me at dinner parties and parties, and all the time I could *tell* that they really liked me!

"But Dean that morning was totally relaxed. He told me all about his ex-wife and his children and his dog and who knows what else. Then, in the end, he took hold of my hand and he said, 'Mandy, I have to tell you this, I really like you. In fact I think you're fabulous.' I told him I liked him, too, which was more than true. But do you know what he said then? 'Every time I've met you at work, I haven't been able to take my eyes off you, but you've always looked so distant and self-contained and remote. I knew that you weren't married, but I always guessed that you had a steady man in your life, or else that you were a totally dedicated career woman who wasn't interested in starting any kind of relationship—or else—and I hope you'll forgive me for this, that you were a lesbian.'

"I couldn't believe what he was telling me. I'd always tried so hard to look smart and sexy, for no other reason except to attract Dean's attention. And he'd always thought that I was a dedicated career woman or a *lesbian*!

"I started laughing, and Dean laughed, too. We literally rolled around the floor laughing. Then I was lying sprawled on my back and Dean was on top of me, and he looked me straight in the eye and he kissed me. It was a fabulous kiss. He ran his fingers into my hair and slid his tongue between my lips and touched every one of my teeth until my whole mouth tingled.

"We rolled over again, until *he* was lying on his back and I was on top of him. I leaned forward and kissed him and he held my hips. Then he ran his hands up inside my sweater and felt my ribs and then he felt that my breasts were bare. I was sitting astride his crotch and I could feel his cock stiffening through his pants. He squeezed and caressed my breasts in both hands, and then he started to fondle my nipples, and my nipples are very, very sensitive—it was like somebody was giving me tiny electric shocks in my breasts. I started to get very turned on, and I could feel my pedal pushers getting wet between my legs.

"Dean pulled up my sweater and took it off over my head. He kissed me and massaged my breasts, and I sat on his lap and pushed my pussy against his cock, around and around.

"He said, 'Mandy . . . I'd love to make love to you . . . but I wasn't expecting anything like this and I don't have any condoms . . . do you want to wait while I go buy some?'

"I said, 'Later . . . there's lots we can do.' The reason I knew so much about it was because only the previous year I'd spent four whole days with my former boyfriend in a cabin near Madison, Wisconsin, totally snowed in. He wasn't HIV or anything, but of course I hadn't wanted to get pregnant. I wasn't on the pill and we'd totally run out of condoms. So we'd improvised . . . and, boy, it's amazing what you can learn about sex when you have to improvise.

"My boyfriend and I had done a whole lot of oral sex
. . . but of course that was something that neither Dean
nor I wanted to risk with each other. But we could use
our hands and we could use our bodies.

"Dean kept on kissing and squeezing my breasts, and
that really turned me on. You wouldn't believe how
many guys give your breasts one or two quick squeezes,
give you a peck on your nipples like they're pecking some
strange woman at a cocktail party, and then dive straight
down between your legs. They don't seem to understand
that when a woman's sexually aroused, her breasts can
be really sensitive, and she adores having them fondled
and kissed. Once, up in that cabin, my boyfriend actually
brought me to orgasm, just by fondling my breasts, and
it was one of the most fantastic orgasms I'd ever had,
because it flooded all over me like some tremendous tidal
wave. I've never managed to have another orgasm
since—not just by having my breasts fondled—but I can
still make my pussy really wet by massaging my own
breasts and tugging my nipples.

"I pulled down my pedal pushers and Dean started
to smooth his hands all the way down my bare back
and around my hips. He squeezed the cheeks of my
bottom, and ran his fingertip right down the cleft and
touched and tickled my anus. I've always enjoyed having my bottom fondled, but I know there are quite a
lot of women who are shy about it, they think it's dirty
or something. They don't realize that most men are
absolutely crazy about bottoms—at least most of the
men that *I've* ever met—and that it's quite clean so
long as you're careful.

"Those are the words a girl wants to hear"

"I climbed off Dean and lay on my back on the carpet, and opened up my legs for him, just enough to be
inviting. He touched the lips of my pussy and twined my
pubic hair around his fingers. Then he slipped his finger
up inside me, right up inside me, until I could feel him

touching my womb. He massaged his finger around and around, and at the same time he kissed my lips and kissed my breasts and whispered that I was fabulous and that I was turning him on like crazy. I mean, those are the kind of words that a girl wants to hear, yes?

"He took his finger out of my pussy and started to stroke my clitoris. He had a lovely, light, quick touch, just flicking the tip with his finger and occasionally running his finger down the shaft. Whenever my clitoris started to get a little dry, he dipped his finger back in my pussy and made it all juicy again.

"I was beginning to feel warm and light-headed and incredibly turned-on, all at the same time. I gripped Dean's cock through his pants and rubbed it slowly up and down, but I didn't want to take it out yet, because I knew that I'd be tempted to take him inside me, and that was something that neither of us could risk, not until we were sure of each other.

"Dean continued to flick my clitoris with the middle finger of his left hand, and then he opened up my pussy-lips with the middle finger and the index finger of his right hand, and slid them right up inside me, right up to the knuckles. He began to massage the front of my pussy, quite strongly and firmly, with his two fingers pressing beneath my clitoris. I'd never been touched like that before, but the sensation was incredible. He was actually massaging my clitoris from *inside* me.

"A feeling came over me like I was totally out of control. The pleasure was so intense that I thought I was literally going to die before I managed to reach orgasm. Then I felt like somebody was gripping my shoulders and shaking me, and I climaxed. I don't know whether I made any noise or not. I don't remember. But Dean made my climax even more intense by opening my thighs wide and preventing me from closing them, which is my natural instinct when I have an orgasm. I looked down between my legs and I was literally squirting out fluid. At first I thought I was peeing myself. I was absolutely soaked. But afterwards I realized I hadn't peed at all. It was just a really wet orgasm, which you can sometimes have if a man massages the inside of your pussy like that. It was amazing. I've had two or three since then, and they're just out of this world. That sudden gush of fluid gives you such a sensational feeling, and it actually leaves you with something to *show* for your climax, like a man shoots out sperm.

"Afterward, I opened up his pants and took out his cock. It was tremendously hard, totally huge, and the end of it was already slippery and juicy. I rubbed it up and down a few times, and I would have done anything to have him inside my pussy, but I knew that I couldn't. I mean, the odds were that it was perfectly safe. He was a clean, intelligent guy, living what seemed like a pretty normal life-style, but he was a divorcee, right, and he must have been doing *something* for sex, and I didn't know who with. He could have been HIV without even knowing it.

"I pushed him gently over onto his back and unfastened his belt and pulled his pants right down. All the time he was stroking my hair and touching my breasts, and I knelt beside him and we kissed like we hadn't eaten for a week. I love kissing, and yet so many men don't seem to be able to kiss and have intercourse at the same time. I had one boyfriend who made love to me practically every single night, yet he didn't kiss me from one week's end to the next. He seemed to think that kissing was something you only did when you first went out with a girl.

"I kissed Dean's neck and his chest and bit his nipples. Not too hard; that can really hurt. All the time I was massaging his cock up and down. It was hot and swollen, and I kept slipping my hand between my legs so that my fingers stayed juicy.

"I kissed him all around his hips and his thighs, and while I was doing that he reached around and fondled my bottom and slipped his fingers into my pussy again.

"I kissed his balls and all around the shaft of his cock. His balls were so tight they were like two hard walnuts. I rubbed his cock harder and harder until the end of it was flushed dark red, and his head dropped back onto the carpet, and he closed his eyes, and I knew that his climax was close.

"I wet my finger with pussy-juice and I stroked and tickled his anus. Then I slid my finger right up inside his ass, as far as it would go, and I massaged him inside his ass. He was so tense that every muscle in his body was hard. He was trying desperately hard not to climax, to hold on a few seconds longer. His thigh muscles were rigid, the cheeks of his ass were really clenched and tight. He was gritting his teeth and even his chest muscles were bulging. But I kept on massaging his cock up and down, up and down, giving it a little sharp tug every time I massaged it downward, so that the skin was stretched. The head of his cock looked like a plum, really shiny and hard. It really took some self-control for me not to take it into my mouth. I kept on working my finger around in his ass, and then I managed to wriggle a second finger in.

"He shouted out loud, and a huge white fountain of sperm came shooting out of his cock, then another, then another. It was all warm and jellyish and all over my hands and halfway up my arm. I don't think I'd ever seen a man shoot out so much sperm in one go. I rubbed it all over my breasts and massaged my nipples with it, and then I took hold of Dean's hands and guided them onto my breasts so that he could massage them, too. Afterward we lay on the floor, drinking champagne and occasionally kissing and touching each other, and it was a totally great experience."

By recounting the whole of Mandy's sexual encounter with Dean, we're leapfrogging ahead of the subject of invitational dressing to some pretty advanced and confident sexual techniques, which we'll discuss in more detail later. For instance, Dean's internal massage of Mandy's vagina had the effect of stimulating that area which is popularly known as her "G-spot," with the result that she had an extremely copious flow of vaginal fluids when she climaxed. And—in return—Mandy's internal massage of Dean's rectum had the effect of stimulating his prostate gland, intensifying his sexual feelings, and producing a very thick and generous ejaculation of semen.

But I thought it worth including at this stage because it illustrates that Mandy was the kind of girl who was sexually skilled, who wasn't coy or embarrassed when it came to giving or receiving sexual pleasure, and who wasn't frightened of being sexually positive. Yet the way she dressed and the way she behaved was *invitational* rather than blatant, and at any time during her sexual encounter with Dean she could have backed off and said, "That's enough."

Chapter 4

What *Really* Turns
Your Man On

Many girls fail to understand that men can be very cautious when it comes to sex. They may act macho, they may talk gung ho, but their sexual knowledge and experience is often as limited as that of the girls they're trying to impress. They're looking for all of those little signs from you that tell them you like them, and that you could be interested in a sexual relationship. And when I say "little signs" I mean "little signs," not fortissimo flirtatiousness.

Jasmine, twenty-three, a dental receptionist from Memphis, Tennessee, told me, "I met Jamie at a charity cookout. I wasn't expecting to meet anybody there, and it came as a good surprise. We spent almost the whole of that evening together, and by the time the evening was over we were dancing and kissing and cuddling and getting really hot. I had to go home with my friends, so we didn't have the opportunity to do nothing else, but Jamie asked me to meet him on Saturday. I piled up my hair and I wore my shortest skirt and my killer blouse. And what happened? He did nothing but fret. We had a terrible afternoon and we didn't do nothing at all but drive around. In the end Jamie said that he didn't want to take me nowhere, dressed up the way I was, specially the places where his friends were. He said I was coming on too strong, and what was he supposed to do about it?"

So, on the whole, a little sexuality can go a long way, especially when you're dating a man for the first time. Mandy's relationship with Dean became very intense very quickly, even though she wasn't wearing clothes that were specifically erotic—such as a miniskirt or a tight top or a body-hugging Lycra dress.

However, when you're going out to excite a man with whom you already have an intimate relationship, you can obviously be much more daring. If you want to turn on your husband or your lover, for example, just by looks alone, there are a whole lot of things you can do to excite him, and have him panting to take you to bed.

Although there will always be times when your man wants you to look immaculately groomed, husbands and long-term lovers will still respond to that tousled, girlish, just-rolled-in-the-hay look.

"Maybe I'll wear panties, maybe not"

Jacqui, twenty-two, a petite blonde from Oakland, California, said, "Every now and then, when Brett gets back from work in the late afternoon, I meet him at the door wearing nothing but one of his shirts. Maybe I'll wear panties, maybe not . . . it's up to him to find out. He likes me to dress pretty when we go out in the evening, for sure, but when I open the door for him and that's all I'm wearing . . . that really turns him on good."

Melissa, a tall, dark twenty-seven-year-old from La Jolla, California, told me, "We have a very private yard that nobody can see into, and so in the mornings I often go water my pot-plants wearing nothing but a baseball cap and a pair of tennis shorts, and when I do that you can bet your last dollar that David will be out on the deck with me in about a minute flat, feeling all roused up and horny.

"One morning in the spring I went outside naked except for my baseball cap and a pair of white socks and Nike training shoes. I was hunkered down, trimming back one of my plants, when David came up behind me, and knelt down, and started running his fingers down my back and fondling my breasts.

"I pretended to be irritated, but there's no way that

you can be really irritated when the man you love is caressing you like that. He kept on cupping my breasts in one hand and stroking my nipples, and running the fingers of his other hand all the way down my back. After a while his fingers strayed down right between the cheeks of my bottom and he touched my cunt. Because I was hunkered down like that, my cunt was open, and he slid his middle finger right up, and wiggled it, and used his other finger to play with my clitoris.

"I closed my eyes and I forgot all about my plants. In the end I was so turned on that I had to drag him into the house and onto the bed. . . . It was still unmade and the sheets were all rumpled but that didn't matter. I pushed him back onto it and I opened up his shorts and I sat on him and I fucked him and it was beautiful. That was the first time I ever made love with my training shoes on."

The key to Jacqui and Melissa's sexy way of dressing (or *un*dressing) was the contrast between an item of clothing as prim and proper as—for instance—a man's shirt or a baseball cap, and partial nudity.

There is a famous poster of a girl playing tennis, her back turned to the camera. She is lifting her small white pleated skirt to reveal that her bottom is bare and that she is wearing no panties. If she were completely nude, the poster wouldn't have half of its erotic effect—and *you* can make use of that same erotic effect time and time again to drive the man in your life really wild.

Here are some favorite accessories—quite innocuous and unsexy in themselves—which women have used to excite their lovers.

Helga, twenty-five, a young blond homemaker from Milwaukee, Wisconsin: "Sometimes I get out of bed in the morning and make John's breakfast naked except for my white cotton apron. That always turns him on so much, he pulls me back to bed and makes love to me before we eat. I guess that's why we always end up with cold food!"

Joan, nineteen, a titian-haired student from Minneapolis, Minnesota: "If there's one thing that always makes a

man go totally weak at the knees, it's when you wear
stockings and a garter belt to bed. And high-heeled
shoes, too—you must wear shoes. But that's all. Don't
wear anything else, unless it's one of those quarter-cup
bras that show your nipples."

Paulette, twenty-eight, a brunette secretary from
New York, New York: "The single most sexually dev-
astating outfit I ever wore was a soft red cashmere
sweater. I bought it at Saks Fifth Avenue and it was
the most expensive sweater I ever owned. I wore it
with soft brown ankle-length boots, and absolutely
nothing else at all. I opened my apartment door for my
boyfriend Paul dressed like that, and he flipped. We
were supposed to go out to the theater to see *Miss
Saigon,* but we ended up on the couch, making love
almost all night."

Jennie, twenty-four, a color processor from Los Angeles,
California: "A black leather jacket and black leather mo-
torcycle boots. Oh—and a black leather cap, too, just
like bikers wear. And what else? A pretty white lacy
G-string that you can *nearly* see through but not
quite."

You probably have plenty of ideas of your own about
erotic dressing. String vests, that allow your nipples to
poke through. Silk teddies and French-style step-ins and
leather briefs. Just remember that men respond strongly
and quickly to visual stimuli—much more strongly and
much more quickly than women. That's why they respond to strippers and pictures of naked women in sex
magazines and even a glimpse of something that does
little more than *suggest* a bare breast or a hint of bare
bottom or a shadow of pubic hair. It is a plain fact of
human sexuality that men are riveted by the sight of
women's bodies, in a way that women will always find it
impossible to comprehend. "What on earth possessed my
husband to want to look at pictures of such cheap, whorish women?" one distraught wife wrote to me, after she
had discovered his collection of sex magazines. "He has
a beautiful wife, a beautiful family, and our sex life has
always been marvelous." But—*men like to look.* They
like to look at women's breasts, they like to look at wom-
en's vulvas. A man can be aroused by a close-up photo-

graph of a woman's vulva even if he has no idea who it belongs to. The shape, the softness, the moistness, the mystery, the apparent vulnerability of it. The thought of kissing it, the thought of sticking his finger into it, the thought of thrusting his penis into it.

A popular German magazine for men is called *Lippen der Lust* (Lips of Lust) and features (according to its advertising blurb) "kissable vaginal lips! Open the page and there they are! Just a kiss away! The juiciest red vaginal lips belonging to the most beautiful young girls! This magazine is devoted to the gorgeous lips surrounding the female sex."

Feminists may protest at what they see as the "sexual exploitation" of magazines like *Lippen der Lust,* as well as striptease and pornography and centerfold poses. But they should try to appreciate that most of this so-called "exploitation" is natural and normal. Men are hugely aroused by looking at naked women, regardless of who they are, but there is nothing cold or mechanical in what they feel. The majority of men respect and like women and their response to erotic pictures of women is a straightforward biological urge—combined (in many cases) with a straightforward sense of curiosity.

Women who love men and who want to be loved by men in return will always understand that *men like to look*. At them, at pictures of other women, at pornography, and at sexy movies. The most faithful lover in the world will still be turned on by erotic visual stimuli, and he will be lying to you if he says he isn't. The trick of handling your man's interest in visual stimuli is to *share* it with him.

You can do this (a) by giving him sexy glimpses of *you* to look at, (b) by expressing an interest in sexy photographs or magazines (in other words, by giving him "permission" to look at pin-ups, and (c) by asking him to show you erotic movies or videos, so that you can share actively in his stimulation.

Always remember that the excitement your man experiences when he looks at erotic videos or magazines is *perfectly natural* and that you have nothing whatsoever to be jealous about. Those pictures are all an aid to sexual fantasy, and he wouldn't dream of trying to contact any of the girls he sees and trying to get to know them personally. He simply wouldn't want to. Meeting any of them in person would destroy the fantasy of a completely compliant woman. He knows that in real life they would be just as characterful and idiosyncratic as you are, and need just as much attention and flattery and day-to-day loving. The point about girls in magazines is that they don't need loving, they don't need wooing. He pays his money and there they are, with their legs wide apart, their smiles bright, silent and never-arguing, even when he examines their vaginas in long and appreciative detail.

But if you want to drive your man really wild in bed, you can learn from the girls in the magazines. I'm not expecting you to turn yourself into the human equivalent of a pin-up photograph—silent and unmoving and uninvolved. But you can arouse your man enormously by exposing yourself to him explicitly and intimately—and you can satisfy his curiosity, too . . . and in return you can encourage him to satisfy yours.

Even the most broadminded of women can find that their lovers' interest in visual sexual stimulation—such as pornographic magazines or videos—is quite difficult to understand and even more difficult to accept. They don't realize that it very rarely represents any kind of threat to their relationship. If you're quick to come to terms with your lover's liking of visual sex—if you treat it as natural and normal and nothing to be ashamed of—he'll have even greater sexual confidence in you, and even greater sexual respect.

Make it work *for* you, instead of treating it as something threatening and negative. It's only paper and printing ink. Take a close look through it, and see if you can detect in it any particular sexual tastes which your lover may feel are unfulfilled. Is there a special emphasis on oral sex, or anal sex? Are the girls dressed in leather or basques or rubber or high heels? Are the girls especially big-breasted? Are they posing in a way in which you would never dream of posing?

Don't worry if you can't detect any obvious sexual theme. Your lover may enjoy looking at these magazines simply because he is sexually stimulated by the sight of naked women, in common with 99.9 percent of all other heterosexual men on the planet Earth. The point I'm making above all is that it isn't a slight on your sexuality if your man responds to pornography, and it certainly doesn't mean that he's betraying you in any way. Men who two-time women don't usually bother with magazines. They go out and two-time them for real.

Let's take a look at Valerie's story. Valerie is twenty-seven, and works for the state legislature in Mississippi. She had been living with her boyfriend John for two-and-a-half years and her love life was "okay . . . but a little routine . . . not exactly in 'the earth moved' league." But then, by accident, she discovered a cache of very explicit sex magazines in his toolbox in the garage.

"I couldn't think of any reason why he might have had them except that he wasn't sexually satisfied with me. They were all well-thumbed, and some of the pictures had marks on them as if John had jerked himself off all over them. Well, you can imagine that I was real upset. I felt almost as if John had been unfaithful to me, and it certainly did nothing for my self-esteem. It was as bad as if I'd found a letter saying 'Valerie can't keep me satisfied in bed.'

"And what seemed to make it worse was the fact that he'd hidden these magazines, kept them a secret."

What happened to Valerie happens to hundreds of wives and lovers. After all, the sales of sex magazines run into millions, and they're not all bought by adolescents or lonely single men. Most women who discover that their men have secret hoards of pornography report similar reactions: disgust and revulsion at the sexual blatancy of the pictures (since a comparatively small number of women have ever had occasion to look closely at a sex magazine), bewilderment and betrayal that their men should feel the urge to look at pictures of other women, and a terrible feeling of sexual inadequacy. Not to mention, of course, the fact that their man has apparently been carrying on a whole secret sex life of his own and never once thought of sharing his urges and his desires with the woman who is supposed to be closest to him.

One woman I spoke to was incensed that her husband had masturbated over pictures of strangers instead of taking her to bed and making love to *her*. "We were trying for children for three years. When I think of all the sperm he ejaculated over filthy pictures instead of up inside me, it makes me so mad I can hardly speak." In spite of intensive counseling, this woman's marriage only barely survived.

But I hope you will have grown to understand from this chapter that men are always strongly aroused by looking at the naked female body, and that their relationship with the girls who pose for pornographic magazines is totally without emotion or involvement. Once a man has ejaculated over a pornographic magazine he will completely lose interest in it and—depending on the circumstances—will often be overcome with shame at what he has done. That is why so many discarded sex magazines can be found in toilets and in bushes or anywhere else secluded that a man has taken them in order to masturbate.

Actually, there is no need whatever for him to feel ashamed. He is simply responding to a perfectly natural and normal urge—an urge which almost all men have from time to time.

It would be absurd to pretend that in cases where men are not fully satisfied by their sexual relationships, they will not seek relief in masturbation, and that they will not use pornography to arouse them while they are doing so. But you cannot assume for one moment that just because the man in your life masturbates, or has a keen interest in pornography, that he considers your sexual relationship to be inadequate in any way.

Out of hundreds of married men that I have interviewed over twenty-six years of sex counseling and research, over 75 percent of them have admitted that they have masturbated during the course of their marriage or long-term sexual relationship. Out of those 75 percent, only 9 percent said that their sex lives were at all unsatisfactory, and many of them said "When I masturbate, I fantasize about making love to my wife."

So why did they feel the urge to masturbate?

There were several answers, the most common of which was "because I enjoy it." In other words, they regarded it as a short, simple physical pleasure, a way of stimulating themselves and relieving emotional or physi-

cal tensions, no more consequential than smoking a ciga-
rette or having a drink (and very much less dangerous).

Quite often, men confessed to having masturbated in
bed while their partner slept next to them—even though
their partner, if woken, would have been quite willing
and ready to have intercourse. They didn't perceive masturbation as the same act as intercourse, and they certainly didn't think of it as being disloyal. It was a solitary
act—an act which required no overt expression of love
or emotional commitment—an act during which all kinds
of erotic fantasies and wishful thinking could be explored
without distraction. In other words, a very *internal* act,
an act of sexual self-absorption, and no challenge at all
to the shared excitement of making love.

Leather or Rubber or Stockings

Thirty-one percent of men who were either married or
in long-term sexual relationships admitted to having
bought at least two pornographic or erotic publications
during the past twelve months. Out of those 31 percent
(which I personally interpreted as a very low figure compared with the estimated sales of sex publications, and
reliable readership surveys conducted for men's magazines), slightly fewer than three percent said that they
looked to pornography as a substitute for sexual inade-
quacies in their relationships.

Another figure was quite telling. More than half of
that 31 percent said they bought sex magazines because
they depicted sexual acts or sexual modes of dress that
aroused them (such as leather or rubber or stockings and
garter-belts), but which they never felt the women in
their lives would agree to try.

They weren't greatly dissatisfied with their sex lives,
but they would have liked a little more erotic variation.
The trouble was, they were either afraid to tell their partners what they wanted, or they *had* asked and been re-
buffed. We can't completely blame women who are
reluctant to try sexual variations. Although sexual education in schools has improved in the past decade (and

especially recently, because of the specter of AIDS), most women are given very scanty information in their sexually formative years on what a man expects out of sex and how to make their love lives interesting and exciting.

Girls are first experimenting with sexual relationships at a younger and younger age. A general medical practitioner of my acquaintance has remarked on the number of girls of eleven and twelve who have obviously experienced sexual intercourse. But at the same time, their sexual knowledge is still limited to a hotchpotch of school biology, playground superstition, and anything they might have glimpsed in an R-rated video.

Sex is physically complex and emotionally challenging. No other activity requires a woman to go through such bodily effort and such powerful physiological changes, while at the same time handling such a storm of feelings. No other activity demands such a reversal of her natural self-protection and modesty. In front of others, she is supposed to be discreet, quietly dressed, and politely spoken. In front of her lover she is expected to open up her most intimate parts and behave like a skillful and shameless whore.

As the socialite wife of one Texas businessman told me, "I made love to my husband an hour before we went out to a party. I spent all evening talking to people, and kissing friends, and it occurred to me that none of them could possibly know that just a short time before, my lips had been closed around my husband's penis, and his come had been running down my chin."

Some women find it confusing and difficult when the man in their lives expects them to be a princess in public but a prostitute in private. But let's go back to Valerie, who had discovered her lover's secret store of sex magazines, and see how the way in which she came to terms with his interest in pornography actually *improved* her love life out of all recognition.

Fortunately—before she confronted John with her discovery—she wrote me a letter telling me what had happened and expressing her bewilderment. We had several discussions, and after a very short while Valerie came to understand that he wasn't being unfaithful. He wasn't desperately dissatisfied. He was simply looking for that extra element of erotic fantasy that makes all the difference between "satisfying in bed" and "wild in bed."

This is why I have complained time and time again about the shortcomings of sexual education in schools, and about parents' unwillingness to face up to the seriousness of their responsibilities and tell their children the full facts of life. There is no harm at all in giving even quite young people the full facts about sex . . . telling them about everything from masturbation to straightforward intercourse to contraception to oral sex. You don't make a child into a pervert or a sex maniac by telling him or her the truth about sex. Sex is the most dramatic expression of love for each other that we have at our disposal. Sex is the key to relationships of depth, excitement and emotional fulfillment. Sex makes people happy. It makes people stay together . . . and better sex education will do more for the stability of our families and our society than all the psychological counseling in the world.

Why are we still so ashamed of sex? Shame brings secrecy, secrecy brings suppression. Suppression leads to dissatisfaction, tension, the breaking down of relationships, marital discord and acts of sexual violence—such as rape and sexual abuse. Why is it acceptable to show a movie on TV in which a man brings out an Uzi and blows a woman's head off, but unacceptable to show a movie in which a man takes out his penis and gives a woman more pleasure than she can bear? You tell me. I don't know. All I know is that I counseled Valerie that John's interest in sexy magazines wasn't at all harmful and that if he was aroused by pictures of naked women she had nothing to worry about.

In fact, the best thing she could do was look through John's magazines, see what it was that turned him on, and use this covertly acquired knowledge to drive him wild.

Valerie said, "It didn't seem to me that any of John's magazines had anything much in common. There were blondes, brunettes, black girls, Asian girls, you name it. But the pictures that seemed to have turned him on the most were the pictures in which the girls weren't completely nude . . . but it was almost like the camera had caught them when they weren't expecting it. There was one picture in which a blonde girl was sitting on the stairs. She was wearing a very short red dress, and of course you could see right up her dress. She wasn't wearing any panties, so you could see her pussy. Naturally she knew the photographer was there. But the whole picture had the look of something which you could have glimpsed by accident.

"There was another picture I remember, in which a girl was curled up asleep—or pretending to be asleep. She was lying on this flowery comforter, wearing nothing but a short nightshirt. It had ridden up at the back so that her bare bottom was exposed and her leg was slightly lifted so that she was showing her bare pussy, too.

"I took your advice and didn't tell John that I'd discovered his magazines. I was angry when I first discovered them, but when I realized that I could use them to my own advantage, my attitude totally changed, totally. I actually felt like I had some kind of sexual power, which was something I hadn't felt in a long time. Instead of feeling cheap and whorish, I actually felt like more of a woman.

"Let me tell you something, I'm proud of being a woman, and I think I'm deserving of equal pay and equal respect and equal treatment under the law. But that doesn't mean that I don't like flirting or romancing or any of the things that make a woman what she is. I want to tease a man, I want to turn him on, and I want to feel that I can woo him and win him.

"Two days after we'd talked, John and I were invited to a big barbecue party. It was mainly a business party, so it was pretty dull. I didn't wear any special dress: just a short black velvet skirt with a shiny purple satin top. I combed up my hair and fixed it with these two mock-diamond barrettes so it looked pretty formal and ornate, if you know what I mean. I don't think that John liked it very much. He always preferred my hair to hang loose. But this *was* quite a formal affair.

"I wore high-heeled shoes with mock-diamond buck-

les, and black stockings, and a black garter-belt, but . . .
no panties.

"I didn't tell John that I was wearing no panties until
we arrived at the party. We were just about to get out
of the car when I said, 'Oh, no . . . I forgot to put on
my panties.' He stared at me and said, 'You're kidding
me! You're not wearing any panties?' And I said, 'I'm
not kidding you, look,' and I quickly lifted up my skirt
so that he caught a quick flash of my pussy.

"He didn't know what to do. He went bright red and
completely confused. But I could tell that it turned him
on. He asked me if I wanted to go back home and put
some on, but I said, 'Don't be silly . . . who's going to
know, except you?'

'I wore no panties . . . but only he knew"

"That was the cruncher. That was what really got him
worked up . . . the idea that I was wearing nothing but
a garter belt and stockings under my skirt, that my pussy
was totally bare, but he was the only one at the party
who knew.

"I had never seen him so jealous or so attentive at any
party. Usually he used to have quite a roving eye. But
that night he wouldn't leave me alone. And after a few
cocktails, in the shadows at the edge of the garden, he
slipped his hand under my skirt and fondled my bare
bottom.

"He was so hot for me that *I* was getting turned on,
too. At one time he was talking to one of his accounts
people, and I stood in the background where nobody else
could see me, except John, and I lifted my skirt, and
rubbed my hand around my pussy, and then I let my skirt
drop back again, and came over to him, and touched his
lips with my fingers, so that he could taste me and smell
me . . . right in front of this straightlaced accountant he
was talking to.

"Later on, when we were standing in line for food, I
whispered to him, 'I want you . . . the breeze keeps tickling my pussy and I want you so much.' Then I reached

around and squeezed his cock through his pants, quite hard, and gave it two or three quick rubs, and he almost came in his pants, right then and there, while he was standing in line for baby back ribs.

"Let me tell you something . . . what you advised me to do was to act like one of the fantasy women in one of his magazines, and I did. John wasn't under any illusions. He knew it was me, and he still respected me and all the rest of it. But just for that one night, I was like a dream girl, too. I was like a stripper or a porno model . . . teasing and willing and very, very sexy.

"I discovered one thing. Acting sexy wasn't demeaning to me as a woman. Acting sexy gave me power, and influence in our relationship, and not least of all it gave me fantastic pleasure. I *liked* being a whore because I was being a whore by choice. I *liked* turning my man on, and giving him the time of his life. For sure, it was over the top. But by the end of that evening, my pussy was so wet with excitement it was literally dripping down my thighs into my stocking tops. I was *aching* to make love. I suddenly understood what you meant when you said that being sexy and whorish is only one facet of being a woman . . . but it is one of a woman's strongest attractions, just like her mind, just like her personality, just like her soul. I realized that I'd been denying myself sexually, and at the same time I'd been denying John, too, because I hadn't allowed myself to show him how sexy I could be.

"I couldn't even wait to get home. After the party was over, and John was driving us home, I couldn't keep my hands off his pants. I could feel how hard his cock was, and I gripped it tight, and rubbed it up and down. But in the end I had to open up his zipper, and tug his shorts down, and take his cock right out. It was so hard, it felt like it was made out of rubber, like one of those dog bones. But it was real wet and slippery, too, and I was squeezing it and rubbing it and it was getting even wetter.

"I dug my hand into his shorts, and I could feel his balls. I felt—what's the word?—so *wanton*. But for the first time in my life I understood that I was grownup, that I was free, that I could do what I wanted to do.

And if I wanted to squeeze this man's balls in my hand and rub his cock, I could do it. Sometimes I think that women totally underestimate their strength in a sexual relationship. If they did a little more of the running, from time to time, not *all* the time, they could have their men literally eating out of their hand.

"I rubbed John's cock quicker and quicker, and then I bent my head down and took it into my mouth. There's a scene in Steve Martin's movie *Parenthood* when Steve Martin's wife tries to do that, and he's so surprised that he crashes the car. Well, John almost did the same, but not quite. No sooner had I closed my lips around his cock than he started to climax. His first shot of come went straight down my throat. I didn't even have time to swallow. I'd never done that before, so it kind of took me by surprise, so my first reaction was to whip his cock out of my mouth. The second shot went all over my lips, and the third one over my cheek, so that my eyelashes were stuck together.

"He slowly, slowly went softer"

"If you'd asked me a couple of months before that night if I would have ever allowed John to come down my throat and over my face, you would have gotten the sharpest *no* you'd ever heard. But this time was different. This time, *I* was in control. John hadn't climaxed into my mouth because *he* wanted to, but because *I* had turned him on so much that he hadn't had any choice in the matter. It might sound like the end result is the same, and I know there are lots of women who don't relish the idea of giving head, and I didn't like it when John tried to push his cock into my mouth and treat me, I don't know, like some kind of receptacle. But I think that any woman can turn the tables by being sexually positive, and that's what I did. So when John shot that come down my throat, it was bliss. I thought, I've done it, I've made you do what *I* wanted to do.

"I rubbed his cock and his come all over my face, I kissed him and I licked him and I sucked him. I took his whole cock into my mouth and while he was driving, his cock slowly, slowly went softer. That was something else I'd never felt before, a man's cock going soft in my mouth. It's beautiful. He might have wished it was hard, to show me how macho he was, but it wasn't, it was soft, and I loved it all the more because of that. I could lick it and suck it and pretend that it was something that belonged to me."

Because Valerie was able to grasp so quickly that it was not only possible for her to take control of her own sex life, but to be able to take control of it virtually overnight, everything worked out more than well. You can do the same. Your whole sexual relationship could be different by morning. But you do have to be prepared to take quite a mental and emotional leap forward. You have to think your way out of your old inhibitions and your old prejudices. You have to turn your perception of your relationship around 180 degrees and say to yourself, "Tonight, we're going to make love this way because this is the way I *want* to make love." Be bold and resolute. Believe me, men may look tough, but they're all susceptible to a woman who not only knows what she wants, but insists on getting it.

Maybe you have a phobia about oral sex. I discussed Valerie's case with several women who had been going through difficulties in their sex lives, and their reaction was almost unanimous. How could she have taken his soft, spermy penis into her mouth . . . yuk!

Women who react in a negative way to the physical realities of sexual stimulation are almost always women who (through no fault of their own) have had a limited sexual education. They have often started an affair or even gotten married without any clear idea of how a man's sexual organs work, or even what they look like. Mary-Lynn, twenty-two, a hairdresser from Indianapolis, Indiana, told me, "Before I got married, I'd slept with two boyfriends, both both times in the dark . . . so that I'd only *felt* them, you know, rather than seen them. I had only the vaguest idea of what a man looked like. I'd seen guys on the beach and Chippendales dancers, and all you can really make out is this bulge with a kind of pointy bit in the front. When my husband appeared on my wedding night with his penis completely erect, I couldn't believe it. I thought there must be something abnormal about him. I was terrified, and my whole wedding night was a fiasco. I spent all night awake, wondering if I'd married a monster.

"It took me a long, long time to get over that first experience, even though I had a very helpful and understanding girlfriend who told me what men were all about . . . and even though I read two of your books about mutual exploration.

"You want my honest opinion? I think girls should be shown videos of couples having sex, right from grade school. I'm not talking about kinky sex videos, I'm talking about straightforward fucking, which everybody does. A young girl should see how big a man's penis can get. A young man should see what a woman's vagina looks like. Why not? We've all got one, we all do it. What's the big secret?

"Sex was very, very difficult for me, and I still have a problem with oral sex, even though my mind tells me that I ought to do it and my emotions tell me that I want to do it. Your first experience of sex is so important. It affects your sexual attitudes for the rest of your life. Young people should be shown everything in a noncommittal way and left to make up their own minds. It won't corrupt them. The worst way to corrupt somebody is not to tell them the truth."

For men, visual stimulation is a highly important part of becoming sexually aroused. Yet there are still millions of women who are shy of exposing themselves to their lovers or husbands, and who would never dream of opening up their legs the way that girls in sex magazines do, and letting their lovers take a long, lingering, exploratory look. As one thirty-five-year-old wife from Scottsdale, Arizona, told me: "I'd rather die than let Gordon look at me like that. I was brought up to believe that a woman's body is her own. A woman has to have her personal privacy." And this from a woman who had already borne her husband four children.

It is this kind of reticence that prevents so many sexual relationships from ever really taking off. When you are involved in a sexual relationship with a man, you should give it all or nothing. If you decide to do that tonight, you'll be startled at the terrific improvement in your loving. You'll also be startled by how affectionate and attentive your partner suddenly becomes . . . in and out of bed.

Giving your sex life everything you've got doesn't mean that you have to start doing things in bed that you really don't like. You have your sexual rights, too . . . and the most fundamental of those rights is the right to enjoy your lovemaking.

Reach across the Bed and Fondle Him

But sex is like a whole lot of other activities in life . . . some of its greatest delights are an acquired taste, and some of its richest rewards can only be reaped through experience and practice. Don't give up on oral sex, for instance, just because you didn't care for it too much the first time you tried. Allow yourself to get used to the idea of it by taking it step by step. Try fondling and kissing his penis before you try taking it into your mouth. Press it against your lips and roll it against your cheeks. A surprising number of women scarcely ever touch their lovers' genitals, despite the fact that over 97 percent of men to whom I talked about "things I wish my lover would do for me" said that having their penis and their balls manually caressed is one of the single most pleasurable sexual favors that their women could give them.

Make a point of remembering to reach across the bed when you wake up in the morning and fondle your lover's cock. Do it tomorrow morning, while he's still half-asleep. Be bold about it. Enjoy his erection. Give him some firm, confident rubbing. Don't worry about having intercourse. . . . See if you can make him ejaculate. Bear in mind that sex doesn't always have to be a trade—"I'll give you a climax if you give me a climax." Sometimes, it's much more exciting and stimulating if one partner concentrates on the other partner's sexual satisfaction without any immediate concern for his or her own needs.

As I said at the beginning of this chapter, men are very rarely as competent or as experienced in matters of sex as they like to pretend . . . or as women expect them to be. I have had literally hundreds of letters from women complaining about their lovers' clumsiness and lack of consideration. But most of the time, their lovers are very far from uncaring. They *would* be better lovers if only they knew how. That's why the woman who has the most exciting and satisfying sex life is the woman who knows all about sex, who knows what she wants in bed, and is prepared to be adventurous enough to make sure that it happens.

More often than not, driving your man wild in bed is achieved by gently educating him in the kind of lovemaking you like. If he knows that he's turning you on, then he's going to be turned on, too.

Let's go back to visual stimulation. We've discussed at some length the way in which men can be quickly and strongly turned on by visual images—by photographs, by videos, by the way you look. I fully understand that, for many women, the idea of displaying themselves sexually to the men in their lives isn't easy. They find it embarrassing. They think that it devalues their feminine mystique. In fact they consider that the whole idea of a man wanting to peer between a woman's legs is vaguely disgusting.

Such sexual reticence isn't easy to overcome. But you *can* overcome it if you have pride in yourself. Pride in your body. Pride in your femininity. And pride in the fact that your lover wants you so much.

For a man, looking closely at the woman he loves is one of the most exciting experiences of his life. He wants to enjoy her, he wants to make love to her, he wants to honor her. He is filled with fascination and pleasure at the sight of her. The first and most significant step forward you will ever make in improving your love life is to show yourself to your lover, openly, and proudly. Let him see you, explore you, touch you, lick you, love you.

Let him open your vaginal lips. Let him see and touch

your clitoris and your urethra and your vagina. Let him stimulate you, let him taste you. Open yourself up to him.

All you will have to do then is lie back, relax, and enjoy it.

5

Show Him What You've Got

Kay, a very pretty twenty-four-year-old window-dresser from Chicago, Illinois, wrote me that she and her boyfriend had very nearly ended a "very intense" three-year relationship over the question of pubic hair.

After a roundabout discussion that had taken in the topics of high-cut swimsuits and centerfold girls and the merits of various depilatory creams "Lenny at last managed to ask me whether I would shave off my pubic hair."

Kay was perplexed, cross, and "in the final analysis, badly put down." She thought that Lenny "after all this time, was telling me that there was something wrong with me, that he didn't like me the way I was."

He first response was to tell him, "I would never ask you to shave off your mustache. Your mustache is part of you. Why are you asking me to shave off my pubic hair?"

Kay had been raised in a straightforward blue-collar environment in Indianapolis, Indiana, and although she worked for a big-city department store she still considered herself "a plain girl at heart." Her relationship with Lenny, a would-be professional saxophonist who worked in the music department of the same store, had been "passionate, fun, caring . . . anything I could have asked for." She had been expecting Lenny to ask her to marry her when he came up with his shocking sexual request.

But what Lenny was asking Kay to do was neither unnatural nor unusual. When I questioned men about their sexual preferences, well over 75 percent of them said that they would like the women in their lives to shave off their pubic hair, either occasionally "so that it grew back from time to time" or permanently.

Some women are afraid that a man who expresses an interest in shaven pubes is suppressing a secret desire for underage girls. But, largely, the opposite is true. It is the sight of a fully mature vulva, completely hairless, with nothing hidden, that most men find so arousing.

These days, the advent of high-cut leotards and swimsuits has meant that most women do a certain amount of pubic depilation. This has met with such obvious approval from their partners, however, that a considerable number now do it for sexual purposes as well, regularly removing most or all of their pubic hair.

Why do men like it so much? Firstly, because it shows them instantly that the women in their lives want to arouse them. Secondly, because it openly displays that part of the female anatomy that really excites them.

In some of the very first sexual advice books that I ever wrote, more than a quarter of a century ago, I suggested to women that they could electrify their lovers by shaving off their pubic hair. Here are four letters from women who followed that advice, and who found that it wasn't just a cosmetic change, but a radical sexual statement that changed their love lives (literally) at the stroke of a razor.

This is Moira, twenty-three, a homemaker from Detroit, Michigan: "To say that our sex life had been going through the doldrums would be putting it mildly. David had been working too hard at the bank because GM had been laying off people right, left, and center, and part of his job is dealing with mortgage arrears, which is very stressful. Sometimes a whole month would go past and I would have another period and realize that during the whole month we hadn't made love once, not even *once*, whereas when we first dated we used to make love six or seven times a week.

"I guess in a way that part of the problem was me, because David always seemed so tired and depressed when he came home from work but I didn't make any effort to be sexy or attractive. It was just dinner, TV and bed, every night, and I never bothered to dress up for him or anything like that. I was talking to my neighbor over coffee one morning and she showed me your last book, *Sex Secrets of the Other Woman*. I have to admit that frankly I found some of the things in it quite embarrassing, and I don't think David would have liked it too much if I'd tried them.

"But I did take notice of what you wrote about grooming, how 'the other woman' always manages to attract men away from their wives because she takes the trouble to have her hair done well and to look extra-good. I went downtown and had my hair highlighted and cut in a bob. I had a manicure and a pedicure, and I gave myself a facial. I felt about a hundred times better already. I bought three new sweaters and some new skirts, and also some really sexy lingerie, a negligee and three G-strings and two bras. I'm quite big-breasted so I can't wear any of those quarter-cup bras, but I found some black see-through bras which I really liked.

"I also read in your book about shaving off your pubic hair. I didn't know whether I should, I was quite shy about it, but in the end I decided I would. I was so nervous about doing it I was shaking! Isn't that ridiculous? I undressed and then I stood in front of my dressing-table mirror and snipped off most of the long hair. Then I went into the bathroom and half-filled the tub with warm water. I sat on the edge of the tub and soaped myself between my legs, and then I used David's razor to shave off the rest of my hair. Absolutely all of it—bald cunt! I rinsed myself (and made sure I swooshed all of the hairs out of the tub) and then I went back to the bedroom and admired my handiwork.

"I have to admit that everything you said about it was true. I didn't look like a little girl or strange or anything. I looked and felt very womanly and also daring that I had actually exposed myself like this, in order to turn on my husband.

"When David came home from work that evening, I had a martini ready for him, like I always do. But I wasn't dressed in my usual jeans and sweater. I was wearing my new negligee, and when he sat down I opened it up for him and did a twirl.

"I was frightened that he was going to think that I was pushing him, that I had gone too far. You know how unpredictable men can be sometimes if they think you're trying to be critical. But he smiled and shook his head and said, "Heyyy, that's pretty!'

"I knelt up on the arms of the chair and he kissed my stomach and then he kissed all around my bare mound of Venus. Then he ran the tip of his tongue up and down on my bare slit. He couldn't get enough of my cunt. It turned him on so much. He kept kissing it and licking it and opening it up with his fingers. I'd never let him look at me like that before. At first I closed my eyes and I could feel myself blushing and my cheeks burning real hot. But he was kissing and sucking me so much, it was so obvious that he adored me, really adored me, so how could I be embarrassed? I opened my eyes and looked down and he was sucking my cunt lips, and his tongue was wriggling around inside my cunt, it was just so sexy.

"I shave my pubic hair all the time now"

"I never would have believed that doing anything so simple would have turned him on so much. But I talked to some of my friends about it who have tried it too and every one of them says that their husbands go wild for it. I shave all the time now and I wouldn't grow my pubic hair back. For one thing it looks so much cleaner and prettier, and who needs it? For another thing David adores it so much. I can see him looking at me sometimes when we're out with friends, and he smiles in a way that he never used to smile at me before, like he's thinking, there's my wife, under that skirt, inside those panties, her cunt's completely bare, and she's done it for me."

Of course, there are men who adore pubic hair and wouldn't dream of having you shave it off. Nina, a nineteen-year-old student at Washington State, is an authentic redhead, and her boyfriend adores her gingery pubic hair. "He helped me to trim it for the summer, so that it wouldn't show out of the sides of my swimsuit, but he kept all the hair that he clipped off, and sealed it in an envelope. He loves it."

Some men like both hair and bare. So sometimes you

can let it grow, but now and then give him the enjoyable surprise of discovering that you've removed it.

But here's another sex secret . . . a surprising number of men who have a preference for women with no pubic hair would find it very arousing if you shave off *theirs,* too. There was an unprecedented response a few years back to a letter in *Playboy* from a girl who complained that her boyfriend's pubic hair was so luxuriant that it made oral sex a very unpleasant experience. Was she right in insisting that he trim it?

The first man I ever met who openly admitted that he shaved his pubic hair was Gunnar, a live-sex performer who worked for Stockholm's Black Pussy Cat Club in the mid-1970s. He and his wife Inge had sexual intercourse live on stage, and both of them were shaved. They were always a tremendous success with the audience—who visited the club not only to be aroused but also to satisfy their sexual curiosity.

Gunnar said, "My mother and father were always keen on naturism. Of course summer in Sweden is very short and so we always try to make the best of it. We used to have a holiday cabin on a lake near Uppsala, a very private cabin, so that we could swim and sunbathe in the nude and nobody would ever disturb us. During the summer my parents would both shave their body hair. They were very fit, very proud of their bodies. By the end of August my father would have a tan like mahogany. I can remember him now, sitting on the little jetty where we used to swim . . . very trim, muscular, with his completely bare penis, no pubic hair at all . . . his foreskin drawn back over his glans because the wind and the open air was always a little arousing.

"My father always told me that when I grew up, I would discover that, for a man, making love without pubic hair is an experience which cannot be matched. The feeling of completely bare skin, there is nothing to match it. When I met Inge she had already been stripping and dancing and posing for magazines, and she found that shaving off her pubic hair made her very popular with audiences and photographers. So not long after we started to sleep together, I shaved off all of my hair, too, and I wouldn't ever grow it again.

"My father was right. The feeling of closeness when you make love is very intense. And because Inge likes to take me into her mouth so much, she prefers the smooth skin. Of course it doesn't make you look like a child. When your penis and balls are so big and developed, it is obvious that you are a man. *Very* obvious."

More and more men are shaving . . . for sexual display, to make oral sex more of an attractive proposition to their partners, and simply for the sake of good grooming. In an age when men are unafraid to make themselves more attractive by taking care of their hair and their skin and the way they smell, removing superfluous hair is only a part of good grooming.

Some women really go for it—although there are others who prefer their men to be really hairy. Melanie, a twenty-year-old student from Arizona State, wrote, "I really go for men who have hairy chests and hairy arms and hairy backs and hairy thighs. My current lover is just like King Kong. I just love to lie back when we're making love and run my fingers through all that hair. He has a deep, dark forest in the cleft of his bottom, and I can really get my hand in there and tug at it, and there's so much shaggy hair around his balls and his cock that I can wind it around my fingers and twist it. Once I actually braided his pubic hair, when he was asleep, but that got him all angry when he woke up. He's all man, totally male, and that's the way I love him."

But here's Gemma, a twenty-seven-year-old ceramic designer from Sausalito, California: "Gerry and I are about as different physically and mentally as any two people could be. But we get along so well. . . . We're in such deeply corresponding life-rhythms that sometimes we can go for days on end without even speaking. We don't have to. Gerry is very instinctual. . . . His formal education was very limited but he has a wonderful sense of color and beauty, not only in art but in music and words, too. He loves poetry even when he can't follow all the intellectual nuances.

"On the other hand my family were always into literature and art and music. I went to UCLA to study art and design. I met Gerry on the beach when I went to visit my cousins one day. He is so physically beautiful that nobody can fail to notice him. He's very tall . . . six feet four inches . . . with dark hair and a very strong face. If you can imagine an Italian Arnold Schwarzenegger, that's what he looks like. His body is like a sculpture. He was doing one-handed pushups when I first saw him, and I was so amazed by how many he was doing that I stopped and talked to him. He asked me if I wanted lunch and he bought me a steak and salad. He said that was practically all that he ever ate, steak and salad.

"We traded addresses but I never thought that I'd ever see him again. But lo and behold about three weeks later he turned up on my doorstep in Sausalito. He said he was visiting friends in San Francisco, but later he confessed that was a lie: He'd driven all the way up from LA just to see me.

"We had a great time that evening. Some friends came around and we all went to one of my favorite restaurants and ate Japanese. Gerry had never tried sushi before, and he really loved it. Later, when everybody else had gone home, I invited him to stay the night, on the couch. I still didn't know for sure whether we were going to be lovers. But there was something about him . . . some inner peace, some kind of confidence, that you very rarely find with academic people. He was proud of himself physically, he wasn't upset that he wasn't Einstein. I guess you could say that he lived in paradise.

"He took a shower, and while he was showering he called out that he couldn't regulate the water. It's a pretty old shower—sometimes it freezes you to death, then it instantly boils you like a lobster. You need a special knack with the faucet.

"I climbed into the shower with him"

"Anyway, I stood outside the shower trying not to look too hard through the frosted glass door, and I shouted out all the instructions. But he still couldn't get it to work properly. In the end, I shouted 'Turn your back!' and I opened the shower door and reached inside.

"But he didn't turn his back. He was the kind of guy who wasn't shy about the way he looked.

"I couldn't help myself from looking him up and down. He was magnificent. He *is* magnificent. He's built like a god. His muscles were all soapy, his stomach was taut and hard, and there was this *huge* cock hanging down, with these balls like baby oranges, completely shaved smooth and bare, so that I could see everything, the thick vein running down his shaft like a tree-root, everything, and the water trickling off the head of his cock and running down his thighs.

"I could have adjusted the faucet and closed the shower-stall door and left. It was my choice. But I didn't. I climbed into the shower with him, and stripped off my soaking-wet blouse, and tugged down my soaking-wet shorts, and put my arms around him, wearing nothing but a little white thong. We didn't say a word, but I kissed him, and he kissed me back, and I ran my hands down his sides and all down his back. His back was so tapered and muscular, it felt fantastic. I gripped his buttocks in my hands, really gripped them tight, dug my nails in, and he clenched his muscles so that they felt knotted up like rope.

"I had never been the aggressor in a sexual encounter before. But having seen Gerry naked, I wanted him so much that there was no stopping me. If you want to talk about wild in bed—yes, I went wild.

"I don't think I'd ever realized before how often men are waiting for responsive signals from women. . . . A lot of the time, they're waiting for women to make the first move. They're not nearly as confident and as assertive as you'd think, especially if you'd never seen anything but movies and TV, where the heroes are always confident and assertive. But they're only confident and assertive because it's in the script. The rest of us have to live our lives according to chance . . . and how many happily married movie and TV stars have you ever heard of? In real life, I mean.

"Gerry was physically proud of himself, very calm and confident about what he was; but he hadn't known how to make that quantum leap between friends and lovers. As it was, he didn't have to. His looks were enough. I kissed his mouth, kissed his nipples, and then I couldn't help myself from fondling that big bare cock. It was already stiff, it was *immense,* it was just as thick as my wrist, and the head of it was almost as big as my hand. I slowly masturbated him, and his smooth, slippery skin was such a turn-on. Because men are almost always hairy, you don't realize how silky and smooth the skin of their cocks is, and how smooth the surrounding area feels. I was fascinated. I couldn't stop stroking and masturbating him, and all the time he was growing harder and harder.

"I pressed both of my thumbs against the head of his cock and gently pried the opening apart, like opening a fig or an orange. He kissed my wet hair and squeezed my breasts. His hands were so large that he could get the whole of one breast in his hand at once. I'll never forget how much that turned me on. The head of his cock was dark reddish purple, but the opening was even brighter red and brimming with clear slippery liquid. I could feel how slippery it was, even under the shower.

"I would have done anything to take his cock into my mouth and suck him, but these days that's one of those no-nos. You just don't dare to do it with anybody you're not sure of. So after we'd been kissing and fondling each other for a while, I turned off the faucet and led him out of the bathroom into the bedroom.

"We were both dripping wet, but we rolled over and over on the Navaho rug on the bed, kissing and squeezing and massaging each other. He stopped for a while to take a Trojan out of the back pocket of his jeans. He was about to put it on, but I said no . . . I'd roll it on for him.

"He knelt on the bed and I opened the foil and took out the rubber. I held his cock tight, and fitted the rubber around the head. I gave him two or three extra strokes for luck, and he literally groaned with pleasure. I unrolled the condom all the way down that shaved-bare cock and kissed all around the root of it and kissed his balls and took his balls into my mouth.

"I told him that I'd seen plenty of women shaved but never a man. He said that a whole lot of body builders did it these days. It was partly because they didn't want to show pubic hair around those little swimsuits they wear and partly because they're very vain and fastidious and partly because it gives them a sexual kick . . . I don't know, like tattooing or something. It's kinky without being harmful.

"I loved it. I sat on top of him that night, and I opened my legs, and he pulled my thong to one side, and without any hesitation he slid himself right up inside me, so far up inside me that I gasped, like climbing into a chilly swimming pool. He held my bottom in his hands and he lifted me up and down on top of him—rhythmically, fast, almost like one of his workouts, but he didn't make it *feel* like a workout, he did it with passion and strength and I felt he really wanted me, really needed me.

"I looked down and there was Gerry's huge bare cock sliding in and out of me. My cunt-lips were flushed and swollen, and I was really juicy, too, so that his cock and his balls were smothered in it. My pubic hair was wet; it looked like dark waves of seaweed.

"I leaned forward on top of him and kissed him urgently. He said that I was fantastic, that I turned him on so much. I reached around behind me and fondled his bare slippery balls. They felt so smooth and tight that I couldn't believe it. I loved fondling them, but I could have taken them into my mouth and swallowed them, too. I felt as if I wanted him sitting on top of me . . . as if I wanted to give him everything. I could have pressed his bare balls against my eyelids, and stuck my tongue up his ass . . . that's how dirty and submissive he made me feel.

"He reached around behind me, too, and caressed my fingers while I caressed his balls. Then he ran his fingertips around my cunt-lips, and caressed my anus. He pushed his finger a little way inside, and rotated it slowly around and around, and the sensation was staggering. Nobody had ever done anything like that to me before, especially not on a first date. As his cock pushed in and out of me, his finger worked its way deeper and deeper inside my anus, until with no warning at all, well *almost* no warning at all, I climaxed.

"It's supposed to make
your breasts bigger"

"I think I yelled out. Anyway, Gerry gave six or seven really deep strokes, and then he climaxed, too. I felt the Trojan bulging.

"He took his cock out at once. It was a drag; one of the best parts of making love is when it's all over and you can feel a man going gradually soft inside you, but it was better to be safe than sorry. I held his cock in my hand and squeezed the last of his sperm into his condom. Then I eased it off and rolled onto my back on the bed and let all the sperm drip out onto my breasts.

"Gerry asked me what I was doing. I said, 'Don't you know? Sperm is supposed to make your breasts grow bigger.' One of those high-school old wives' tales. A girl called Laura told me about it, and she had the biggest breasts you've ever seen in your life. I massaged my nipples with Gerry's sperm, and smoothed it all over my neck. I guess it was a kind of substitute for not allowing him to climax inside my cunt—a way of showing him that I still wanted his sperm, even though we were practicing safe sex. It smelled wonderful. A little bit rubbery, because of the condom, but there's no smell like the smell of a man's sperm. I adore it. And you're the first person I've ever confessed that to.

"I think it's a different world for women these days, because of women's rights, because of AIDS, because of the whole change in women's role in society. That first time with Gerry was the first time that I had ever taken the lead in a sexual relationship with a man, and believe me, my heart was beating so fast! But it worked and I enjoyed it. I wouldn't do it every time. I do expect a man to be positive and dominant. But sometimes men are slow on the uptake, or a little shy, and it doesn't do any harm to show them that you really want them."

Cara, now twenty-two, a brunette photography student from Santa Cruz, California, first learned about the intensity of men's sexual curiosity when she was just fifteen years old.

"I matured quite early. I had my first period when I

was eleven and by the time I was fifteen I was into a 36D cup. I was pretty popular with the boys at school but I didn't know anything at all about sex . . . not much, anyway, apart from what they taught us in biology class.

"We were real poor in those days. My dad had died in an auto accident when I was seven years old, and my mother had to bring us up on her own . . . that's my brother Eddie and me. Eddie's two years older.

"Anyway, one night I was undressing for bed when I heard a noise outside of my room. I covered myself with my bed cover and opened the door, and there was Eddie standing outside. He was wearing nothing but a shirt, and he was trying to cover himself up with his hands. But his cock was hard, and it stuck right out and he couldn't really hide it.

"I asked him what he was doing. He was so red in the face! But before he could answer, Mom called something from her room. Eddie whispered, '*Please,* if she finds me like this she's going to kill me!' He ducked into my room and hid behind the door, so that when Mom looked out she didn't see him.

"When Mom had gone back to bed, I asked Eddie again what the hell he was doing outside my bedroom door with no pants on. He went all red again, but in the end he said he'd been looking at me. He didn't have a girlfriend in those days. He was real shy, and being so broke he didn't have a car, so of course none of the girls was interested in him, even though he was very good-looking.

"He said he'd been jerking off. He'd done it two or three times already, and he was real sorry and if I didn't tell Mom he wouldn't do it again.

"I'd heard about boys jerking off but didn't really understand what it meant. I guess I was just curious. But Eddie and I had grown up very close. I mean we shared baths together until we were eight or nine. Because of that I didn't feel embarrassed. I didn't even feel as embarrassed as *he* did.

"I asked him to show me. He couldn't believe his ears. He said 'What? I can't show you that. You're my sister.' But I said, 'Well, you've been looking at me undress and you've been doing it.' He said, 'That was different. You didn't know about it then.'

"I said, 'If you don't show me, I'll go out of this room right this instant and tell Mom what you've been doing.' You can see who was the bossy one in our family! So finally he gave his cock two or three rubs, although he wasn't very enthusiastic about it, and he had gone all floppy.

"I said, 'Supposing I undressed? Would that help?' I thought this was all fantastically exciting. We were so close that it didn't occur to me that brothers and sisters shouldn't have anything to do with each other sexually.

"Eddie didn't say anything. But I slowly dropped the bed cover and stood in front of him wearing nothing but my bra and panties. I said, 'Go on, jerk off, show me how you do it.' I reached behind me and unfastened my bra and let it drop to the floor. Then I cupped my breasts in my hands and squeezed them, the way that you see strippers doing it.

"Eddie slowly began to rub himself, and his cock rose up hard. I thought it was fascinating. I'd never seen a boy really hard before. I couldn't believe how big his cock was. I asked him if I could touch it, and he said, 'Sure.' I touched the head of it very gently and then ran my fingernails all the way down to his balls. I had never touched a boy's cock before. I couldn't believe how hard it was; yet the skin was so smooth. I couldn't stop touching it and feeling it. It was so warm, so alive. I pressed it against my cheek and it felt fantastic. Eddie closed his eyes and said, 'Mmmmm.'

"I said, 'Do you like that?' and he said, 'You don't have any idea.'

"He kept on rubbing himself, quicker and quicker. I did a kind of dance for him, kind of a belly dance, and then I slowly tugged down my panties. I lay back on my bed, naked, and Eddie climbed on the bed next to me and touched my breasts. He touched and kissed my nipples and my nipples really tingled, that's the only way I can describe it. When you talk about it cold, you know just to a tape recorder, it sounds terrible that a brother and a sister could have done this, but we loved each other, we were fantastically close, and we were friends.

And the last thing in the world we wanted to do was hurt each other, or do anything really wrong.

"I held Eddie's cock in my hand and rubbed it up against my breasts. His cock was wet, and it made my nipples wet, too. Kind of slippery. I slowly rubbed his cock while he ran his fingers down my sides and between my legs. He touched my cunt—and until he touched it, I hadn't realized that I was wet, too.

"He said, 'Let me see,' and so I opened my legs wide so that he could look. Why not? He was my brother and I loved him, and my growing up was something I wanted to share. He stroked my cunt with his fingertips; then he opened my cunt-lips wide apart, so that he could see everything. He touched my clitoris, which made me shudder. Then he touched my pee-hole, and rubbed the tip of his finger against it, and said, 'This is where you pee from, hunh?' That felt really strange; but nice, too—one of those feelings you can't explain. Then at last he opened up my actual cunt and slipped his finger inside. He said, 'You're so wet, it's unbelievable.'

"I was embarrassed, to tell you the truth. Not because I was showing my brother everything I'd got, but because I was wet.

"But he said, 'That's good. That shows that you're sexy.'

"He kissed my forehead and said that I was the most fantastic sister that anybody could dream of. He kept on stroking my cunt, very lightly, very gently, it was like being touched by a butterfly.

"We both knew that what we were doing was something we had to keep secret. Maybe it was wrong—I don't know. We knew for sure that it would be wrong for us to have intercourse. But I loved Eddie's body, I loved his cock, I loved the feel of him, and I knew that he loved touching and looking at my cunt, and even today I can't see the harm in it. I loved touching and stroking his cock so much; I couldn't keep my hands off it. Holding the head of his cock between my fingers, squeezing out a little juice. Feeling his balls in the palm of my hand. It was beautiful, and nobody can tell me that it was really wrong.

"I was frightened and delighted and turned on"

"That first night, I kept on rubbing him and rubbing him, and in return he kept stroking my cunt. Then he stopped stroking me, and his stomach muscles went really tense. I rubbed him two or three times more, and then suddenly he was splashing this warm white sperm all over me, all over my breasts, all over my hands, it was everywhere. It was amazing. I could actually see it shooting out of his cock, right out of the hole. I was frightened and delighted and turned-on, all at the same time. I didn't even know whether to stop rubbing him or not: that's how little I knew about sex.

"But I touched his cock with my fingers, so that my fingers were all spermy, too. And I rubbed his sperm onto my forehead and my cheeks, I don't know why. Like makeup, I guess. Like blooding somebody, after their first hunt. Like war paint.

"That was the end of our first time together. Eddie didn't really know how to jerk off a girl. In any case, I think we were both kind of frightened by what had happened. But two or three days later, when Mom was out working, I invited him back into my bedroom, and I lifted up my nightdress so that he could see that I was naked underneath.

"I lay back on the bed and opened my legs. Eddie took off his clothes, and he knelt at the end of the bed. He kissed the insides of my thighs, and then he kissed all around my cunt, and then he ran his tongue down the length of my cunt and slipped his tongue right inside my vagina.

"I guess there are many women who might be disturbed at the idea of having their own brother's tongue inside of their vagina. But Eddie was sensitive, gentle, and all he was doing was learning and exploring. I enjoyed it. I found it exciting. But it was all the more exciting because I knew he was my brother, and that we wouldn't be making love.

"He climbed up on the bed and kissed me, a very brotherly kiss. Then I slipped down beneath him, and took his cock into my mouth. It was very big and hard, and I licked all around it. I stuck the tip of my tongue into the hole at the end of his cock, as deep as I could go. Then I sucked him all the way down the length of his shaft and took his balls into my mouth and sucked his balls. It was exploring. It was finding out. I pushed him over onto his back and I licked all around his balls and then I licked his asshole. It was tight and it was clean and it was beautiful. I ran my tongue all around it and then back up the seam of his ball-sack, and then up his cock, and then swallowed the head of his cock. It was then that he climaxed, and I could have taken my mouth away but I didn't. He filled up my mouth with sperm, and I swallowed his sperm—one, two, three swallows—and then I rubbed his cock all over my face because I loved him so much, not as a lover, but as a brother.

"We never had intercourse together, not once. But for two or three months we spent night after night together, feeling and touching and masturbating together. I guess we just grew out of it, after a while. Eddie found a girlfriend, Winona, and about six weeks later I started dating a really terrific guy named Paul—who's still a good friend of mine.

"I think I'm quite a good lover, because I think I understand what men want. They want to see, they want to look. Also, I know what *I* want, and if I have any kind of sexual fantasy, you know, I'm not ashamed to tell my boyfriends about it. Just because you've been to bed with hundreds of men, that doesn't make you a good lover. What makes you a good lover is understanding what turns men on. Exploring turns them on. Finding out about a woman's body turns them on. Eddie used to sit there for half an hour, just looking at my cunt and touching it and feeling it. He used to love doing that, and I used to love him doing it."

Cara was extremely lucky, inasmuch as she benefited from her sexual relationship with her brother. Most siblings who become sexually involved suffer from emotional and sexual problems for many years afterwards, and often find it very difficult to have normal relationships with other people. This is quite apart from the well-known dangers of incestuous pregnancies.

While I can never recommend or condone incestuous sex, Cara learned from her relationship with Eddie that most valuable of sexual lessons—that true sexual closeness comes from giving all of yourself to your lover. That means opening yourself up mentally, emotionally, and physically.

Of course there are times when you will have to use your own judgment of your lover's personality before deciding to give him your sexual all. Sometimes, a man may not be anything like as serious about you as you are about him, and *vice versa*. But when you *do* meet a man whom you can love and trust, and with whom you wish to reach the very highest peaks of erotic excitement, don't be coy, don't be shy. Show him what you're made of.

Time and time again, I've talked to women who have told me, "I wouldn't. *dream* of telling my husband that," or "You've always got to hold a little bit of yourself in reserve."

This nervousness about committing themselves wholeheartedly to their sexual relationships is what makes the love lives of so many women only 75 percent as exciting as they could be. They're always keeping a part of their sexual desire hidden. Because they're afraid of it. Because they think it's undignified. Because they think that it's dirty.

Sometimes they keep their true desires to themselves because they're afraid that their lovers will take advantage of them.

But let's look now at some of your secret sexual desires . . . and how some women have turned their fantasies into red-hot reality.

6

How to Make Your Sexual Fantasies Come True

Everybody has secret sexual desires which they are reluctant to confess even to their most intimate lovers. This is because we use our imagination as a way of stimulating ourselves sexually—and at the height of sexual arousal our fantasies can often be far more extreme than we are prepared to admit by the cold light of nonaroused day.

Many women keep their fantasies to themselves because they are afraid that their lovers will consider them perverted or bizarre or disgusting. Sometimes they themselves consider that their thoughts are perverted or bizarre or disgusting, and are ashamed of them.

Some women are afraid to tell their lovers about their secret sexual desires in case their lovers interpret their confession the wrong way—and think that they're complaining that they're not sexually satisfied. I've come across cases in which men have reacted angrily and even violently when the women in their lives have admitted having an erotic fantasy. In each case, the man's bewildered response was, "So my lovemaking hasn't been good enough for you, then? Why didn't you say so before?"

Men can be hypersensitive about their sexual performance. They think that they're always supposed to be perfect in bed and that they're supposed to know everything there is to know about sexual technique. In actual fact, good lovemaking has to be learned—by experience, by study, by clear and open communication between lovers. It takes years to make a good lover, but because of their macho attitudes most men refuse to believe that they don't know everything about sex. At a very early stage in their sexual development, they close their minds not only to plain and simple information about lovemaking skills, but to the needs of their lovers—both the obvious needs and the less obvious needs:

• Women need physical stimulation and regular climaxes in order to be sexually satisfied.
• They need affection, warmth, reassurance, security, and a sense of masculine strength.
• But they also need a sense of excitement—even a sense of sexual danger. They need creative and colorful sex—the sex of fantasy and romance.

If the man in your life is a routine and unexciting lover, he has forgotten that you too have strong erotic desires and your own erotic fantasies. Maybe he never really knew. So many men in long-term sexual relationships internalize their lovemaking and go to bed with their lovers in search of nothing more than the speedy release of their own physical tensions. They fuck, they go to sleep. They don't think for a moment that the women lying beside them are left unsatisfied, if not physically then emotionally. They don't think for a moment that they have shifted their lover's erotic imagination into top gear, and then left them with their wheels spinning.

Unfulfilled, frustrated, *misunderstood*.

If that sounds suspiciously like *your* love life—and believe me, there are many, many women who suffer the same frustration every day—then it's time for you to do something about it. You may argue that it's your lover's responsibility to make your sex life fulfilling. But if he *won't* do it or he *can't* do it, or if he simply doesn't understand what it is that needs doing and how it's going to be done, then it's time for you to take control.

You can do this discreetly, without making your lover feel that you've suddenly turned into a bossy, overbearing dominatrix (mind you, there are men who would *adore* a bossy, overbearing dominatrix!). You can guide your lovemaking in such a way that it satisfies *you*—while at the same time intensifying *his* pleasure.

The crux of the problem is that very few men are brought up to understand that sex is an emotional and imaginative adventure as well as a physical thrill. Of course men feel emotions as much as women. They fall in love. They feel rapture. They cry.

They have erotic imaginations, too. Many men are capable of reaching a sexual climax by thinking erotic thoughts alone, without even touching their penis.

But they do have difficulty in combining emotion, imagination, and physical stimulation into one explosive act—which, after all, is what good lovemaking is all about. And it's not surprising. Making love successfully is a damned sight harder than almost any human activity you can think of. At a Swedish seminar on sexual behavior, I once compared a man's role in sexual intercourse with learning to fly a helicopter in a hurricane with no instruction manual—a helicopter that would only fly if it was convinced that you adored it.

Fortunately, women are beginning to realize that *their* role in successful lovemaking is equally important—if not *more* important. Because of the nature of the sexes and because of the nature of the act of love, a sexually well-educated woman can do far more to improve an intimate relationship than a man can.

The sexual act is *penetrative*—in other words, the man's penis penetrates the woman's body—vaginally, orally, or anally. A woman's body cannot be penetrated without either permission or coercion. Since coercion (i.e. rape) is unlikely to lead to a close and satisfying relationship, the only way in which a man can happily make love to the woman in his life is with her implied or explicit permission and her active cooperation.

This is why your sexual responses and your sexual knowledge hold the key to a satisfying relationship. If you are always reluctant to have intercourse, unless cajoled—if you wrinkle your nose up at the thought of oral sex—if you totally reject the idea of anal penetration— then your love life will remain as routine and tedious as ever. One person's sexual responsiveness excites another person's sexual responsiveness. Your lover's sexual excitement will be very much greater and his penis will be very much harder if you show him that he is turning you on and that you *want* to make love.

All women have erotic fantasies but very few women will admit to it. I took part not long ago in a fascinating radio discussion about women's response to pornography. With the benefit of anonymity, woman after woman called the radio station and confessed to having graphic and extreme sexual fantasies. "Not just blurry, romantic fantasies about a perfect relationship." They also admitted that they had a tremendous interest in pornography, particularly written pornography in which the characters were realistic and involving. But they were interested in pictorial erotica, too. Their most frequent complaint: male pinups are never shown with erections, which was what they really wanted to see. "I would just like to have a long, hard look at a long, hard cock," said one girl of twenty-five. (One answer, of course, is for women to buy gay men's magazines, which clearly show men with hard penises . . . but gay men's magazines cannot readily be bought by women without difficulty and embarrassment.)

All of us have erotic fantasies which for one reason or another we are unable to fulfill. Sometimes these fantasies will be physically impossible (such as the woman who told me she wanted to be carried around the office while impaled on her boss's erect penis) or physically intolerable (such as the woman who fantasized about being fistfucked up to the elbow by a famous WWF wrestler). Sometimes we will know for sure that our partners would never consent to them. Quite often, it is better that many of our erotic fantasies remain fantasies—and that we accept them for what they are, which is simply an imaginative way of exciting ourselves. Again and again, women have told me about masochistic fantasies—about having their nipples pierced, or rings or diamond studs in their vaginal lips, or tattooes all over their bodies. One lovely young girl told me that she fantasized about having lighted cigarettes stubbed out on her anus. But these are sexual variations which are better unfulfilled. Dream about them, by all means. Tell your lover about them. But I very strongly advise that you shouldn't do anything in the heat of sexual excitement which will leave permanent marks or scars or disfigurement.

Many people—both men and women—have vivid and enduring sexual fantasies. They fantasize about performing sex in public . . . or being tied up . . . or wearing bizarre clothes . . . or making love to famous people.

Sometimes, sexual fantasies might seem frightening or
threatening. But they are all in the mind. Not only are
they completely harmless, they can often enhance your
sexual relationship and give it new life. Your mind is
your own, just as your body is your own, and if it pleases
and excites you to dream some extreme and dirty
dreams, then go ahead and enjoy them.

Here are three women who came to me because they
had overwhelmingly erotic fantasies and didn't know what to
do about them. They were embarrassed, ashamed, and
thought that they might be sexually perverted. In each
case, however, I was able to reassure them that their
fantasies were perfectly normal, perfectly acceptable, and
that they could actually use them as a basis for pepping
up their love lives.

"You can see right through their gowns"

This is Marion, thirty-two years old, blond, an
accountant from Schaumburg, Illinois: "I have variations
of the same erotic fantasy over and over. I arrive at a
party in a large, opulent mansion. There are scores of
young, handsome men around the place, all dressed in
tuxedos. There's music playing, strange music, and some
of the guests are dancing. I notice that some of the
women are wearing filmy evening gowns and that you
can see right through them—you can actually see their
nipples and their pubic hair. I can't stop looking at them.
How can they walk around showing everything like that?
But they don't seem to be self-conscious, they keep on
dancing.

"A manservant comes up to me carrying a black velvet
band on a silver tray. He says it's my blindfold. He tells
me that I have to put it on and follow him through to
the bedroom. I do what he says—not because I feel in-
timidated, but because I want to see what's going to happen next. Of course I *know* what's going to happen next,
because I've thought through this same fantasy over and
over. But I can still manage to think about something

new and unexpected, so there's always a tingle of anticipation.

"I put on the blindfold and I can't see anything at all. Actually, in my mind, I can see myself, and everything that's going on around me, but I think the idea of being completely blindfolded is very erotic. The thought that people are touching you and you don't know who they are. You don't know if they're ugly or handsome. You don't know if they're black or white. You don't even know if they're men or women.

"Anyway, the manservant takes me by the hand and leads me through to the bedroom. He sits me down on the edge of the bed and takes off my shoes. I can't see anything but I can feel fluffy carpet under my feet. Then suddenly, somebody else unzippers my dress at the back and somebody else unfastens my necklace. There must be at least three people in the room, maybe more. I can hear them breathing, I can feel them moving about. The manservant tells me to stand up, and I stand up. Then somebody else takes off my dress and helps me to pull it over my head. From the gentleness of her hands, it feels like a woman.

"Now I'm standing blindfolded in the bedroom wearing nothing but bra and panties and garter belt and stockings. Nobody touches me for a while; then I feel fingertips gently pinching my nipples through my bra. Somebody kisses my hair and strokes my back. Then somebody kisses my lips. It's definitely a man, I can feel his bristles. He licks all around my lips and my teeth, and then he thrusts his tongue right down my throat. Somebody else unfastens my bra, and my breasts are bare. I try to cover them up with my hands, but two more people gently take hold of my wrists so that I can't. Then I feel two people kissing and sucking my breasts, licking my nipples. One's a man and one's a woman; at least I think so.

"Then somebody's kissing my inner thighs, a third person. I can feel soft curly hair so I think that it must be a girl. She clamps her mouth over the crotch of my panties and breathes warm air into my pubic hair. Then she starts sucking my panties until they feel really wet, and slipping her tongue underneath the elastic and licking my pubic hair. After a while she pulls my panties to one side and starts licking my pussy. She sucks my clitoris and gently bites it . . . then she opens up my pussy-lips with her fingers and licks right inside.

"I'm getting very excited and turned-on by now. I can't see who's touching me. I can't see who's caressing me. I can feel a man standing behind me. I can feel his breath on my bare shoulders. I can feel his hard cock bobbing against my back. He reaches around and squeezes my breasts, while the man and the woman suck at my nipples.

"There must be five or six people around me, because suddenly I feel a man's hand cupping the cheeks of my bottom and dipping his finger into my pussy to make it slippery. The girl with the soft wavy hair keeps on licking my clitoris, while the man works his finger in a corkscrew motion up into my bottom . . . right up to the knuckle. The girl slides her finger inside my pussy, and she massages her finger up against the man's finger, right through the skin that seperates my bottom and my pussy.

"I'm getting so turned on now that I can scarcely stand up. But then I hear the bedsprings creaking. Two men must have stood up on the bed, because now they're touching and rubbing my face with their cocks. They roll them against my cheeks, and then they both push their cocks into my mouth, two cocks at once, I almost choke. One of them takes his cock out, but then the other pushes his cock right down my throat, so that his hairy balls are dangling against my chin, and I have to breathe through his pubic hair.

"All the time, the other man is still working his finger up my bottom, then another finger, then three fingers, churning my ass around and forcing himself deeper and deeper. The girl's licking my clitoris like a hysterical butterfly. Her tongue's whipping it up so that it's totally stiff.

"Then I can feel more men, two or three more, forcing their hard cocks in between my thighs and the tops of my stockings. One of them climaxes, and I feel his come sliding down my thigh, right inside my stocking. Then another one climaxes, and another.

"Then the man with his cock in my mouth climaxes, too, and comes right down my throat, and his friend climaxes over my face. I'm close to climaxing, too. My whole body feels as if it's being swept away on a huge warm tidal wave. I feel blind, helpless, wonderful.

"I start to shake with an orgasm. But as I do so, they whip the blindfold off my face, and I see for the first time that there's a whole crowd of people watching me—people who must have been watching me all the time. It's too late to stop myself climaxing. I stand there gasping and shuddering, my face and my body dripping with come, while they watch me and kiss each other and fondle each other, and I realize that I've been their entertainment. They've been watching me just to turn themselves on. They didn't care about me at all."

Literally scores of women have told me about fantasies that closely resemble Marion's. In each case, they have been naked in front of dozens of prurient eyes—either posing or masturbating or making love. It seems clear that many women have a strong element of exhibitionism in their sexual makeup, and that they are very aroused by the idea of showing themselves off sexually to an audience.

This doesn't mean that they would *really* enjoy it. It's just the idea of it that turns them on. But I talked to several girls who dance for a famous nude review in London, and they all told me that even after months of performing, they were still excited by the idea of men wanting to look at them dancing naked. "It gives you a funny feeling of power," said one of them. "But at the same time you feel like you're sort of a slave, too."

This is the whore/princess fantasy . . . actually quite a healthy combination of sexual domination and sexual submissiveness.

It's one of those fantasies that translates well into reality . . . one of those fantasies that are easily acted out and which can give your sex life a whole lot of extra excitement, with no emotional or physical risks.

Marion experienced her fantasy so frequently that she decided to try it for real. She asked her husband Ned to blindfold her and then to do whatever he wanted to her.

What she found most exciting was that (once she was blindfolded) Ned was far more uninhibited and passionate than he had ever been before. She put this down to

the fact that she was blindfolded and that she couldn't
see what he was doing, but it went a little deeper than
that. By suggesting an erotic game like "blindfold," she
had actually given Ned permission to indulge himself in
some of his *own* fantasies, and of course he took the
opportunity very readily.

As you will have noticed all the way through this book,
the importance of sexual permission comes up time and
time again. A woman's body is her own, and these days
there is far more awareness of her sexual integrity than
ever before. On the whole, men have always been much
more sexually cautious than you might think, and now
(with the legal specter of date rape and even marital rape
hanging over them) they are more sexually cautious than
ever. Even married men look to their partners to give
them the signals that will indicate how far they can go
. . . so if you really want to go wild in bed, you will have
to make sure that you give those signals loud and clear.

One Woman Will Take It in Her Mouth

A thirty-four-year-old realty saleswoman from Sacramento, California, wrote me a letter complaining that
her husband of thirteen years had never attempted oral
sex. I wrote back asking if she had made it clear to him
that she wanted it, and that if she hadn't, she should.
She wrote back two weeks later and declared herself
"satisfied . . . blissfully satisfied." All that had been necessary was the coquettish question, "Why don't you kiss
my pussy?"

All right . . . you expect men to be knowledgeable and
masterful in the bedroom. You expect them to pick you
up in your arms like Rhett Butler picking up Scarlett
O'Hara, sweep you up the staircase at Tara, fling you
down on the bed, and make passionate love to you. You
expect them to know when you want your breasts caressed. You expect them to understand when you want
to make love in the open air.

But the reality is that—most of the time—they *don't*
know. Every woman's sexual tastes and limitations are

different. One woman will happily and eagerly take her lover's penis in her mouth; another will do it only when she's finally feeling happy and excited; another can't do it at all. One woman will enthusiastically accept her lover's penis in her anus; while others will find it almost impossible. A woman's sexual tastes depend on her personality, her upbringing, and her previous sexual experiences (particularly her very first sexual experiences). The only way that her lover is going to be able to discover her tastes is if she tells him . . . or at the very least gives him explicit indications of what she is prepared to do.

The women who get the most exciting sex—the women who don't go to sleep feeling frustrated and short-changed—are the women who actively show their lovers what they want, and who are prepared to be a little more daring.

Safe sex is nothing to be scared of. The very worst that can happen is that you feel a little sore the next morning. If you're truly close to the man you love, you will be prepared to try anything and everything—at least once, anyway. After all, if you don't like it, you don't have to do it again.

Marion said, "Once I'd been blindfolded, Ned caressed me through my clothes . . . feeling my breasts through my dress. He kissed me and ran his fingers through my hair in a way that he hadn't done for a long time. He was really eager, really romantic, the way he used to be when we first dated. He unbuttoned my blouse and spent a long time massaging my breasts through my bra. I'd forgotten how sexy that could be. It was just like heavy petting at high school. I suddenly found that my pantyhose were wet and that Ned was turning me on.

"He took off my blouse and at last he unfastened my bra. I couldn't see anything at all, not even a chink of light. It's amazing how intense your sense of touch becomes when you can't see anything, how erotic it is. I like making love with the light on, you know, but sometimes it's more intense in the dark, when it's just feelings. I guess it makes it a little more mysterious in the dark, and maybe mystery turns me on.

"He lay me back on the bed and he kissed my breasts,

and for the first time in a long time he took my nipples deep into his mouth and rolled them against the roof of his mouth with his tongue, and he was gently sucking them at the same time. Then I heard him take off his clothes. I couldn't be sure that he was completely naked, but I heard the rustling. He sat astride me on the bed, I could feel his hairy thighs on either side of me. Then he massaged his cock against my nipples; I could feel his wetness, and I could feel his hairy balls on my breasts. He squeezed my breasts together with his hard cock in between them, and slowly fucked my cleavage. Then he lifted himself higher up and touched his cock against my lips. I tried to catch it with the tip of my tongue, tried to lick it, tried to suck it, but he kept bobbing it out of my reach.

"He massaged my cheeks and my neck with his cock. He had never done anything like that before. I grasped his cock for a moment and squeezed it, but then he went further down the bed, kissing my breasts again, kissing my stomach. He unfastened my skirt and tugged it off me. Then he rolled down my pantyhose. He kissed the inside of my thighs, just like the girl in my fantasy. Then he kissed and licked my pussy . . . not the way that I'd imagined it, but big, broad strokes of his tongue.

"I had never reached a climax so quickly. I mean, one minute I was thinking 'this is great, Ned's really doing what he wants to do.' The next minute, it hit me, and I was literally screaming out loud with an orgasm.

"What I'll never forget is, Ned fucked me then and there, right then and there; he didn't even wait for me to finish my orgasm. I was jumping and shaking on that bed like you couldn't believe, and he was pushing his cock into me, fucking me hard. He had never fucked me like that before, not like he really meant it, but that night he meant it, he was fucking me like a whore, like somebody who was blind, like somebody fantastic, like somebody really sexy who he couldn't get enough of. I wanted it to go on forever. I had another orgasm and then another and then another. They were like a drum-roll, like an earthquake, they wouldn't stop. Then Ned climaxed, too; he shouted out, and that was the finish of it. He took off my blindfold and we lay side by side and just looked at each other and kissed and grinned, like a couple of cats who had gotten the cream.

"Acting out that fantasy had liberated both of us, sexually. It had really set us free. Ned would never have made love to me like that if I hadn't asked him to blindfold me, and I never would have known what it was like to have a multiple orgasm. I mean, I had *five*!—at least I think it was five.

"It was really difficult for me to suggest that we act out my fantasy. But when we did, it made me realize that there was a whole new dimension to our sex lives which we hadn't even begun to explore . . . and which we wouldn't have explored, if I hadn't suggested it. My advice to any woman who's keeping a secret sexy thought in her head is to try acting it out, as far as she's able."

Marion was talking good sense. Just because sex is an intimate and private activity, that doesn't mean that it has to be a *secret* activity—at least, not between the two people involved. Making love well is more difficult than, say, playing golf well—and yet how often do you see a man checking his watch and telling his office colleagues, "I have to cut this meeting short. I have to get home and put in some lovemaking practice"?

It's Time for Sex Without Guilt

It's time that we all grew up, as far as sex is concerned. It's time that we were well-educated about sexual techniques and sexual variations and contraception, as well as how to protect ourselves against sexually communicated diseases, especially AIDS. It's time we realized that sex is exciting, stunning, and the very best way of telling the people we love that we love them. It's time that we taught our children about recreational sex as well as sex for the sake of having babies.

It's time that we enjoyed sex without guilt. Time that we let our fantasies loose, and our imaginations go wild. It's time that we realized that *nothing* two loving people do together can be dirty or bizarre, no matter how much we personally may not want to do it.

Let me give you an example—from Linda, twenty-four, a library assistant from Darien, Connecticut. Linda wrote to me five times before she finally came out with what was troubling her. It was a fantasy—a fantasy on which she had elaborated night after night, week after week, year after year. She prefaced her letter by saying that it was "gross." But it turned her on, and she had to tell somebody about it, if only to be reassured that she wasn't perverted.

"I've had this fantasy in various different forms ever since I was fifteen or sixteen years old. It was then that I was walking in the woods near my home when I came across a boy pissing up against a tree. He hadn't seen me. He wasn't doing it to shock anybody. He was simply standing in the sunlight pissing against a tree. I could see his cock in his hand, I could see the piss coming out. I watched him until he'd finished, and then he walked away.

"I had dreams and fantasies about it for weeks afterwards. Then about a year later I saw a photograph in a magazine of a baseball team in their locker room, changing. Some of the men were bare-chested and some of them wore nothing but shorts. Somehow I got the two images all mixed up in my mind.

"I started to fantasize that I was the cleaner for a baseball team, I had to scrub out their locker room and clean out their baths and their toilets, but I had to do it naked. I kept imagining myself on my hands and knees, totally nude, scrubbing the floor, while they all came in from their baseball game, sweaty and dirty and swearing, and took off their clothes, too.

"They would all be really handsome, with dark hairy chests, and they'd all stand around me while I scrubbed the floor of their toilet. Then one of them would hold his cock in his hand and start pissing on the floor in front of me. When I tried to complain, he would piss all over my hands. Then the rest of the team would piss on me, too, all these men pissing all over my hair and my face and my back, and two or three of them would stand behind me and piss up between my legs.

"I would be dripping with hot piss. My hair would be soaked, piss would be dripping from my nipples. I would

feel so humiliated, like an animal. But if you can understand me, it would be fantasy piss, not real.

"They would all take hold of me, six or seven men,
and turn me over onto the toilet floor. They would all
have hard-ons. Two of them would open my legs up
wide, and I would be so frightened that I would piss too,
right up in the air, all over myself, and one of the baseball players would smear his hand between my legs and
then massage my breasts and my stomach, so that I was
all wet and slippery.

"Then they would all kneel down between my legs,
one by one, and fuck me. They would all be swearing
and saying filthy things to me. No point in trying to protest, and in any case it was all a fantasy and I loved it.
The floor would be swimming in urine and all my hair
would be spread out in it. I would rub it on my face and
on my breasts, and all the time the team would be fucking me, one after the other."

I wrote back to Linda and reassured her that sexual
fantasies involving urination were extremely common and
nothing to be ashamed of. As sexual expression has become more liberated, I have noticed an increasing tendency for sex videos and sex magazines and even
mainstream romantic novels to feature what we call "wet
sex."

Urination is very closely linked to sexual display, and
for couples to urinate openly in front of each other can
be a very liberating experience. Childish, perhaps. But
almost all of us are "childish" when it comes to sex, and
any experience that frees us from shame about our bodies
and our bodily functions is welcome.

The fresh urine of a healthy person is completely sterile and harmless, and it appears from the letters I receive
that there is an increasing interest in "wet sex" as a prelude to lovemaking. A new brochure from one of Eu-
rope's biggest suppliers of erotic videos shows that over
half of their features include urination. "Black sex god-
dess Jeannie in leather and studs takes a golden shower
and gets a mouthful of come." "Robert and Carol pee
on each other as a prelude to anal sex." "Laura stretches
her pussy wide with a speculum and pees on the floor."
"Mistress pees on the slave's cock." "Big-breasted Suzie

likes to decorate in the nude. She gets dirty with the paint roller then pees in a bucket." "Lottie and Inga fist-fuck themselves. Max arrives and pisses on their breasts and comes on their faces."

Of course these are quite extreme sexual acts which are performed in front of the camera in order to excite an audience . . . which is not the way that most of make love. But a very high percentage of prostitutes find it profitable to offer "golden rain" as part of their sexual services. And I have received numerous letters from ordinary men and women who find wet sex exciting. The reason they find it exciting is because it is a "forbidden" act, even though it is completely harmless. But many of them also find that it brings them a fresh physical intimacy with their lover, and—as one thirty-two-year-old woman described it—"a feeling that, at last, I could do absolutely anything I wanted . . . that I was totally free of embarrassment about myself, forever."

Linda contacted me after some weeks and said that she had realized her fantasy for the first time. "It was frightening and exciting both at the same time," she said. "Once you'd explained to me that my feelings weren't perverted or weird, I decided to express them for real.

"I first 'let myself go' when my husband Jack was on a fishing trip with his friends and I had the whole of Saturday to myself. I lay in bed idly masturbating and thinking about my baseball-team fantasy. Then I went to the bathroom, took off my pajamas and climbed naked into the empty tub. It was a very hot day so I didn't freeze!

"I lay back in the tub, stroking my breasts with one hand and gently massaging my clitoris with the other. I kept thinking about my fantasy over and over. I have to admit that my heart was fluttering. Then, when I was getting close to my orgasm, I let myself go, and I just peed. It was incredible. I had never known that if a woman pees lying on her back, how high up into the air it goes. I opened my cunt wide with my fingers and I could watch it gushing out of me, which was something I had never seen before. It splashed all over my stomach and my breasts, and I lay back in the bath and massaged myself with it. I had a strange orgasm, a very gentle kind of rippling sensation, and more pee spurted out. Then I just turned on the shower fixture and washed myself.

"At first I felt ashamed, and I promised myself that I would never do it again. By the time Jack came home that evening, however, I had mostly gotten over my shame, my feeling that I was a 'dirty girl,' which I think was more because I had masturbated than the way in which I had done it, if you understand me. Jack would have been pretty upset if he had known that I had masturbated. He would have said, 'I'm here any time you want me, why do you have to masturbate?'

"Anyway, that night, when we were getting ready for bed, I came into the bathroom wearing nothing but my pajama top and sat down on the john right in front of Jack. He looked surprised but he didn't say anything. I said to him, 'Come here, give me a kiss,' which he did. My heart was beating about a thousand to the minute! I reached into his pajama pants and took hold of his cock and stroked it until it was stiff and came right out of his pants. I don't think even then that he realized what I was going to do.

"I kissed his cock and licked and sucked the end of it. We were both into oral sex, I mean that side of our sexual relationship was very open and intimate. Jack said, 'You're feeling sexy tonight.' It was then that I started to pee. I opened up my legs wide and I took hold of Jack's hand and drew it down to my cunt, so that I was peeing all over his fingers. I think he was shocked at first, but his cock went even harder, and I could tell that he was turned on, too. He said, 'What's this?' but I just kissed him and said 'Go ahead, enjoy it, and why don't you do it, too?'

"He said, 'What?' and I said 'Piss, let me see you piss, too.' I held his cock and he started to piss, but because he was so stiff he could only piss it out in jets, you know, one jet at a time. I aimed his cock between my legs and he pissed onto my cunt. The very first time you feel your man doing that to you, it's amazing. It's blissful. You feel these warm jets right between your legs, on your clitoris, on your cunt, he even pissed on my asshole, too.

"I lifted his cock and he pissed over my pajama top; by then he couldn't stop himself. Then I aimed his cock to my mouth, and he pissed onto my tongue and between my teeth. I didn't swallow any, I just let it run down my chin. It didn't taste of anything much, just bitter-sweet.

"After that, we were both so excited we got right on the bathroom rug and we fucked until we were both screaming. We kissed and clawed each other and I hadn't known any kind of ecstasy like that since before we were married. I mean we were going at each other like wild beasts. In the end, Jack was kneeling upright on the rug and pumping me up and down his cock, and I was climaxing over and over, I wanted him to stop and put me down, but he wouldn't. We finished up lying on the bathroom floor, totally exhausted.

"You know what it did, though? It brought back that hot, excited feeling that we'd forgotten about. That sexual hunger you get when you first fall in love . . . when you can't get enough, you think you'd like to eat your lover alive."

Does Linda still have her baseball-team fantasy? "Unhuh. Now if I have any pissing fantasies at all, I have a fantasy about Jack. I guess that's the way it should be, too. We don't do wet sex that often, only when we're feeling kind of playful. But it's like the very last barrier came down between us, we're two people who can do *anything* in front of each other, and enjoy it.

"I'm a woman . . . I can show myself off"

"I also learned that I'm a woman, and that the way I pee is nothing secret or shameful. I can do it openly, the same way a man does. I can show myself off. I'm not just 'wetting the ground,' the way some chauvinistic writer described it.

"About a month ago we spent a weekend up in the mountains. We went for a long walk, and on the way back I needed a pee. Instead of waiting until we got back to the hotel, or going behind a tree, the way I would have done before, I lifted my skirt and said to Jack, 'Put your hand in here.' He slipped his hand into the front of my panties, and I deliberately wet myself. While I was peeing, he slipped his finger into my cunt and massaged me, and that was so sexy I felt like standing there forever, in the woods, with wet panties and my husband's finger right up me."

There is a whole book to be written about wet sex. Most sex writers (if they mention it at all) sniffily describe it as a "perversion," but the simple fact is that urination for sexual pleasure is no more perverted or dangerous or unusual than oral sex or anal sex, and it is certainly a great deal less perverted than sex which involves violence or coercion or the infliction of pain. Women and men are equally fascinated by sexual urination, and it strikes me as far wiser to give sensible advice about it than to condemn it.

If you are interested in a wet sex session, cut down on rich foods for a couple of days, if possible, and drink plenty of mineral water. This will cleanse and freshen the system, and make your urine less pungent and acidic.

There is no harm in swallowing a small amount of fresh urine. Plenty of explorers have survived in arduous conditions by drinking their own urine. But avoid drinking too much, and *never* drink the urine of somebo'y whose HIV status is unknown to you.

Above all, wet sex should be playful and fun and exciting. It is often associated with other "forbidden" sexual fascinations, such as rubberwear and bondage and enemas. But the sooner couples are able to talk about such fascinations openly, the sooner they will lose their stigma of being "perverse." Everybody has different sexual tastes and different sexual fantasies, and they are no more perverse than different tastes in music or food or comedy or any other kind of human stimulation.

A thirty-three-year-old wife from Omaha, Nebraska, wrote me a desperate letter because her husband had asked her to sit astride him and pee on his genitals before they made love. You would have thought from the tone of her letter that he had asked her to murder somebody. I had to write back and ask her, "Where's the harm? If he wants you to pee on his genitals, then why not do it? It only shows that he loves you and that you excite him and that he wants to try something a little new."

There is no rule-book which defines "normal sex."

There is no moral law which says that oral sex or anal sex or wet sex or any other kind of sex is wrong or perverted. The only kind of sex which *is* undeniably wrong is the kind of sex in which one person's sexual tastes are imposed on another person against their will, or sexual activities which cause unacceptable pain or permanent physical damage or the transmission of any sexual disease—from gonorrhea to HIV.

In my opinion, sex has become far too political. As we approach the millenium, this is the age when men and women should stop arguing about each other's "self-esteem" and do their best to harmonize closely. In other words, they should stop squabbling and striking politically correct poses, and learn to address each other's physical and emotional needs. This should be an age of sexual openness—not the openness of hopeful naivete, like the so-called "free love" of the 1960s; nor the hedonistic self-indulgence of the 1970s, which eventually led to the rapid worldwide spread of the AIDS virus. This is an age when we should take the trouble to learn all about our bodies and our sexual responses, to understand the needs and desires and fantasies not only of our lovers but of *ourselves*. This is an age in which we should become sexual experts. The end result can only be happiness and sexual satisfaction.

Sexual expertise is not the same as sexual license. Sexual expertise is the means by which couples can learn to make the very best of their existing relationships, rather than seeking new thrills in somebody else's bed. Sexual expertise means being a little more daring—dressing up a little more sexily from time to time, being flirtatious, trying out some of your favorite fantasies, trying out some of *his* favorite fantasies.

Sexual expertise means swallowing your inhibitions and learning to love like a real lover. Sexual expertise means opening yourself up—your fantasies, your desires, your dreams, your whole body. Self-respect is in. Self-respect has *always* been in. Feminine integrity is in, too. But what is most definitely *out* is coyness, shyness, reserve, and prudery.

Almost all of the sexual problems that I am asked to resolve (and these amount to several hundred every year) have to do with sexual inexperience and sexual reserve: "My wife won't . . ." "My husband never . . ." "I thought my lover knew all about sex but . . ."

I have had scores of letters from long-married couples who have only just realized after twenty or thirty years that oral sex wasn't disgusting or taboo. I have had scores of letters from men and women with vivid sexual fantasies which they haven't had the courage to describe to their lovers. Most poignantly of all, I still receive letters from women who have *never* experienced orgasm after years of marriage or living with a man, and who ask me to tell them "what it's like" and "whether it's necessary."

The key to driving your man wild in bed is driving *yourself* wild in bed. Do what *you* want to do—you're not a whore, or a slave, except if you choose to play the part of a whore or a slave. Your excitement will excite him.

Now let's take a look at some more fantasies.

Chapter 7

Even More Erotic Fantasies (And How to Make Them Come True)

Many women have erotic fantasies in which they are raped, tied up, beaten, and otherwise sexually humiliated. Although these fantasies sound like strong sexual meat when they are described in black and white, they are quite common and perfectly normal—even for women who are self-possessed, strong-willed and independent-minded.

The idea of being forced to submit to the sexual pleasures of a ruthless man is a very powerful mental aphrodisiac for many women. You have only to read "bodice-ripping" historical fiction, slavery, and harem novels, and to see movies like *9½ Weeks* to realize what a common female fantasy this is.

However—if you are aroused by masochistic fantasies, that doesn't mean for a moment that you are truly masochistic, or that you are anything other than a smart, imaginative, independent lady. It simply means that you are conjuring up harmless erotic images for your own excitement, and that you respond to exactly the same kind of sexual stimuli as millions and millions of other women.

You may be interested to know that a high proportion of *men* have erotic fantasies not about rape or pillage or having their wicked way with vainly protesting women. Quite the opposite. They daydream of being tied up and whipped and humiliated by a cruel and unforgiving dominatrix. Monique von Cleef, one of the most successful prostitutes I ever knew, told me that the men who came most regularly to her house in the Hague for masochistic sexual services were captains of industry, police chiefs, and politicians.

The fantasy of being sexually helpless is a very potent stimulus for all of us—both men and women. It is recreational as well as highly erotic.

But there is a great deal of difference between erotic fantasy and erotic reality. In a sexual fantasy, you can of course perform all kinds of bizarre sexual acts without the risk of injury, infection, embarrassment, pain or emotional involvement. Probably one of the greatest sexual fantasies of all time was Pauline Reage's novel *The Story of O* in which a girl is systematically whipped, chained and branded and sexually humiliated. Her vaginal lips are pierced, she is forced to have oral sex with whoever her master commands, and her anus is trained with successively larger dildos until she can accommodate a man's erect penis without difficulty.

I asked a number of women to read *The Story of O* and tell me what they thought of it. In spite of the fact that its heroine is treated as a sex object, without even a name, almost 90 percent of them said they found the story "highly erotic" and a "major turn-on." Many of them confessed to having very similar fantasies of their own.

This reaction was further evidence that women are perfectly capable of distinguishing between sexual fact and sexual fantasy. Not one woman said that she would have enjoyed in real life any of the humiliations to which O was subjected, but they found it arousing and entertaining to fantasize about them.

If you are tempted to turn your erotic fantasies into reality, then you should think very carefully about the considerable difference between imaginary turn-ons and real turn-ons. Whipping and handcuffing and nipple-piercing might be erotic to think about, but in reality they are extremely painful and potentially dangerous.

Before you think about dabbling in bondage or masochistic sex, you should ask yourself one serious question: do I really know and trust my lover?

If you don't know the man in your life very well, or if you have any suspicions at all about his temperament or his sense of responsibility, I advise you very strongly not to admit to him that you have any masochistic fantasies—and not to try any sexual games involving tying up, hand-cuffing—or anything else which might lead to you being left helpless. While bondage can be very exciting, it is always better to be safe than sorry. If you don't happen to like the way that a sexual encounter is turning out, you should always be able to vote with your feet—which you certainly won't be able to do if your ankles are lashed to the bedposts.

No matter how extreme your fantasies may be, always make sure that you are physically and mentally prepared for what might happen if you bring them to life and never be afraid to say "stop, that's enough." At the risk of repeating myself from previous books, I advise that you always observe the rules of bondage religiously.

1. However realistically played out, both partners must consent to bondage.
2. Never fasten anything around the neck.
3. Never restrict breathing.
4. Never leave a tied-up person on their own.
5. Never play bondage games unless you are totally sober.
6. Agree beforehand to an instant release signal which must always be honored without hesitation.
7. I would add my own rule, which is that you should never play bondage games unless you are completely satisfied that you know your partner very, very well, and that you can trust him (or her) implicitly.

And remember, you should never attempt any kind of self-bondage. As a clinical psychiatrist wrote: "A woman may get harmless pleasure from being blindfolded, tied to the bed and tantalizingly masturbated, but for her to subject herself alone to restricting bonds, to the application of painful stimuli to her body, or to devise some apparatus that restricts her breathing, is highly dangerous."

But—having mentioned the cautionary side of bondage fantasies, they do have their exciting side, too. Greta, a twenty-three-year-old flight attendant from Denver, Col-

orado, told me that one of her most arousing fantasies
was that she woke up in a strange city to find that there
were two masked, naked men in her hotel room.

"They are both very tall and very muscular. They have
superb well-developed chests and broad shoulders and
very narrow hips. Both of them have huge hard-ons, so
big that I think they must have been exercising their
cocks, too. Their balls are as big as oranges. But they
both wear black masks that completely cover their faces
except for their eyes, and neither of them says a single
word.

"That's one of the things that turns me on. They're
totally silent and expressionless, so I can never tell if
they're excited or not. They're ciphers, really—muscular
men's bodies and huge hard-ons with no real personality
at all. Kind of like a Chippendales performance going on
inside of your head.

"Before I can do anything or say anything, one of them
grabs my feet and the other one grabs my hands. They
pull my legs apart and strap my ankles to the end of the
bed, then they strap my wrists to the head of the bed.
One of them tears off my nightdress with his bare hands.

"For some reason, I don't scream out for help. Maybe
that's because I sense that they want to have their way
with me, but they don't actually mean to hurt me. One
of them climbs onto the bed and kneels over my face.
He seizes hold of my hair in case I try to turn away.
Then he massages his huge hard-on all over my face.
Then he forces his balls into my mouth, so that I'm practically choking. I suck and lick his balls, and then he
pushes his cock into my mouth and starts to move up
and down, in a very controlled muscular way, very slowly
sliding his cock in and out of my lips.

"He thrusts his cock really deep into my throat, so
that his balls keep bouncing against my chin. When he's
pushing his cock in deep, I feel as if his cock has blocked
out the whole world. I begin to get tremendously
aroused, and I start to suck his cock and roll my tongue
around it.

"Meanwhile the other guy has been kissing and squeezing my breasts and sucking at my nipples. After a while
he works his way down and starts kissing my hips where

I'm really sensitive, and the insides of my thighs, too. Then he licks and kisses my pussy, and starts doing that thing that I always love, which is when a man gently sucks the whole of the flesh of my pussy into his mouth, and flicks my clit with the tip of his tongue at the same time. I start to get seriously aroused, even though I don't know either of these men, and they won't talk to me, and for all I know they're all ugly and pockmarked underneath their masks.

"After he's licked and sucked me, the second guy opens my pussy with his fingers and pushes his cock into me. He's huge, really huge. I've never had a cock so big before. If the other guy's cock wasn't halfway down my throat, I would probably scream. He supports himself by holding on to the other guy's shoulders, and then he starts to fuck me in the same slow pumping-iron kind of way. I keep wanting him to push himself into me harder, and faster, but he won't. He just keeps sliding this massive cock in and out of me, right out of me every time, so that I can feel all the wetness, and the head of his cock rubs against my pussy lips every time, and each time I get a pang of panic that he might not push it back inside me again.

"Then gradually their rhythm builds up faster and faster. They work together, the two of them, the same rhythm. And still they don't say anything. I'm going crazy by now, straining at my straps. I have an orgasm and then another orgasm but they don't care, they just keep on pumping. Then at last they climax, both together. One of them fills my pussy up with sperm, the other one fills up my mouth. A mouthful of fantasy sperm is always better than a mouthful of real sperm, because real sperm always takes quite a lot of swallowing, you seem to be swallowing it and swallowing it and tasting it in your mouth for ages afterward, whereas fantasy sperm is warm and smooth and tastes like eggnog."

There are several interesting aspects in Greta's fantasy. It is, of course, a masochistic bondage fantasy, but not a very extreme one, and well within the parameters of normal, pleasurable sex play. Although technically Greta's fantasy was about being raped, the unpleasant elements of real rape were completely lacking. The men were forcible without being violent. They caused her no physical harm, and she "sensed" that they weren't going to hurt her. In fact she didn't scream, she didn't put up any show of resistance, and she was very quickly aroused.

The men's anonymity is a very interesting factor. They didn't speak, their faces were masked. In fact they were little more than human sex machines. This anonymity indicated that Greta was largely satisfied with her relationship with her husband, and wasn't seeking a romantic affair, or a man who would offer her any kind of emotional entanglement. She was simply aroused by the idea of being sexually stimulated while she was completely helpless.

Helpless she might have been, but her imagination made everything else in this whole scenario quite acceptable. To be strapped to a bed and sexually assaulted by two masked men in a strange hotel room would (in reality) be a nightmare rather than a fantasy. But these men were obviously clean, skilled and talented lovers, and even if there was a slight hint of danger (maybe, behind their masks, they were *ugly*!) they were never *revealed* as ugly, and this was nothing more than a way of giving herself an extra erotic *frisson*.

She even changed the taste and consistency of semen to suit her fantasy.

This was especially fascinating, since over the years I have received scores of letters from women who say that they would love to practice oral sex on their lovers, and that they would adore it if their lovers climaxed in their mouths, but they wouldn't or couldn't do it because they simply didn't like the taste and/or the consistency of semen.

Some women love it, and say that they can't get enough of it. A nineteen-year-old newlywed from Pasadena, California, said that she liked her husband's sperm so much that she would lie awake after they had made love, dipping her fingers into her vagina and licking them. "And I always give him head when he wakes up in the morning, so that I can taste his come in my mouth for the rest of the day." A twenty-six-year-old from White Plains, New York, said that she occasionally masturbated her boyfriend while he was watching baseball on TV, and collected his sperm in a champagne glass, which she would then slowly drink while she masturbated herself. "I love it . . . I love the way it slides down your throat."

But on the whole, these women are exceptions. Although most women are highly aroused by the appearance and the feel and the smell of sperm, not very many of them particularly enjoy swallowing it—although they will occasionally do so in a state of high sexual excitement, or to please and satisfy their lovers.

It Doesn't Make Your Breasts Grow Bigger

You can acquire a taste for semen, just as you can acquire a taste for oysters, and there's no harm in trying. Semen is nothing more than a mixture of fructose, which is a simple sugar, a number of enzymes, bicarbonates and phosphates and high concentrations of vitamin C. Perhaps if you swallowed enough of it you could stop yourself catching colds! Contrary to popular myth, however, semen doesn't make your breasts grow bigger or make you put on weight. The only time that it may be wise to avoid swallowing it on health grounds is when you're heavily pregnant, since sperm is suspected to contain chemicals which could have the effect of triggering labor.

But it's about time that the writers of sexual "how-to" books acknowledge that the majority of women—even if they like fellating their lovers—are not great lovers of semen, and that many more women would perform oral sex much more readily if they knew that there was little or no risk of their partner ejaculating in their mouth.

Dr. Eric J. Trimmer, medical editor-in-chief of *The Visual Dictionary of Sex,* says nothing more enlightening than "semen ejaculated into the mouth or even swallowed is harmless: it has a faintly salty, pungent taste." *The Encyclopaedia of Love & Sex* says "The woman faces the additional problem of the man's ejaculation.

The amount of liquid that this involves is usually wildly overestimated because a little liquid spilled manages to spread itself over an unbelievably wide area, making it seem much more than it really is. How much semen the man will ejaculate depends on how long it is since his last orgasm, but a rough guide would be a teaspoonful. And swallowing it will certainly not poison anyone, despite what old wives' tales say. Taste, of course, is another matter. (A woman) may notice a mild, slightly salty flavor, and some women find that semen stings the back of the throat a little as it is swallowed."

I can't say that a woman has ever complained to me about semen stinging the back of her throat. But Marilyn Chambers, star of the 1960s porno epic *Behind the Green Door,* once remarked that the longer she kept a load of ejaculated semen in her mouth, the chewier it became, almost like gum.

My old friend Xaviera Hollander, the famous Happy Hooker, had her own idiosyncratic way of describing semen. Recounting a sex session with a young virgin named Phil, she said: "I proceeded to slide my lips over his huge penis until I reached its base. I could feel his balls literally vibrating and seem to grow in my mouth and my hands. Phil began to moan. My baby was so turned on both emotionally and physically that he couldn't contain his passion any longer—and now I was experiencing the jism shooting out of his cock into my mouth. It was warm and plentiful. I half-swallowed it and half-dribbled it onto his belly. It was thick and virile and certainly looked fertile enough to produce many babies. I hadn't seen sperm like that, so thick, in a long time. It was the first semen from a virgin boy into the mouth of a woman. It almost reminded me of yogurt."

So . . . if you can imagine a brand of salty, pungent, stinging, chewy yogurt . . . !

Quite a number of women find that they acquire a taste for semen (or at least a greater tolerance of it) when they become more adept at oral sex. There is a physiological reason for this. As they become more experienced and more confident at fellatio, they become more sexually aroused when they are doing it. Contrary to popular misconception, people who are highly sexually aroused are actually less alert to sensory impressions than people who are not so stimulated. As we near orgasm, all of our sensations are concentrated deep within our nervous system, and our ordinary senses tend to fade. The pupils of our eyes dilate and we can see only straight ahead of us. Hearing falls away. Our senses of smell and taste are considerably diminished—so when a highly aroused woman *does* swallow her lover's semen, she will be less likely to taste it than when she was not so excited. Nor will she be so conscious of its sticky consistency.

The loss of sensation during the period of maximum sexual arousal also releases psychological blockages in the nervous system. People who normally stutter find that—during sexual arousal—they lose their speech impediment. Similarly, women who normally gag when anything is thrust deep into their mouths—even women who find it difficult to swallow a small pill—are capable of taking a fully erect penis right into their throat. (They also find anal penetration much easier.)

Time and time again, I find that the problem with oral sex is rooted in just one clumsy sexual act by a woman's present or former lover. Of course oral sex is highly arousing for a man, but men should remember that women are not so quickly stimulated. To have an erect penis pointed at their mouth like a loaded .38 when they have not yet been tickled and kissed and gently turned on is, for many women, both off-putting and even threatening.

Read My Lips: No More Forcible Oral Sex

Worst of all, many men hold their partners' heads when they climax, making it impossible for the women not to take their full ejaculation down their throats. Such clumsy lovers should be force-fed a quart of yogurt twice a day for a month, because they are not only behaving crudely and insensitively, they are probably destroying the woman's enjoyment of oral sex forever. Read my lips: no more forcible oral sex. Just one deeply upsetting experience with any sexual act can make a woman inhibited for the rest of her life. So men, remember—all sexual acts, from the simplest to the most extreme, should always be performed with as much skill and care and imagination as you can muster.

And when I say imagination, I mean: although your thoughts are very much concentrated on your own sexual excitement, try to put yourself in your lover's place. She's a woman: arouse her gradually, arouse her gently, take her up on a magic carpet. The Apollo rocket can come later, when she's really turned-on.

For women who enjoy oral sex but who don't enjoy swallowing, the solution is very simple . . . and often it gives their lovers just as much excitement . . . if not *more* excitement, because it's obviously much more visual. When your man is close to climaxing, take his penis out of your mouth and aim his ejaculation over your face or your neck or your breasts. You can actually let it spurt onto your lips without having to swallow any of it.

Carole, twenty-three, a jewelry artist from Sante Fe, New Mexico, said: "I've never shied away from giving my husband head, but I have to admit that swallowing sperm is something that I find pretty difficult. I have done it two or three times, but only when I've been very aroused. I'm one of these people who can't even swallow a Tylenol without gagging!

"I found that the answer was to take my husband's cock out of my mouth just before he climaxed—or just when he started to climax. I can almost always tell when he's just about to come, and even if he isn't, it doesn't take more than a few rubs with my hand to bring him off. Then I point his cock at my nipples, and let him climax all over my breasts. I massage his cock around and around, until my breasts are smothered in sperm. *I* enjoy it, he loves it, and we're both happy."

Having digressed for a moment to discuss one of the more critical aspects of oral sex, let's get back to Greta, and how she made her masked-men fantasy come to life.

"I wanted to get that same feeling of helplessness," she said. "But of course I didn't really want to be fucked by two strange men. The odd thing about most of my fantasies—even the fantasies in which I'm being fucked by six or seven men, or even more—is that *all* the men are Richard, my husband. I guess I should have married sextuplets, right?

"But when you suggested a way of acting this fantasy out, it worked really well. In fact it was incredibly exciting and satisfying, and that little extra touch with the hairbrush made it a terrific turn-on for Richard, too. In fact, I think that made it for him."

When Greta first told me about her fantasy, it occurred to me that the bondage element of her fantasy was not deeply masochistic. In other words, she didn't feel the need to be trussed up so tightly that she was totally unable to move. She wasn't looking for humiliation. All she really needed was to feel that she was helpless and unable to escape, so that she didn't have to take any of the responsibility for what happened to her next. This is a very common sexual feeling amongst both men and women, particularly if they are embarrassed or slightly ashamed about their sexual tastes. Once they are strapped to the bed, or tied up with rope, they can thrill to the pleasure of being tickled or massaged or masturbated or mildly abused, without feeling the slightest bit guilty about it.

And even the straightest and most conventional of men—once he is confronted with the opportunity of doing whatever he wants to a "helpless" woman—will rarely pass up the chance of being a little more sexually inventive. *She* will shed her inhibitions because (once she's tied up) she is no longer responsible for what happens to her. *He* will be more adventurous because he will feel that—if she has willingly submitted to bondage, if she has *allowed* him to touch her and feel her and excite her in any way he chooses, then she must be agreeable to almost anything.

The crux of Greta's fantasy—the element that made it really arousing for her—was the men's total silence and anonymity, their masked faces, their refusal to speak. Also, the fact that they were completely naked, too, so that they were threatening and vulnerable at the same time.

"It took me a long time to get around to explaining my fantasy to Richard, but eventually I managed it. His reaction was quite different from what I'd imagined it would be. He wasn't shocked; but to begin with, he didn't seem particularly excited, either. He just nodded and said, 'Okay . . . if that's what you want to do.'

"He didn't say anything more about it for a couple of days, but then one Wednesday evening, when I was sitting up in bed watching TV, he suddenly came into the room totally naked, except for this black leather mask. It covered his whole head, except for his eyes, and it had zippers on it. It was really scary. I laughed at first, and said 'Show time!', but then he came up to the bed without saying a word, and even though I knew that it was him, even though I knew that it was Richard, I began to feel frightened. In fact I felt more frightened in real life than I had in my fantasy.

"I said, 'Where on earth did you get that mask? It's really scary.' But he didn't answer. Instead he forced me back onto the bed, and sat astride me. He took a leather strap and buckled my left hand to the bedpost. I laughed and tugged at it, but when I realized I couldn't undo it, I started to struggle. Still he didn't say anything, and the whole thing was starting to get kind of unnerving, if you know what I mean.

"He buckled my right wrist to the opposite bedpost. It's a kingsize bed, so my arms were stretched wide apart. Then he twisted around and buckled my ankles to the foot of the bed. I tried to kick him but he was too strong.

"Once I was spreadeagled on the bed, he climbed on top of me, and slowly unbuttoned the shirt that I was wearing. I could see his eyes but behind that mask they looked totally expressionless and cold. It was like seeing somebody's eye looking through a hole in a changing room or a shower cubicle, you know, a peeping Tom. Really eerie, and it made me feel very vulnerable and exposed, and *naked,* too. I had fantasized about this, but when it was real it was about a hundred times more frightening and about a hundred times more erotic.

"Richard stroked my hair and twined it around his fingers. Then he touched my cheeks. He couldn't kiss me. All he had for a mouth was a zipper. But he stroked my lips and he ran his fingertips around my teeth, and then pushed them into my mouth. He had never done anything like that before, and it was very strange and exciting. He was breathing harshly all the time. You know, like Darth Vader. I kept begging him to say something—anything—but he wouldn't.

"He fondled my breasts, massaging them over and over, and rolling and tugging my nipples between his fingers. Then he sat up, and massaged my breasts with his cock. He had done *that* before, but he had never done it so slowly and so—what's the word?—lustfully, I guess. Lasciviously, that's it. Like he was really enjoying every second of pressing his cock against my nipples, and burying it deep in my breast-flesh. I was enjoying it, too, but even if I hadn't been enjoying it, I wouldn't have had any choice, would I?

"He mounted my face, and rolled his cock against my nose and my cheeks. He pressed his balls up against my mouth. They were tight and hard and the sack was wrinkled. I kissed them and licked them, and ran my tongue down the line in the middle of them. Then he tugged apart the cheeks of his ass, stretched them apart, and I tongued his anus.

"The whole thing seemed to go on for hours. Sometimes I felt okay, sometimes I felt panicky, but every time I started to feel panicky, Richard would give me some sensation that I couldn't resist, a feeling that would make me glow. He touched me everywhere, absolutely everywhere. He caressed my breasts, he ran his fingers down my legs, he fondled every one of my toes. He pressed his cock up against my navel, and massaged it around and around, until my navel was slippery with cock-juice. Then he touched and stroked the inside of my thighs, higher and higher, until I was almost crazy with anticipation. I lifted my hips off the bed and reared them up towards him, because I wanted him so much. But all he did was delicately trace the outline of my pussy with his finger, and then gently touch my clitoris, so gently that I could hardly feel it, and I kept aching for *more, more, more*!

"I pleaded with him to fuck me, but he went on slowly fingering me. He opened my pussy and slid his finger inside, and that was better than nothing, but I needed his cock. Then he slid another finger inside, and another. My pussy was so wet that it was actually making a squelching noise, and that turned me on even more. I mean, I could even *hear* how turned-on I was.

"He pushed his whole hand up inside my pussy, right up to the wrist, and slowly churned it around. All the time he was stroking and fingering the neck of my womb, so that my whole insides were moving like some kind of slow-motion earthquake.

"I had an orgasm then. It just swelled up and swallowed me. I was shaking and crying out, and pulling at the straps, but there was nothing else I could do, I was helpless, and because I couldn't have all of the spasms, the orgasm seemed to go on and on and on.

"Richard took out his hand, and started to massage my anus. Again, he took such a long time doing it, he squeezed it and fingered it, and then at last he forced one of his fingers inside. I gripped his finger tight with my muscles, but then he forced another finger inside, and stretched it open. He reached across to the night table, and picked up my hairbrush, my really soft-bristle hairbrush, and he pushed the handle right up my anus, the whole handle, right up as far as the bristles.

"He slid it in and out a few times. Then at last he climbed up on top of me, and touched my pussy with his cock. If my hands had been free, I would have gripped hold of his ass and I would have pulled him right into me. But I was helpless and I had to wait. He pushed himself into me a little at a time, half-inch by half-inch, until I was practically crying with frustration. I screamed 'Fuck me, damn it! Fuck me!' but he still pushed it in real slow.

"He fucked me and it was heaven. He was moaning, too, underneath that mask, because he was pretty close to climaxing. Also, every time he pushed his cock into me, his balls were brushed by the soft bristles of my hairbrush, which was still sticking out of my anus. He told me afterwards it was more sensation than he could normally stand.

"Suddenly he tensed up like a clock-spring. He started to push himself into me in a very strange, jerky way. Then he let out this muffled shout underneath his mask, and I actually *felt* his cock swell up and pump out his load, I actually *felt* it filling me up—and that's something that I don't feel very often.

"We've only done the strapping-up bit one more time, but that was without the mask. The mask is okay in fantasy but a little heavy to take in real life. We've done the hairbrush thing a few times, though. I like it because I like the feeling of something up my ass when I'm making love, and Richard likes it because of those brushy bristles! I think they ought to sell hairbrushes as sex toys!"

Every woman has her own private fantasy—from the deeply romantic to the strongly perverse. As I have said before, sometimes it's better if a fantasy *remains* a fantasy. Trying to act it out would do nothing more than spoil a perfectly good mental stimulus—a stimulus which can be much more beneficial to your sex life if it stays inside your mind, an unrealized longing. Some fantasies, if acted out, would be harmful or dangerous or simply not arousing at all.

Here are some examples from letters that I have received recently:

- "I have a fantasy that I am tattooed with exquisite pictures from head to foot. My head is shaved and all my head and my face are tattooed. I have dragon scales tattooed all the way down my back so that— from behind—I look like a human reptile. My eyes are surrounded with tattooed feathers, like an owl's eyes. Even the inside of my mouth is tattooed. My stomach is tattooed with beautiful scenes from all around the world . . . Oriental palaces and gardens . . . forests and waterfalls. My sex is shaved completely bare, and surrounded by the tattoo of a man's hand, as if he's reaching between my legs and holding my sex between his fingers. My legs are tattooed with twining creepers and blossoming flowers . . . I have to go naked everywhere . . . people stare at me. I frighten them and excite them at the same time."

- "I'm an animal trainer in a circus. I'm one of the most famous circus acts in the world. I perform in a cage of lions and tigers, in front of thousands of people. I'm nude except for a top hat and a tailcoat and very high heels. I crack my whip at the animals and they do whatever I want. I have a power over them that is almost magic. But they are very dangerous animals, too, man eaters. They would kill anybody who didn't know how to control them. The highlight of my act is when I command a huge shaggy Bengal tiger to climb on a platform and rear up on his hind legs. I snap his penis with the tip of my whip until it rises. His penis is bright red, and huge, the size of a man's arm. With all the spotlights shining on me, I climb onto the platform and slowly lower myself on the tiger's penis, my hips rotating around and around. I grip the tiger's fur tight. He's hot and muscular and his fur smells rank. I ride him harder and harder, and he growls dangerously and scratches my bare bottom with his claws."

- "I dreamed this first, after my first day at my new aerobics class . . . I remembered the dream and it became a regular fantasy. I don't really understand why it excites me to think about it, because I've never done anything like it, and I wouldn't *want* to do anything like it. I've never told my boyfriend about it. He'd be *very* suspicious about me if I did. So this is the first time that I've told anybody.

"She pushes her thigh between my thighs"

"I arrive at this new aerobics class. It's very classy and modern and the sun's shining through the windows and everything. Then I discover that everybody has to exercise in the nude. They're dancing and stretching and toe-touching, all of these nude girls, and you can see absolutely everything. I'm very shy at first, and I don't want to do it, but they tell me that if I don't like it after the first session I don't have to come back. I start dancing in the nude and I discover that I'm really good at it. Along with another girl, I'm the best in the class. She and I dance together in front of the mirror. She has an incredible figure. She's blonde—blue-eyed, tall, with amazing breasts with huge wide nipples, which I've always wanted. She starts dancing really close. We dance something like the tango together, our breasts touching and bouncing together. She runs her hands down my sides and pushes her thigh between my thighs, and then I do the same to her. I can feel her pubic hair on my skin, and her cunt like a warm wet kiss. We start to caress each other and kiss each other, real kissing with tongues down throats. We fondle each other's breasts and nipples. Everybody applauds and says we're amazing."

The beauty of fantasies is that they allow us to picture ourselves in sexual situations that, in reality, would be impossible or dangerous or undesirable. No woman would really want to be tattooed all over, although there is a strong sexual lure in tattooing to which many women succumb—even if they have nothing more extensive than a butterfly on their left buttock, or a hummingbird on their right breast.

Personally, I am very much opposed to any kind of piercing or marking or scarring which is done for sexual purposes. Almost all of those women I have known who have been tattooed—or who have had their nipples pierced for rings or their vaginal lips pierced for rings or studs—have later expressed regret at what they have done.

No woman would really like to have intercourse with a tiger. The woman who recounted this fantasy has been divorced for a year and a half, and admitted that she had "read about women who train their dogs to please them sexually," and had on two or three occasions manually stimulated her own German shepherd. I was able to explain to her that her feelings were not at all uncommon, although very few women go as far as to have intercourse with their pets. (If they do, incidentally, there is no risk of any kind of pregnancy, and no health hazard.)

Many women have fantasies of lesbian encounters: from kissing to mutual breast-fondling to full graphic lovemaking. Again, these fantasies are very common, especially at physiologically critical stages in a woman's life—when she reaches puberty, when she becomes pregnant, as she approaches the menopause. Lesbian fantasies are completely harmless and are not indicative in any way of any hidden homosexual tendencies. Many men have homosexual fantasies which are equally harmless.

You simply wouldn't *want* to act out your most extreme sexual daydreams. Many of them would be sexual nightmares.

But we have clearly seen that—with judgment and care—you *can* use some of your favorite fantasies and use them to drive your man very wild in bed. Some fantasies can very successfully be acted out, in whole or in part, with wonderfully erotic results.

One of my favorites came from twenty-one-year-old Susan, a nursery school assistant from Chicago, Illinois. Every few weeks, she dresses up for her husband Richard in her bridal veil, complete with floral headdress, a white lace basque, white stockings and white satin shoes. She even takes a fresh bridal bouquet to bed.

"It's like being a new bride every time," wrote Susan. "Life with Richard is just one wedding night after another. I love it because it's so romantic. Richard says he loves it because he can deflower me, over and over. We know it's just a game, but we love it."

8

How to Handle Your Man ... in Every Way

When it comes to the physical side of lovemaking, one worry seems to come up time and time again: how do I actually touch my lover's thing? Am I being too timorous? Am I being too rough? Am I rubbing it the right way? Should I be rubbing it at all? Can I bite it? Squeeze it? Suck it?

Does he like me to touch it when he's driving/reading a book/watching TV/taking a shower? Does he like me to squeeze his testes or not? If he does, how hard should I squeeze them?

To many women—even to women who have been living with men for years and years—the male sexual organs are still a mystery.

If you learn to handle your lover's sexual organs expertly, however—and if you know when to touch them, and how, and for how long—you will be able to transform your sex life so dramatically that you will wonder how you ever got along before. And that's no exaggeration.

For the fact is that most women don't have the foggiest idea how a man's sexual organs work, how to handle and stimulate them, and (most critical of all) what to do with them once they've actually managed to produce an erection. Once it's hard, what do you do? Do you have intercourse immediately? Supposing you've managed to give him an erection at a time and a place where you can't have intercourse immediately? Do you progress to oral sex? Supposing you can't possibly do that, either? Do you masturbate him to a climax? Do you take your hand away and let his erection collapse? If you do, will he be seriously frustrated? Will it actually hurt him? Will it affect his virility? And so on, and so on, etcetera, etcetera, ad infinitum.

Let me say here that most *men* don't have the foggiest idea how a woman's sexual organs work, nor how to handle and stimulate them, so I'm not being sexist. But let's leave *his* lack of technique until later. Once you have the confidence and the competence to stimulate your lover's sexual organs, you will be better able to show him how to stimulate yours—in just the way you like it.

The best way of improving your handling technique is to have an obliging lover lying next to you whose sexual organs you can use for practice. That way, you can be sure of getting an immediate response to everything you try—such as *"mmmmm"* or *"ouch!"*

It's also possible to buy dildos that are remarkably life-like replicas of male sexual organs—including one that sports its own foreskin. These can help you to perfect the way in which you handle an erect penis, but they don't go flaccid, the way that real penises do, and they won't teach you much about nervous response.

The first thing to understand about your lover's penis is that—in spite of its silky textured skin—it is remarkably resilient, and will stand up to all kinds of vigorous manipulation without pain or discomfort (in fact, quite the opposite). Many women are very cautious about handling their lover's penises too robustly, with the result that they never quite manage to give them the strong, consistent stimulation which they enjoy the most.

If your lover is amenable, the clearest way for you to understand how vigorously you can stimulate his penis is for him to show you how he masturbates (or, at least, how he *used* to masturbate before he met you, and you satisfied his every sexual craving). If he tells you that he never masturbated in his life, he's lying, but he's probably too modest to show you. See if you can persuade him some other time.

As you will probably know from previous books, your lover's penis is made up of three columns of porous tissue. At the top and sides of the penis are the two *corposa cavernosa*, which are attached at their base to his pelvic bones. Underneath runs the smaller *corpus spongiosum*,

which also forms the wedge-shaped *glans,* the head of
the penis.

Blood vessels open into all three of these columns of
tissue, and when your lover becomes sexually excited,
blood pours rapidly into them and fills them up. But the
vessels leading *away* from them are almost totally closed.
The very visible result is that your lover's penis becomes
stiffer and very much larger, and stays that way.

Erection is an automatic action caused by nervous signals from the spinal column. Automatic, in the sense that
a man cannot willfully stiffen his penis in the way that
he can flex his biceps. If only he could!

But external stimuli can also encourage erection, as we
have seen. If the nerve receptors on your lover's penis
are stimulated by fingers or tongue or almost anything,
he can achieve an erection. He can also achieve an erection without any physical contact being involved. Erotic
sights, erotic smells, erotic ideas—they can all bring on
a hard-on.

One of the results of erection, in uncircumcised men,
is that the glans of the penis is uncovered. The skin of
the glans, particularly where it joins the shaft of the
penis, has many highly sensitive nerve receptors. Consistent friction of these nerve receptors—either by hand or
by tongue or by rubbing against the inside of the vagina—is what eventually brings a man to a climax.

During sexual arousal, your lover's "accessory" glands
inside his body are preparing the cocktail that will spurt
out as semen. His sperm will have been developing in
his testes, at the rate of hundreds of millions every day,
to be stored in *ampullae.* They will then be mixed with
fluid from the seminal vesicles, the prostate gland, and
two further glands known as Cowper's and Littre's glands.
The resulting fluid gives the sperm a medium to swim
in—as well as food and oxygen to keep them alive and
kicking—although they don't start up their frantic tail-
thrashing movements until they're actually ejaculated.

An early sign of arousal is the leaking-out of a thin,
clear lubricating liquid from the opening in the glans.

As your lover becomes increasingly excited, you will
notice his breathing-rate increases—from twelve to sixteen breaths a minute to forty or even fifty. His body

muscles will begin to tense up, and his face and his chest may redden. His heart-rate will increase from 72 beats a minute to 110 or 180—or even faster if sexual tension is very high.

Some women are worried that their lovers will suffer a heart attack during sex—especially if they already have a history of cardiac trouble. Doctors are still undecided whether the "exercise" involved in sexual intercourse, and the resulting increases in pulse and blood pressure, are beneficial to those with heart problems or not. But the lower a man's presexual heart-rate, the less it will rise during sexual stimulation—which supports the current medical view that maintaining good physical condition is important for preventing heart attacks, since the healthier a man is, the lower his heart-rate.

As your lover is stimulated more and more, he will reach a stage during intercourse where he clutches at you, and thrusts deeper and faster into your vagina. Just before the instant of climax, he will push himself forward as hard and as deep as he can. He has reached the point of *ejaculatory inevitability,* when nothing in the known universe can prevent him from ejaculating.

All of your lover's secondary sex organs expel their fluid into the urethral bulb at the base of his penis in preparation for ejaculation. His urethral bulb then rhythmically contracts—rather like the rubber bulb at the end of an eyedropper—and two large muscles in the floor of his pelvis contract, too, adding extra power to his ejaculation. Semen shoots out of his penis in two, three or four spurts.

The first spurt of semen will have sufficient kick behind it to send it anything up to two feet (unless there's something or somebody in the way).

The remaining spurts will diminish in power and in quantity of semen as your lover's climax ebbs.

Immediately after his ejaculation, your lover's sexual interest will fall away sharply. You can continue to caress his penis, for sure, but you should do it only gently, since he may very well find any strong stimulation to be irritating or even painful. This *resolution* phase doesn't last for very long, but it is often a cause of misunderstanding and sexual frustration, especially if you haven't reached *your* climax yet.

Give him a little time to recover, and your patience will pay off. If you've been having intercourse, my advice is to keep his penis inside your vagina. Not only is it the most comfortable place for his penis to be, but there will be a far greater chance of him keeping at least a partial erection, and very quickly becoming ready for a second climax. If he takes it right out, however, his erection will die away altogether, and his interest will be much more easily diverted (to watching TV, or having a drink, or getting up and going to the bathroom).

If you've been masturbating him, then keep his penis enclosed in one hand, while gently caressing his glans with the fingertips of the other hand. And when I say gently, I mean *gently,* using his sperm as a lubricant. You can add to his pleasure by caressing his balls, too, and massaging sperm all over them. Make a point of running your fingernail down the central "seam" of his scrotal sack. You can lightly caress his perineum, too, which is the area between his scrotum and his anus. This gentle postclimactic massage will keep him in a state of semiarousal, and may soon bring him back to full erection.

A man's testes are quite sensitive and should be handled carefully. There are few sensations more off-putting for a man than to have his balls squeezed too hard right in the middle of lovemaking. One rule of thumb is to apply no more pressure to your lover's testes than you would to your own breasts, but you can get a much more accurate idea by caressing his balls and asking him how it feels. Nobody knows where that fine line between pleasure and pain lies better than he does.

Many women are uncertain about how to hold their lover's penis, and how to stimulate it most effectively. Because of that, they are often reluctant to touch it at all. When they *do,* their caresses are frequently ineffective (in other words, they don't excite the nerve-endings properly) or they stop their caresses just as their lover is beginning to grow aroused.

There is an old schoolyard story that if a girl handles a man's penis she must bring him to climax or else it could be physically dangerous for him. I suspect that this story was originated by horny young men who saw an opportunity to frighten their girlfriends into having sex with them. There is no truth in it at all. But if you don't caress your lover's penis in the right way, there *is* a danger that he will find your lovemaking unsatisfying or even irritating. You'll be driving him wild in bed all right— wild with frustration.

The commonest mistake that most women make in handling their lover's penis is to grasp it too far down the shaft. When it's hard, of course, a penis has a good solid tree-trunk feel to it which women enjoy—but the lower part of the shaft has comparatively few nerve-endings and is therefore much less sensitive than the head or glans. You can rub it furiously for quite a long time and produce nothing more than a vaguely pleasurable sensation—which, because it is only vaguely pleasurable, at a time when your lover is keen on reaching a sexual climax, is usually more frustrating than exciting.

The most sensitive area of the penis is around the rim of the glans, where it joins the shaft—especially the opening of the penis, and just below it, along that little bridge of skin called the frenum. Although every man masturbates in his own idiosyncratic way, many men can bring themselves quickly to a climax with nothing more than finger and thumb—simply by placing the index finger against the frenum and the thumb against the upper side of the glans, and rapidly rubbing up and down. They will not apply a great deal of pressure—it is the quick, persistent stimulation of the nerve endings that produces the climax. Many women who realize that the glans is the most sensitive part of the penis spoil the effect of their discovery by rubbing far too hard.

You Can Use Deeper, Harder Strokes

As you rub, you can *occasionally* squeeze quite hard, just by way of varying your stimulation, and showing your lover that you are not just mechanically jerking him off. And as he becomes more powerfully stimulated, and nears his climax, you can use deeper, harder strokes, and press more forcefully on his frenum area.

It can take quite a while for a man to reach a climax through manual stimulation, so don't give up three-quarters of the way through because you're worried that you're not doing it correctly or because you're worried that you're not turning him on. If his penis is rigid, if his muscles are tensed, if his breathing rate is increasing, and he seems increasingly self-absorbed, then you're turning him on all right, and you'd probably be surprised how close he is to ejaculating.

The short cut to improving your cock-handling technique is to ask your lover how he holds his penis when he masturbates (or, if he's shy about admitting that he still occasionally jerks off, how he *used* to hold his penis when he masturbated). You should remember that a high proportion of men masturbate throughout their lives—including men who are happily married, and have terrific sex lives. They do it as a way of giving themselves momentary pleasure and relief from stress, and although they may be embarrassed about it and keep it secret, it hardly ever represents a threat to their love-life. In fact it often improves the stability of their love-life, because it relieves those sexual tensions which—unrelieved—may have led to adultery or visits to prostitutes.

Mary, a forty-two-year-old homemaker from Boston, Massachusetts, wrote me a long letter after discovering a hoard of pornographic magazines in her husband's desk—magazines which bore obvious traces of his having masturbated over them. She said: "At first I questioned my own attractiveness and the whole basis of our relationship. I really believed that our marriage was over. But then I began to think about it more rationally, and rationally I had to admit that we still have a wonderful sex life, and that Dick has never seriously flirted with any other women. I read two or three of your books, and from them I grew to understand that Dick's interest in pornography was simply that and nothing more—an interest. Sex magazines fascinated him and aroused him and he masturbated. That was all. Perhaps I was jealous that he wasted his sperm on a photograph of another woman, when he could have given it to me. But as you so rightly said, it's impossible for a man to be unfaithful with a photograph. I'm not saying this was easy to understand. I don't think women can ever completely understand it, because their response to pornography is so different. But I realized in the end that our marriage wasn't at risk and never had been.

"In the end I took a deep breath and told Dick that I had discovered his 'hoard.' I told him that I didn't mind at all, except that he should have shared his interest with me, instead of keeping it secret. He was angry at first. After a while, though, he said he was relieved and even pleased. These days, he reads his magazines openly, and occasionally buys or rents a pornographic movie, too. Sometimes we're both stimulated, and we use a magazine or a movie as part of our lovemaking. Sometimes he lies next to me and masturbates. I still feel a little 'daring,' but I know Dick adores me, and I've come to realize that his interest is no more a betrayal of our marriage than if he spent weekends away from home, fishing. He likes sex, he likes me, so why should I worry?"

Mary's tolerance of her husband's masturbation is (regretfully) unusual. If more women were prepared to accept and even encourage their lover's self-stimulation, particularly when they didn't feel like having sex themselves, a great deal of the sexual frustration in modern relationships would be avoided. Masturbation does nobody any harm, and often (as a way of defusing tension and giving the simplest of pleasures) does people a great deal of good.

I have never seen mentioned in any sex book anywhere the most basic difficulty that a woman faces in handling a man's penis. For the most sensitive and arousing stimulation, the ball of the thumb should be placed on *top* of the glans, applying broad and steady pressure, while the fingertips stimulate the underside of the glans, tickling the frenum and the highly responsive *meatus,* which is doctor-speak for the hole in the end of a man's penis. Many men enjoy the lightest scratching of the frenum with the tips of the fingernails, and the gentle stretching-apart of the opening.

The problem is that it is quite physically difficult for a woman to hold her lover's penis in this way—especially if she's facing him. What usually happens is that she ends up grasping his erection "the wrong way round"—that is, with the ball of her thumb pressing on the frenum and her fingers on the less sensitive top of the glans, or curled around the shaft, which (as we know) is *very* much less sensitive.

Even when she's lying close beside him, she will find it very awkward to twist her wrist around to hold his penis in the thumb-on-top-fingertips-underneath position—and will usually grasp it sideways, so that she is unable to apply nearly as much stimulating pressure as she ought to be.

This results in masturbation which may admittedly feel quite good—but not nearly as good as it could if the penis were to be held in the ideal way.

So how can you learn to hold your lover's cock in the way that he likes it the best—the way which gives you fingertip control, and the ability to quicken or delay his ejaculation, whichever you want?

The answer is really quite simple, but it's surprising how many women have never learned to arouse their lovers like this. *He* lies on his left side, with his left leg drawn up and his right leg straight . . . and the important thing is that he props himself up slightly on a cushion or a folded-over pillow, allowing your left hand to slip around his waist without his full weight bearing down on your forearm.

You're Going to Stimulate Him with Both Hands

The secret is that you're going to masturbate him with both hands.

For a man, stimulating your vulva with both hands is comparatively easy. While his right hand freely massages your clitoris, for example, he can put his left arm underneath you and reach around your hips with his left hand to slide his fingers into your vagina. The movement in his left hand will obviously be slightly more limited, because of the weight of your body on his left arm, but most men are strong enough and most women are light enough for this not to be seriously hampering.

If you tried to put your left arm underneath your lover's body without any kind of support, however, you'd probably feel crushed. Not only is he heavier, he's bigger, and it would be much more difficult for you to reach the end of his penis . . . even if you could reach it at all.

Cuddle right up behind him (the touch of your nipples on his back will add to his stimulation . . . as will the tickling of your pubic hair or the feel of your smooth-shaven mound of Venus against his bare buttocks). Curl your left arm around his waist and take hold of his cock with your left thumb pressed firmly on the glans just above the ridge where the glans joins the shaft. Make sure that you leave the frenum and the opening uncovered, because that's where your right hand is going to come in.

Reaching around him with your right hand, you will be able to use your fingertips to touch the sensitive underside of his glans and his balls. Your right hand will have complete freedom of movement, so you will be able to tickle and caress him all the way up his shaft, and give him delicate fingertip circling motions around the opening of his penis which (as he nears his climax) will drive him really wild. Your control will be almost 100 percent, because your fingertips will be able to play his hardened cock like a musical instrument . . . running down the shaft when his excitement grows a little too quickly . . . running back up the shaft to the frenum and the glans when his excitement begins to subside.

At the same time, your left hand will keep up a steady, strong, masturbating rhythm, squeezing the shaft hard and applying varying degrees of thumb pressure to the top of the glans. With very little practice, you should soon be able to masturbate your lover as quickly or as slowly as you wish. You will be able to choose to the second when you want him to ejaculate, or if you want him to ejaculate at all (maybe you'd prefer—once he's highly stimulated—to have him enter you and ejaculate inside you).

There are all kinds of variations you can use to make this masturbation technique into an erotic art form. You can hold a silk handkerchief or a pair of silk panties in your left hand while you strongly massage your lover's shaft. Margaret, a twenty-six-year-old realtor from Fort Worth, Texas, said that she often masturbated her husband in the morning with a pair of her panties, so that he would fill them with sperm. "I can put them on after he's left for the office, and they're still wet. I can smell his come all day, and every time I go to the bathroom it turns me on. By the end of the day, I just can't wait to see him again."

You can squirt a dollop of KY or any other intimate lubricant into the palm of your left hand, and make your masturbation really slippery. Or you can use massage oils, which come in a whole variety of aromas, from sandalwood to cherry.

Some men will be extra excited if you masturbate them while you're wearing latex gloves, or if you wear rubber thimbles on the ends of your fingers, of the kind used by bank tellers to count bills. Rhoda, a twenty-seven-year-old librarian from Albany, New York, told me that her husband was particularly turned on if she masturbated him with a glutinous, crunchy mixture of Rice Krispies and clear honey.

With your left hand, you will be able to grip your lover's shaft quite tightly, and you will increase his pleasure if you masturbate him with a downward tugging motion, so that at the end of each stroke you are slightly stretching the skin between the glans and the shaft. Keep tickling and massaging with those right-hand fingertips and put the clear natural lubricant that will well up from his penis to good use, circling it around and around the hole in his cock.

Your right hand can stray downward sometimes, and caress his scrotum and his perineum and his anus. But keep up a steady, gradually quickening rhythm. In this position, you should be able to masturbate him for quite a long time without tiring. Just remember, though—you *will* frustrate him if you bring him close to a climax and suddenly stop. So before you start manipulating his penis, it's better to have some idea of what you feel like doing: whether you want to masturbate him to orgasm; whether you want to masturbate him just to make him harder, with a view to intercourse; or whether this is a preliminary to your going down on him and fellating him to orgasm.

If you don't really feel like sex—if you're tired, or out of sorts, or if you're masturbating him for no other reason than you're feeling guilty that you haven't made love for quite a while—then it's better not to start hard, intense masturbation of this kind. You can show him you love him sexually by caressing his cock and his balls very gently, very lightly; by kissing him, too; and by telling him how you feel. There is nothing emptier in an intimate relationship than sex that is performed out of duty, rather than passion.

The main purpose of this chapter has been to take away some of your doubts and fears about touching your lover's sexual organs. So many women shy away from handling their lovers intimately, whereas they should caress and fondle them and simply *look* at them as often as they wish. Very few men dislike the idea of being frequently caressed. In fact, 74 percent thought that more intimate touching would improve their sex lives "substantially."

There is nothing like experience to cut through myth and misconception. Even today, I am still receiving letters from young women who have no clear idea of the size of the male penis, and who are worried that—when it comes to making love—their vaginas are going to be far too small.

I have letters from wives of several years' standing who have never caressed their husbands' penises with their hands, let alone their mouths—wives who have never seen their husbands naked. It still happens, even today.

But every woman in a sexual relationship has a right to look, to investigate, to ask, to touch, to caress, to fondle, to lick, to taste—to do whatever she wishes. As thirty-two-year-old Philipa, from Seattle, Washington, wrote: "I didn't really understand men's balls until I took one of my lover's balls into my mouth, and very gently explored it with my tongue. I took a long time doing it, I wanted to relish it. I felt as if I had the whole of his manhood at my mercy. I suppose I could have bitten it. But he wasn't afraid and I wasn't afraid. When it comes to a man's cock, a man's cock is a man's cock; it's him and nobody else. But a man's balls contain the future of the human race and the whole reason why men and women love each other—just as a woman's womb does. I think men's balls are wonderful. I always lick them, always suck them. It's like sucking destiny. It's like sucking the future."

You should never think that—once you've started fondling your lover's genitals—you have some kind of obligation to continue. If you start deliberately masturbating him—then, yes, I think you ought to continue, until he's come to a climax, just as he should do the same for you. But you should be able to stroke and touch and lick his penis and his balls and anywhere you like, without feeling that you *have* to get involved in an act of masturbation or intercourse.

A sense of relaxation and openness is critical to any good sexual relationship. You should be able to look at him and fondle him, and he should be able to do the same to you. You would like to spend some time caressing his penis, unembarrassed, with the light on. When was the last time you lay in bed with your legs apart and allowed him to do the same to you?

Even at times when you don't feel like making love, you should make a point of touching and fondling your lover intimately. Stroke his penis the same way you would stroke your cat. Sex can be expressed on many different levels at all times of the day . . . from extreme perversity, to out-and-out fucking, to the gentlest of touches. Make sure that you express your sexual feelings for your lover at all times, and in every imaginable way.

Wake him in the morning by caressing his cock. Slip your hand into his pajama pants while he's cleaning his teeth. Squeeze his cock through his jeans while he's watching TV/mowing the lawn/putting up shelves.

In other words, show him that you love his cock and that you're not afraid to touch it and fondle it. That's one of the fundamental steps that any woman can take toward being the wildest of lovers.

9

To Serve and Protect

In a sexually outspoken society like ours, with information on birth control so freely available to everyone, it is almost beyond belief that women are still having unwanted pregnancies.

Recent figures show that over *half* the pregnancies in the United States are unplanned, and that over 70 percent of these so-called "accidental" pregnancies happen because the couple have taken no contraceptive measures whatsoever—not because their birth-control method has let them down.

There will always be those moments when passion overtakes prudence, and a couple will risk unprotected intercourse. But these days, there can be absolutely no excuse for an unplanned conception, except if a condom should genuinely break (which they scarcely ever do).

Choosing a contraceptive is a much more individualized matter than most women realize.

Take Karen, for example, a twenty-two-year-old assistant in a smart fashion store in Dallas, Texas. Karen had been married for nearly two years to Grant, a successful young accountant, but they both wanted to wait until they were financially secure until they had children.

To begin with, Grant used condoms, but both of them found that rolling on a sheath before every act of intercourse was destroying the spontaneity of their lovemaking, and Grant complained that wearing a condom was "like swimming in your socks."

Karen went to her doctor, who prescribed a contraceptive pill. This worked well for a while, but after seven months Karen found that she was becoming depressed and lethargic, and that she was beginning to put on weight. She had always been proud of her figure—and she needed to look slim and smart for work. Could she try something else?

She had read about the loop, or IUD, and wanted to try that. She had heard that the loop was simple and effective, and that once it had been inserted by a doctor, it required no further preparation.

Karen's doctor, however, explained that she never prescribed the loop for women who had not yet had children. This was because for reason or reasons unknown, women who have not yet had children have a tendency to expel the loop out of their vagina without realizing it—so that there is a constant risk that they will continue to have intercourse without knowing that they are no longer protected.

She asked about the rhythm method—which involves making love only on those days of the month when a woman is thought not to be capable of conception—but the rhythm method is highly unreliable, and at the age of twenty-two, Karen was at her most fertile. The risk of accidental pregnancy was too high.

The so-called "withdrawal method"—when the man takes his penis out of the woman just before he ejaculates—was also discounted by Karen's doctor as far too unreliable, not to mention frustrating. Regular use of the withdrawal method can lead to all kinds of sexual difficulties, not the least of which are premature ejaculation (on the part of the man) and an inability to reach orgasm (on the part of the woman).

Eventually, Karen chose the Dutch cap. This is a rubber dome which is fitted over the neck of the womb and held in place by a light spring around its rim. Karen had originally considered it too messy, particularly since it is usually used in conjunction with a spermicidal cream, and she didn't like the idea of fitting it in before love-making. But her doctor trained her to fit it properly and securely, and explained that she could insert it before she went to bed. A condom, of course, can only be fitted over an erect penis, so it always has to be put on just before the act of making love.

Karen was satisfied with her Dutch cap, and used it for over three years before having children.

After only a few months, she was relaxed enough to put it on in front of Grant; and a little later she let him fit it on for her. Like many couples, they learned to use their method of contraception as a means of foreplay. Karen loved Grant fingering her deep inside, and she found the sensation of him moving the neck of her womb "incredibly arousing."

Let's take a look at some of the main methods of contraception.

Believe it or not, the withdrawal method is probably used more widely than any other method of birth control. While withdrawal can be frustrating and messy, it is better than no contraceptive method at all, and it has no physical side effects. In the last century, it was thought that it could cause "pelvic congestion" which could lead to cancer, but there is absolutely no truth in this at all.

The rhythm method—sometimes known as the safe period—involves predicting the day of the month on which a woman will ovulate, that is, shed her egg from her ovary. Since the egg is only fertile for a short time, it is assumed that once that time has passed, there is no possibility of conception until the next ovulation.

The rhythm method is biologically sound, and if every woman's menstrual cycle went like clockwork, it would have a high rate of success. But unfortunately, the onset of the next menstrual cycle is notoriously difficult to predict with accuracy, and if a woman's is very irregular—that is, if there is more than a week's difference in the length of her cycles—then there will probably be only two or three days every month when she can really be regarded as "safe."

The Thermometer Method

Some women attempt to predict their ovulation with greater accuracy by using a thermometer. This is because a woman's body temperature rises marginally after ovulation—by about a half of a degree Fahrenheit. Once she has detected this rise in temperature, it should technically be safe for her to have intercourse. But many women experience "false" rises in temperature, particularly if they have a head cold—which renders the method very risky.

The temperature method is about twice as effective as the calendar method, but in spite of the fact that they both have the approval of the Vatican, neither of them can be considered medically reliable.

Now we come to the "artificial" methods of contraception. The most popular of these is the condom, or rubber, or sheath. The condom is cheap, portable, easy to fit, and one of the most effective methods of birth-control ever.

The invention of the condom is attributed to the Italian anatomist Gabrielli Fallopius in the 16th century, as a device to prevent the spread of syphilis. Today, the condom still has the quality of protecting users against sexually transmitted diseases, especially AIDS, and for that reason it is far and away the most desirable form of birth control for anyone who indulges in casual sex.

There is a schoolyard story that every hundredth condom has a pinhole in it, but this is total nonsense. Modern condoms are made under the most rigorous conditions and scarcely ever break. Condoms can fail to protect you if the man allows his penis to go soft while it is still inside your body—thus allowing semen to escape from the ring at the base of the condom and leak into your vagina.

But, properly used, a condom is still a girl's best friend. I have read reports of sex clubs in New York and other big cities where condoms are now being regarded as unfashionable and unnecessary. But I cannot emphasize strongly enough the importance of using a condom when you are having sex with somebody of whose sexual and medical history you are not 101 percent sure.

Instead of allowing the fitting-on of a condom to interrupt your lovemaking, make it part of your foreplay—as Karen and Grant did with her Dutch cap. Many condoms are flavored now, which makes them far more pleasant to fit over your lover's erection with your mouth. Take the condom out of the packet, and insert the "bulb" in your mouth—pressing it with your tongue against the roof of your mouth to ensure that you keep all of the air out. You can then roll the condom over your lover's penis simply by deep-throating him.

Condoms come in a dazzling variety of colors and shapes and textures—mint-flavored, ribbed, extra-thin, black, red, raspberry, extra-strong. But do make sure when you buy a novelty condom that it meets approved safety standards. Some of the wackier prophylactics are intended to be sex toys rather than serious contraceptives.

If you regularly enjoy anal intercourse, it is worth choosing an extra-strong condom. It will cling more securely to your lover's penis, and there will be less chance of it breaking under the greater stress of anal penetration.

The Dutch cap, or vaginal diaphragm, can be almost as effective as a condom, provided it is properly fitted and used sensibly. It does, however, have its drawbacks—not the least of which is that a woman has to insert it well before she has intercourse, otherwise she has to stop in the middle of lovemaking and go through a rather ungainly procedure to put it in.

The Dutch cap should be used in conjunction with a spermicidal cream or jelly—in other words, a chemical that will destroy all of the sperm which come into contact with it—and if a woman wishes to have intercourse more than once, she should put in some more spermicide before she does so.

Incidentally, spermicides on their own are not enough to guarantee that a woman will not get pregnant. There are various types on the market, including pastes, creams, and pessaries which dissolve inside the vagina. The greatest success has been reported from aerosol foams. But whichever spermicide you choose, *don't* rely on the manufacturer's claims that you can safely use it by itself, without the need for a condom or a diaphragm.

In the early part of the 1960s, the intrauterine device (IUD) became hugely popular as a cheap form of contraception. An IUD is made of flexible plastic, and comes in a variety of shapes and sizes (loops, bows, spirals, rings, and coils). A doctor inserts it into a woman's uterus by stretching it out into a long, thin shape and passing it through the cervical canal. Once inside the uterus, it resumes its normal shape.

The fitting of an IUD can be slightly uncomfortable, but once it's inside, it's undetectable, apart from a fine thread which hangs down into the vagina. This enables a woman to check that the IUD is still in place. Theoretically, an IUD can be left inside the uterus for years, although it should be checked by a doctor at least once every twelve months.

It may seem strange, but nobody knows exactly how IUDs prevent you from becoming pregnant. The story goes that Arab camel-drivers used to insert a small stone into the womb of any female camel they wanted to keep sterile, and apparently they still do so today.

One theory is that the IUD stimulates the wall of the uterus to produce a substance which prevents the egg from embedding itself in the lining.

To begin with, IUDs were seen as the magical solution to every woman's contraceptive problems. But thirty years of practical experience has shown us that they can have side effects—sometimes quite severe.

Most women complain of greater period pains and heavier periods after the first insertion of an IUD. Some IUDs can cause an irritation in the uterus, and a subsequent infection, in which case they have to be removed.

Still more women find that—after the insertion of an IUD—they become very much susceptible to backaches and minor illnesses. These days, use of IUDs has reached a plateau, with as many being lost or removed every year as there are inserted.

For those women who find that an IUD suits them, however, its success rate as a contraceptive is very high, second only to the pill. Research work continues to produce an IUD which causes no side effects and which is not so readily expelled from the uterus.

The oral contraceptive (the "pill") is still very popular, although not as enthusiastically acclaimed as it was in the 1960s. Its obvious plus points are the ease with which it can be taken and its effectiveness.

There are two basic types of pill—the *combined* pill and the *sequential* pill. Both of them use two hormones—an estrogen similar to that found in the body, and a powerful synthetic progestogen.

In the combined pill, the two hormones are taken together for twenty-one days. In the sequential pill estrogen is taken first, followed later in the cycle with a combination of estrogen and progestogen. Both pills have the effect of suppressing the release of the mature egg from the ovary, so that fertilization cannot occur.

The combined pill is the more effective of the two, although the sequential type is still a very reliable contraceptive indeed.

The problems with contraceptive pills are (a) the simple fact that women forget to take them; and (b) their side effects.

A startlingly large percentage of women who are taking oral contraceptives miss one, two or even more pills in every cycle. Sometimes this is due to plain forgetfulness: sometimes there is a more complicated reason. Some women harbor feelings of resentment that the entire responsibility for contraception should be theirs. Other women want to become pregnant much more than they will care to admit.

Whatever the reason, a woman's lover should be considerate and understanding—as he should be in all matters of sexual health care. Preventing unwanted pregnancies is the joint responsibility of both the man and the woman, no matter which method you choose, and there should be no shyness or secrecy about it.

Some women say that the pill makes them feel depressed, or that it gives them headaches, or causes sporadic bleeding at odd times of the month. Some report that it makes them put on weight. On the other hand, many women find that it makes them feel happier. This feeling of happiness, of course, may partly be due to their relief at not having to worry any more about the risk of getting pregnant.

If you have any unpleasant side effects when you are taking the pill, your doctor can usually sort out your problems by prescribing a pill with a different dosage of estrogen or progestogen.

The only clinical disorder with which the pill is definitely linked is thrombosis (blood clotting) and this appears to have occurred mostly in women who are already susceptible to it.

Of course, neither IUDs nor the pill have any effect

whatsoever in preventing the spread of sexually communicated diseases. You may have a coil or a loop, you may be on the pill, but if you are planning on having intercourse with somebody whose sexual history is unknown to you, or whom you suspect of having more than one lover, or of being bisexual, or of injecting drugs, then it is still *essential* for your own protection that you use a condom.

When you consider how many pregnancies are unplanned, it's really time that we took birth control more seriously. Sex without the fear of accidental conception is much more exciting, in any case. Look on your chosen contraceptive method as part of your pleasure, instead of an awkward interruption. Discuss it with your lover—how you feel about condoms, how you feel about IUDs. Contraception isn't a downer—it's a way to enhance the freedom and the excitement of mature, responsible sex.

Now—fully protected and ready for anything—let's take a look at some of the wilder things that a mature and responsible lover can get up to.

10

Wilder Still and Wilder

Your sexual pleasure is limited only by your imagination and by what your body and mind can safely accept.

If you can take the plunge, and openly tell your lover what you feel and what you want, there's a whole new world of sexual excitement waiting for you. Not next week, not tomorrow, but tonight.

There's only one safeguard you should bear in mind. While lovers should be open and honest with each other—sharing each other's sexual fantasies, sharing each other's sexual tastes—they should never get involved in any sexual act which is seriously painful or permanently damaging or which one partner enjoys to the shame or pain or humiliation of the other.

Like most sex counselors, I'm very liberal in my opinions about sexual tastes. I've advised and assisted literally hundreds of couples for more than a quarter of a century. I've talked to couples whose sexual activities would make the hair of a so-called "normal" couple stand on end. I've talked to women who have willingly had intercourse with dogs and pigs and horses. I've met men and women who have forced four-inch diameter dildoes into each other's anuses, and then made love.

I've corresponded with men who have wanted to dress up in rubber. Men who have wanted to handcuff their wives and pretend to rape them. Women who have been unable to reach orgasm unless they were spanked.

There isn't a single sexual variation that has escaped my attention. But extreme sexual variations are not the key to real and lasting sexual excitement. *Real and lasting sexual excitement comes from finding one person who*

*really turns you on, and working on that excitement with
enthusiasm and commitment.*

One of the problems that I hear most frequently is:
our sex life seems to have gotten into a rut. We're both
bored at bedtime. What do you think about swinging and
swapping?

Well, I have to be honest. Twenty-five years of counseling experience has shown me that swapping and swinging and orgies and group sex may be highly erotic at
the time. Having sex with somebody new is always very
exciting. But—ultimately—swapping sexual partners is
self-defeating. In the end, those who conduct their sex
lives like bees buzzing from flower to flower are those
who end up with no nectar at all.

The statistics on divorce and separation and psychosex-
ual problems bear me out. More than that, a thousand
personal experiences bear me out. That's why I've written a book which is designed to show you how you can
enhance your sex life by showing even more commitment
to your existing relationship, rather than suggest that you
go looking for somebody new simply for the sake of a
novel sexual experience.

These days, swapping and swinging and orgies are
made all the more dangerous by the threat of AIDS.
But, in their way, they've *always* been dangerous. They
may have looked like a convenient escape for couples
whose sexual relationship has been deficient in some
way. Instead of confronting their sexual problems, they
have gotten themselves involved in superficial sex with
other people.

I have read more letters of woe and bewilderment
about partner-swapping than I can count. "I thought she
loved me . . . but I opened the kitchen door, and there
she was, sitting stark-naked on the counter, with her legs
around the neck of this tall blond bearded guy I'd never
been introduced to . . . and his big red dick was shoving
in and out of that cunt that I thought was mine . . . and
to make matters worse, she was wetter than I'd seen her
in years. . . ."

There's no doubt about it. If you neglect your love
life, if you assume that your partner's always going to
get excited by the same old thing, if you don't *work* at

your sexual relationship, then it's going to grow stale. And when I say *stale,* I'm talking year-old pumpernickel. Working at your sexual relationship means:

1. Making the best of what you already know about sex.
2. Asking your lover what he enjoys the most, and doing it.
3. Showing your lover what you like the most, and showing plenty of appreciation when he does it (you can scream, if you like—but no faked orgasms!).

Point (1) is probably the most important point of all. So many women assume that just because they're relatively inexperienced, they're not very good at sex. The reason for their feelings of doubt and uncertainty is that nobody has ever showed them how to fuck properly. Millions of people watch baseball. They talk about tactics; they talk about teams; they discuss technique in the pickiest of detail. If players make a mistake, they *learn,* and they never do it again. Baseball is a matter of open public debate.

But in spite of the fact that *millions* more people have intercourse every night than have ever played baseball since the game was first invented, we still won't talk openly about the techniques of sex. Most of the time, we don't *know* the techniques of sex. Do they tell you about sex on TV, the same way they tell you about baseball? Of course not! It's up to us! We're supposed to have acquired the most expert of sexual skills, through some mystical process of grade-school mythology plus high school biology plus articles in *Cosmo* telling you to take Vitamin E if you suffer from postorgasmic headache, and what to do if your boss keeps coming on strong.

So do we tell our children that sex is not only the greatest expression of love there is, but amusing, recreational, exciting, natural, healthy (providing you use the proper precautions) and free?

Not very often.

And we won't often admit it to ourselves, either.

Too Many Women Accept a Passive Role

So, let's change all that and learn the physical and emotional pleasures of loving the same person for a very long time—and yes, the difficulties, too, and how to get over them. At the very worst, let's put sex on the same par as baseball.

2. "Asking your lover what he enjoys the most and doing it" is almost as critical. Too many women accept a passive role in lovemaking, expecting their husbands or their lovers to guide them. The truth is that very few men have a comprehensive knowledge of sex and sex technique, and that very few men are naturally good lovers. A good lover is a lover who not only consistently pleases his partner, but who consistently pleases himself as well. We're talking about balance here . . . sexual give and take. And there are not many men who are capable of doing that. Men who appear to be "charming, sexy and satisfying" to women can often be sexually very frustrated themselves, because they simply don't know how to tell the women in their lives that *they* have needs, too.

On the other hand, many men who report that they are "satisfied" or "very satisfied" with their sex lives are often seen by women as "brutish, off-hand and unloving . . . never caring what *I* want, or whether *I'm* satisfied."

"Asking your lover what he enjoys the most and doing it" is your first step toward close sexual communication. You might have to tease him a little, nudge him a little. "Come on, what's your wildest erotic fantasy?" But when he tells you, you should do your best to include it in your love life . . . provided it isn't dangerous or sadistic or puts you at any kind of physical or emotional risk.

Happily, the sexual fantasies of most men are very easy to satisfy.

"I'd like to make love to a woman wearing a scarlet basque and scarlet stockings."

"I have this fantasy of standing naked in this kind of Tarzan tree-house, looking out for natives, while this totally naked woman sits at my feet and slowly, slowly sucks my cock."

"I'm employed at a high school . . . in biology class, I have to stand naked in front of all these young girls and masturbate, so that they can see how the male sexual organs work . . . under their desks most of them are wearing no panties, and they're playing with themselves . . . sliding their fingers into their own pussies . . ."

"It's our wedding-day . . . she's still wearing her bridal veil and her white wedding dress . . . but underneath the wedding dress she's wearing stockings but no panties. . . . Her cunt's plump and completely hairless. . . . She opens it up with her fingers and inside she's as pink and sticky as sugar candy. . . . I sit her on my lap and slowly slide my cock up into her. . . . She's a virgin, so she's very tight. . . . The sun's shining through the bedroom window, and shining through her veil, too. . . ."

"I have to do housework for this beautiful dominant woman. I am never allowed to wear any clothes, only a tight leather strap around my balls, with a ring attached to it so that she can clip a dog leash onto it, and take me around the yard for walks. She has black hair, black eyelashes, and she wears a black leather biker's jacket and black leather thigh-boots with stiletto heels, but that's all. Every night I have to kneel in front of her and polish her boots, but I'm not allowed to touch her. When she thinks I haven't cleaned the house properly, she whips me. Sometimes she whips my cock until it's hard, and I have a climax. She makes me kneel down and lick my own sperm from the floor."

"I'm a lodger in this bordello full of pretty young whores. All the girls like me and accept me as one of the household. They don't mind if I watch them dressing and undressing, and they're always asking me to wash their backs when they're sitting in the tub . . . and they like me soaping their breasts, too. Sometimes four or five of them will get into bed with me in the evening, to watch TV or play cards or just talk . . . and they'll be stroking and caressing me . . . and they don't mind if I touch them, too. . . ."

"I'm driving along the freeway and this girl has her head in my lap and she's licking and sucking my cock. . . ."

"I walk into a bedroom by mistake and there's a fantastic-looking girl lying on the bed asleep. Her nightdress has ridden up, so she's exposed from the waist down. I sit on the bed next to her and gently stroke and finger her cunt. Even when I push my fingers up her cunt she doesn't wake up . . . she just stirs and smiles in her sleep. I work another finger into her ass, as far as it will go, and then I slowly masturbate her . . . all the time she thinks that she's dreaming, because she doesn't open her eyes once. . . ."

"Jane and me are walking in Yosemite. It's a hot sunny day. Jane says she has to go, but it's too late and she fills her panties. She's upset and crying so I kiss her and put my arms around her. I reach around and squeeze her panties and realize what she's done. I tell her to kneel doggy-fashion on the ground and I pull open her dirty panties at the back. I push my cock into her asshole while it's still hot and slippery, right up to the balls, and we fuck and fuck and smear each other, until I finally shoot my whole load right into the back of her panties, too. It's filthy and it's messy but we get real turned on. Afterwards we swim in the lake and wash ourselves clean."

"I have this recurring fantasy that I'm arriving somewhere in the Far East, like Thailand or Cambodia or somewhere, and a very handsome Thai woman takes me upstairs to this room overlooking a courtyard which is my apartment. There is a young girl of about sixteen or seventeen there, wearing nothing but a red silk scarf tied around her waist. She's exquisite, very graceful and charming. The woman says that this girl will take care of me and do anything I want her to do. That afternoon I come back and draw the blinds, and ask the girl to take off her scarf and make love to me. She's gentle and silent and she does everything I ask. I lie back on the bed naked and I ask her to lick my cock. She kneels between my legs and licks it really slow, her tongue curling around the head until it's red and glistening. She never takes her eyes off me. Then I tell her to climb on top of me, which she does, and my cock disappears into the black silky hair around her pussy. There's no rush, no panic. Just this amazing sense of peace and tranquillity, and of being allowed to do whatever you want."

Others Have Fantasies of Whips and Spiked Heels

Some men have erotic fantasies that are surprisingly misty and romantic. Others have fantasies that are surrealistic—involving costumes and settings and sexual acts that are almost impossible. Still others have fantasies that are sadomasochistic—fantasies of whips and spiked stiletto heels and instruments of torture—or fantasies that seem downright filthy.

Whatever sexual variations a man *imagines,* however, it doesn't necessarily follow that he has any desire to act those variations out for real. As we have seen before, almost all of us use erotic fantasies to stimulate ourselves during sexual arousal, even though many of these fantasies (if we thought about them calmly and clinically when we *weren't* aroused) would be quite out of character for us.

But a very high proportion of men have admitted to me that they would never dream of telling their wives or lovers about what goes on in their erotic imagination. Their usual response: "She would be totally disgusted. She would probably never speak to me again."

That, unfortunately, is a very telling indictment of women's failure to show that they really wouldn't mind at all if the men in their lives told them what was going on in their fantasies. In fact, you should make it clear to your man that you would positively *love* to hear about his dirtiest and most exciting thoughts.

Encouraging your man to tell you what he fantasizes about is one of the first steps to really close sexual communication, and to driving your man totally and regularly wild in bed. After all, how can you possibly know how to drive him wild if you don't know anything about his sexual tastes?

It's true that his lovemaking will give you some pretty strong clues about the kind of sex that turns him on the most. Is he strong and thrusting in bed? Or does he enjoy lots of gentle foreplay? Does he use his mouth and his tongue a lot? Or does he scarcely ever kiss you? Does he talk dirty to you while he's making love to you, or does he prefer silence? Does he lavish a lot of sexual attention on your breasts? Does he show an obvious interest in anal sex? Does he expect you to make the running, or is your lovemaking always done at his pace?

Sexual actions speak loud and clear, and you can learn a great deal about your lover's fantasies just by analyzing his lovemaking techniques. But not everything. Some of his techniques may simply be the result of his ignorance or inexperience. One wife complained to me, for example, that her husband always rubbed her clitoris so hard when they made love that she always ended up sore and frustrated. When I talked to her husband, it very quickly became clear that he had no idea how to caress her clitoris properly. He was under the impression that the harder he rubbed, the more excited she would become—not realizing that her clitoris was a highly sensitive organ which became even more sensitive during sexual arousal.

Simple sexual ignorance has also been displayed by men who have bitten or chewed their lover's nipples so hard that they inflicted real pain; or men who have consistently failed to perform any kind of foreplay whatsoever, and then wondered why their lovers never reached an orgasm; or men who have never taken the trouble to make sure that their lovers are satisfied.

The result of this ignorance and lack of communication is always the same: boredom, dissatisfaction, frustration . . . and very often the breakdown of the relationship, or the seeking by one or both of the partners of sexual excitement elsewhere. But there is no point in either a man or a woman seeking sexual excitement elsewhere unless they have made a spirited and wholehearted attempt to improve their existing love life. And even if *that* fails, they should at the very least make sure they have understood what went wrong and learned by their mistakes, otherwise they will be carrying the same sexual ignorance and maladroitness into every relationship into which they ever enter.

Men don't automatically know how to make love just

because they're men. They shouldn't expect to know how, and women shouldn't expect it of them.

Good lovemaking comes from what I always call the KISS factor—a combination of Knowledge, Imagination, Sharing, and Sensitivity.

You should acquire knowledge about sex from your parents, from school, from books like this, from erotic and sexually oriented literature and movies, and from experience. With sex, it's never too late to learn. And you should learn as much as possible—not just about your sexual organs and five comfortable positions for making love—but about other people's desires and perversities. The more you know about sex, the better a lover you will be—and the less shockable.

When you're making love, you should not only apply your knowledge but use your imagination so that every act of love is different and exciting. We've seen plenty of ways how!

You should share everything—both your mind and your body. Surrender yourself to your partner's desires. And I mean *completely* surrender yourself. If your man has an urge to do something erotic to you, why be shy? He's doing it to please you, not to hurt you. Why not let him enjoy it? And why not take the trouble to discover what his fantasies are, so that you can share them?

Then there's sensitivity—being alert to your partner's responses and needs—putting yourself in your partner's place. Those men who climax and then turn over and go to sleep without bothering to bring their partner to an orgasm are not only selfish and clumsy, they're missing out on a whole world of highly arousing sexual activities as well . . . post-climactic sex play, which (if skillfully and patiently done) can lead to yet more full acts of very satisfying lovemaking—second or even third climaxes for the man, and literally countless orgasms for the woman.

Obviously, there's a time and a place for asking your man what his fantasies are. You can ask him while you're driving to the mall to do the weekend marketing, but you probably won't get a very satisfactory or comprehensive answer. Confessing to your erotic fantasies can be a very stimulating experience, too, so it's usually better to do it somewhere intimate, where imagination can easily and quickly become reality.

Lovemaking in the Great Outdoors

All of the ten erotic fantasies recounted by men earlier in this chapter were told to the women in their lives . . . and every couple subsequently made some attempt to bring them to life. They didn't necessarily perform them like high school plays, but they tried to act out the most erotic aspects of them. The results weren't uniformly successful, because some of the couples were shyer and more sexually inhibited than others—and some of the women admitted that they had been shocked by the extremity of their men's sexual fantasies and found it difficult to come to terms with the discovery that their "gentle, affectionate, ordinary" partners had been daydreaming of sexy underwear and lovemaking in the great outdoors.

Here was how the women described what happened:

"I adored his fantasy of wearing a red basque and red stockings. . . . I managed to buy some and we made love while I was wearing them. . . . The funny thing is that the first time I wore them, he was too excited to keep his hard-on . . . but I've dressed up that way a few times since, and it keeps on getting better and better. . . . I'm going to try some black underwear next. . . . It turns him on, so where's the harm?"

"He wanted me to act like Bo Derek in *Tarzan,* I think . . . only even more so. But I have to say that I didn't feel at all comfortable, acting out a fantasy like that. It seemed embarrassing to me, rather immature."

"I thought his fantasy of masturbating in front of a whole class of young girls was pretty radical. We didn't have a whole class, only me, but I sat in a chair with my skirt pulled up around my waist, massaging my cunt, while he stood in front of me stark naked and masturbated. I was surprised because I learned a lot, just by watching him. I'd never seen him masturbate before and I was amazed how quick and how hard he rubbed himself. No wonder I'd never been able to masturbate him myself. In the end he stood in front of me and climaxed, and I opened up my legs so that his sperm dropped onto my pubic hair and my open cunt. I liked his fantasy: I found it a turn-on."

"I haven't enjoyed an evening's lovemaking so much as I did when we acted out his wedding-day fantasy. I still had my white veil from our real wedding, of course, and I also wore a white satin dress that I'd bought for a dinner party late last year. Underneath I wore white stockings with frilly white garters, and that was all. I was kind of dubious about the pubic shaving. Quite a few of my friends do it regularly and say that their husbands really like it, but I never have. I guess I didn't want to look like a little girl. Anyway, I did it, and I was actually pleased with the way it looked and the way it felt, and I've kept on doing it ever since. . . . He carried me up to bed just like he was carrying me over the threshold. . . . He kissed me like he hasn't kissed me for a long time . . . very tender, but very passionate. He undressed and sat on the edge of the bed, and I lifted my dress and sat on his lap. His erection was gigantic. He touched my pussy and stroked it, and then he gently parted it with his fingers, like it was the first time that anybody had ever done it to me. Then he lifted me up and gradually lowered me onto his cock. The extraordinary part about being shaved was that I could see every detail of it . . . his cock sliding in between my pussy lips, all the way in. He made me feel like a virgin that evening. I've always been a little bit innocent and naive. Kind of scatterbrained too. I think that's one of the things he likes about me, one of the things that turns him on. . . . I rode up and down on his lap in my bridal veil, and then I suddenly found that I was having an orgasm. . . . I couldn't stop myself. . . . For the very first time in a long time we came almost together . . ."

As I have said many times before, there is no particular virtue in having simultaneous climaxes, and there is no need for lovers to make a special effort to try to come at the same time. In the early days of a sexual relationship, when your erotic responsiveness is at a very high pitch, the mere feeling of your lover climaxing may well be enough to make *you* climax, too, and so simultaneous climaxes are much more frequent than they are later on in your relationship, when you have grown more accustomed to each other's touch.

But while simultaneous orgasm can be immensely exciting, it is not always the most satisfying way of achieving a climax. Quite often, each of you will derive far deeper and more long-lasting pleasure if one of you works to bring the other to a climax, and then the roles are reversed. While your lover is licking your clitoris, for example, you can lie back and relax and swim in a warm sea of pleasure and contentment, waiting for that orgasmic wave to break over you—without having to worry about whether you're both comfortable in that particular position or whether he's holding his climax back in order for you to catch up or whether you're really going to have an orgasm at all or just pretend.

More faked orgasms can be attributed to the myth of the simultaneous climax than any other cause. You don't need to fake orgasms—and, in fact, you shouldn't. You're shortchanging yourself, and you're being sexually dishonest. Your lover should be sufficiently mature and well-informed to understand that there will be occasions when you can't reach a climax or don't particularly feel the need for it. If you can't reach a climax and don't want him to continue stimulating you, all you have to do is say so. It won't mean that he hasn't pleased you, or that he isn't a good lover. It will simply mean that it is your choice not to have an orgasm on that particular occasion. If he *still* doesn't understand, read him this paragraph out loud.

His turn will come when you ride up and down on him, or give him a superior demonstration of oral sex, or give him a warm, flowing climax by massaging his prostate—of which more later.

Let's go back to the fantasies, and in particular to the fantasy of the "beautiful, dominant woman." Here's what the wife of *this* particular fantasist had to say:

"I was thunderstruck when he described his fantasy of being a servant to a dominant woman. Of course I'd heard all about men like that, who like being whipped and humiliated and treated like slaves. But he's such a normal guy. He's so outward-going, so well-adjusted, so *normal*. He's a thoughtful lover and a good friend and it never would have occurred to me in a million years that he could have had a fantasy like that. I was upset about it at first, as you can imagine. But then I told myself: no, it doesn't really change anything. It doesn't change the kind of guy he is, and it doesn't alter anything we've done together. I still love him . . . and, after all, this slave stuff is only a fantasy. I mean, President Carter said he'd lusted after other women in his head, right? But he hadn't actually done anything about it, had he? So in the end I took the view that all of this slave stuff was just the same . . . just a figment of his imagination. When I thought about it, it wasn't any worse really than a fantasy that I used to have, of modeling very erotic fashions, clothes that showed my breasts, dresses that you could see through. . . . Anyway, we played out this slave fantasy one morning and to my total surprise it was very, *very* erotic. I think that I got into it even more than he did. I wore a soft green suede jacket and black suede thigh-boots and nothing else at all. God knows what any of my friends would have thought if they had looked through the window and seen me! He was completely naked except for a black studded strap which I buckled between his legs and around his testicles. We laughed a little at first: nervousness, I guess. But then we really got into the spirit of it. I made him get down on his hands and knees and wash the kitchen floor. Then I made him clean the bathrooms and clean the windows and polish all the furniture. Most of the time he had a huge erection, and even when he wasn't fully hard his penis was quite swollen . . . it obviously turned him on, and it turned me on, too. I kept coming up to him and flicking him with a thin leather strap, just enough to give him a red mark on his bare bottom. When he was finished I walked around and inspected everything while he had to kneel on the floor. I strapped his thighs for leaving polish-marks on the table. Then I bent over a chair and said, 'As a punishment you have to fuck me.' By that time, both of us were pretty well worked up, and we fucked like tigers. I can remember screaming. I'd never been so excited in my life, not sexually. It was all so weird and dangerous and erotic. His penis felt enormous, and I swear that when he climaxed I actually felt it bulge. Then, afterwards, I stood with my legs apart and made him kneel down and lick all of his come from where it was running down my thighs and out of my vagina and everything. He was kneeling between my legs with his tongue up inside my vagina when his penis rose up again and he actually shot out some more come, like a spontaneous climax. We don't play this game too often. I think if our whole sexual relationship depended on us dressing up and playing mistress and slave then we would both be in danger of losing touch with our real selves. But I'd like to do it again, one day, when we're both really, really ready for it. It's quite a turn-on just thinking that we've done it, and that we might do it again."

"They can watch us make love"

This woman's remarks were very interesting, because it is very often the *thought* of a sexual act rather than the act itself which is the greater aphrodisiac. If you can persuade your lover to tell you his fantasies, you can either act them out for real, wholly or partially, or you can simply whisper embellishments to his fantasy in his ear while you're making love. Such as: "You can fuck me in front of a whole roomful of people. . . . They can watch while you push yourself into me. . . . Other women can reach between our legs and fondle your balls and play with my clitoris. . . ."

Here's the woman whose lover liked to imagine that he was the welcome guest in a houseful of whores:

"I liked his fantasy, yes. . . . I thought it was boyish and kind of romantic, the idea of a young man staying in a bordello. We talked about it a whole lot, whether we could act it out, but obviously we couldn't create the same atmosphere as a real bordello. But we discovered what the kind of key to the whole fantasy was . . . he liked to take care of girls, I mean the idea of being around them while they bathed and dressed and everything was something which turned him on. So one afternoon I let him bathe me. . . . He soaped my breasts and my back and between my legs. . . . Then he rinsed me and wrapped me in a towel and dried me. After that he sprayed me with perfume and shook talc on me. . . . He dressed me in stockings and a garter belt and then he made love to me. . . . It was very different from usual, very dreamy. . . . I felt like I was inside some kind of historical movie. . . ."

"He said that he's always fantasized about a girl giving him head while he drove real fast on the freeway. Well, I sure didn't mind trying that. I opened his jeans while he was driving at ninety-five miles an hour, and I took his cock into my mouth and gave him a real deep sucking. I found that I wanted to take him deeper and deeper into my throat; I'd never wanted to do that before. In the end I had to lever his whole cock and his balls out of his jeans. The head of his cock was actually in my throat; I could massage it by doing this slow gulping. I don't care to swallow his come, so I took his cock out right at the end. He didn't mind, though. He came all over my face and my hand and he thought that was out of this world."

"I lay on the bed pretending to sleep with my white silk nightdress pulled up around my waist. He knew I was pretending, of course, but I didn't open my eyes once, and I breathed deep, as if I was asleep, and somehow that made the fantasy quite real. He came into the room and sat on the bed beside me . . . then, as I 'slept,' he stroked my thighs and all around my hips and my stomach . . . very lightly, gradually trailing his fingers closer to my cunt. He ran his fingertips down my lips and touched me between my thighs. Then he opened my lips a little, and I knew that he was looking at me, looking inside my cunt. He opened me wider, and then gradually stretched my lips as far apart as they would go. It was then that I felt his tongue run all the way down from my clitoris, touch my pee-hole, and then slip into my cunt. He licked me for a while and then very quietly left. That night, however, we made love so closely and warmly that I couldn't believe it. It was just like it used to be when we first dated. I suddenly understood that I'd managed to excite him again, and that was something I hadn't managed to do in quite a long time."

"I completely refused to soil my pants for real, and he didn't push it, because he knew that it was one of those fantasies that was better off being a fantasy than trying to act it out. I know there *are* people who enjoy that kind of thing, and I don't despise them. In fact, I might suddenly feel brave enough to do it one day. But not just yet. All the same, I'm glad we talked about it, and we turned each other on quite a lot just by discussing it. Also, the next morning, I called him into the toilet and sat with my legs very wide apart and let him watch me doing it. I don't think that there should be any secrets between lovers, none at all. I don't believe in that thing about women keeping themselves a mystery. The mystery of a woman is what she is; you don't have to create mysteries by being secretive and hiding yourself from the man you love. If he has a burning curiosity to watch me going to the toilet, why should I make a fuss about him? It's better to show him. He says he can still remember every detail of it and it turns him on like you wouldn't believe."

There are very few women who would have the courage and composure to do what this woman did: and she would have been quite within her rights to refuse to have anything to do with such an extreme fantasy. There are times when everybody has a right to personal privacy, no matter how intimate and open their sexual relationship might be. But I have included her lover's fantasy and her response to it, because between them they are a remarkable example of how a woman can deal with a man's most extreme sexual thoughts, and yet retain her dignity and her self-respect.

An interest in watching women defecating is not nearly as uncommon as you might think. Almost every issue of the glossy Swedish sex magazine *Sex Bizarre* has pictures of girls defecating in extreme close-up . . . sometimes over men's faces or chests or penises.

In his first-class study of Japanese sexual behavior *Pink Samurai*, author Nicholas Bornoff describes a very specialized Tokyo club. "In a spacious room hung entirely with black velvet, wealthy scatologists congregate around a long lacquered table bearing only a large, polished silver tray in the center, which reflects a single spotlight. Having paid substantial sums of money for an occasion lasting some ten minutes, the guests sit in high-backed chairs as though attending a banquet.

"A hush falls as a breathtaking beauty in a dark silk kimono glides across the room and steps noiselessly up onto the table, gradually lifting the hem as she walks like one in a trance towards the gleaming platter. Pausing a moment and gazing into space, she raises the garment over her hips to reveal complete nakedness beneath. As all eyes become riveted to the intimacies reflected in the tray, she defecates. Slowly getting to her feet, she gradually drops the kimono again, steps regally from the table and disappears.

"The deposit has an aroma like incense. She had been fed with certain foods perfumed with aromatic herbs."

Bornoff also describes the S/M shows in the Japanese *nudo* theaters, in which naked strippers offer themselves to the audience for a communally administered enema. "She crawls around the stage backwards, proffering her posterior to ritual postulants like a cat in heat. Once an outsize syringe has been emptied and refilled many times over from an aquarium hauled on stage by the pantomime torturer, the bursting stripper squats over it to relieve herself of gallons of water. In order to ensure that no scatologist should be disappointed by the production of only a jet of clear water, some strippers send dozens of rectally concealed marbles clattering into the aquarium."

His Utter Submission

While these are both rather extreme examples of ways in which some men seek to indulge their sexual fantasies, it is commonly recognized that almost all men are aroused to some extent by the idea (if not the actuality) of wet sex. All kinds of deep theories have been propounded, from the notion that it reminds men of their early childhood, to the idea that it is a way in which a man can show his utter submission to the one he loves.

My own theory (based on talking to some very normal and happy couples about it) is that it can occasionally give a sexual relationship a touch of being "dirty and forbidden"—a highly stimulating sensation which is often lost in the respectability and day-to-day familiarity of a long-term relationship or marriage.

Elaine, twenty-six, a homemaker from Portland, Oregon, wrote: "Before I read your book I had dreamed but never dared. You showed me that all things are possible between two people who love each other without embarrassment or shame. I had never attempted oral sex before, and the weekend after I read your book I 'went down' on Bradley for the very first time. That drove him wild, all right! I wasn't very good at it to begin with, but I got better, and I'm still getting better all the time. Then a week ago I really let myself go. He was shaving in the morning when I came into the bathroom, lifted my dress, and sat on the john. I was only wearing panty hose underneath and I opened my legs and said, 'Look!' and peed straight through them. He was shocked but also excited and he went to the office *very* late that day. If you want to know the truth, you have allowed me to feel 'naughty' again—and it's so exciting!" (The exclamation points are hers.)

The closest and the happiest sexual relationships that I have come across have been those in which the man is highly attuned to the woman's sexual sensitivities—to her changes in mood, to her sense of romance, to her varying sexual needs—and in which the woman is prepared to listen to any sexual desire which her partner may express, no matter how extreme it may sound. Whether she's willing to fulfill that desire—well, that's up to her. But couples very often find (as this woman did) that *talking* about a sexual fantasy is often enough to satisfy it. Sometimes, in fact, it's more exciting to talk about it than it is to *do* it.

A couple from Phoenix, Arizona, told me about their bondage fantasies . . . how they would tie each other up and whip each other. She would pierce his foreskin with a silver ring, and *he* would pierce her vaginal lips with a silver padlock, to which he alone would have the key.

A couple from Eureka, California, described their lovemaking in front of all of their friends, how they would strip naked and perform oral sex and every conceivable sexual variation while their neighbors and their business associates looked on.

A couple from Indianapolis, Indiana, told me that they frequently picked up stray sexual partners . . . hitchhikers, truckers, hookers, salesmen, anyone who took their fancy. They would take them back to their home and make "fierce and dirty love."

In actual fact, all of these fantasies had remained fantasies. None of them had been acted out for real. Yet they all contributed to the sexual excitement of the couples involved, and enabled them to express their innermost desires in the context of mutual affection and mutual understanding.

The tenth and last fantasy that I mentioned in this chapter—the fantasy of being looked after by a young Oriental girl—gives us some very valuable pointers to the way in which you can drive your man wild in bed.

You see, in complete contrast to the feminist view that all men are potential rapists, almost all men are in fact looking for a sexual encounter in which they have to bear none of the responsibility for what happens. Women's erotic fiction is full of rape and conquest, but men's erotic fiction is full of stories about nymphomaniacs who approach men "absolutely begging for it."

One of the major reasons why men are aroused by pictures of nude girls is because the girl is offering her body without any of the complications or embarrassments of having to be wooed and seduced. One of the major reasons why women are not aroused by nude pictures of men is because they are not particularly turned on by a man who is so submissive that he is prepared to take off all his clothes and offer himself like a lamb. (Another major reason is that nude men in mass-circulation magazines cannot be shown with a full erection, and a man without a full erection is obviously a man who is not sexually aroused.)

Eventually, you can strike a happy balance between the way you want to be loved and the way your lover wants to love you. But if you're looking to turn your love life around in one night flat, then you're going to have to think about turning him on first. In fact, you're going to have to do most of the work—for starters, anyway.

It's going to be up to you to set the sexual pace in your relationship, because if he's like most of the men I know, he's going to need guidance, reassurance, stimulation—and, most critical of all, he's going to need your *approval*.

There are a whole lot of sexual desires and fantasies inside of your lover's mind that he hasn't told you about. This is 100 percent true of all men. If he's there beside you now, show him this sentence and challenge him to deny it.

All you have to do is find out what his desires really are, and satisfy them—even, as we've said before, just by *talking* about them. I really don't expect you to defecate on a polished silver plate.

Make your relationship an anything-goes zone, as far as sex is concerned. One proviso, of course—the famous Masterton Rule of Sexual Respect. Never force your partner to take part in any sexual act that he or she doesn't enjoy, or that either one of you finds painful or degrading. In a good sexual relationship, you're one person. Respect your partner as much as you respect yourself.

There are some sexual acts (such as oral or anal sex) which many women initially shy away from. My rule of sexual respect doesn't mean that, just because you don't like the idea of them now, you should *never* try them. All exciting sexual relationships involve learning and growing and sharing. If you communicate well—if you articulate every reservation as well as every fantasy—then you will help your partner to learn and to teach, and the two of you will grow together.

To change and improve your sex life *pronto,* however, you can't wait for your man to make all the moves. With some men, you'll still be waiting when you're ninety. You'll have to show him that you're eager to put some zest into your lovemaking by coming on a little stronger than usual . . . suggesting sex in the middle of the afternoon, climbing into the shower with him, giving him "accidental" peeks as you dress and undress.

Try some new perfume. Take some time out to glamorize yourself a little more. Take a deep breath and buy some very erotic underwear—although you can look plenty sexy without resorting to see-through nylon and lacy frills. Jennifer, a very large-breasted brunette from Charleston, South Carolina, told me that she could turn her husband into a howling wolf just by walking around the house in a pair of old frayed jeans—provided that was *all* she wore. And Aileen, a twenty-three-year-old redhead from Pittsburgh, Pennsylvania, said she improved her sex life "at a stroke" by occasionally greeting her husband in the nude when he came home, and by remaining nude all day "one or two Saturdays a month."

This sort of open erotic teasing isn't always possible—especially if you have children around the house—but there are plenty of other things you can do to show your man that you're interested in sex and that you approve of *his* interest in sex.

Before you launch into a full-blooded erotic assault on your partner, however, it's worth spending a little time thinking about *why* you need to perk up your sex life. If it's become dull or routine or even nonexistent, there may be some physical or psychological difficulties that need to be ironed out first.

Human sexual relationships are complex, unpredictable, and charged with emotion, especially when you're dealing with a man's sense of virility. The very last thing you want to do is to make an existing problem even worse. So here are some of the most common difficulties, and how to deal with them.

11

How to Cure His Sexual Hangups

One of the most frequent complaints I hear from women is that their lovers are disinclined not only to discuss their sexual desires but their sexual difficulties. I was recently in correspondence with a newlywed wife of twenty-four from Philadelphia, Pennsylvania, whose husband had been unable to achieve a full erection ever since they were married. She was growing desperate—not only because she was sexually frustrated, but because she was worried that her new husband may not really love her, or might be suffering from some physical or psychological illness.

However, her husband adamantly refused to discuss his repeated sexual failure with her and refused to seek the help of a doctor or psychiatrist or sexual counselor.

Regrettably, this refusal to communicate is not at all unusual. Many men feel that they are supposed to know all about sex and that they should be infallible in bed—always satisfying their partner, always achieving a mega-erection. When things go wrong, they refuse to face up to the problem, refuse to discuss it—and by doing so, they make matters much worse. They put themselves into a state of panic, and they seriously upset their partners at the same time.

Most of the time, a man's failure to achieve erection has its roots in very simple and easily solved problems. The most common of all is stress at work—anxiety about promotion, anxiety about money. Sometimes the problem is simple exhaustion, in which case a weekend's rest and a good proprietary tonic can work wonders. Alcohol is another common cause of erection failure—that well-known syndrome "brewer's droop"—and its effects tend to be longer-lasting as a man grows older and his liver loses its youthful capacity for dealing so speedily with intoxicating drink.

The problem is that once a man has had *one* bad experience in losing his erection (or failing to get an erection at all), he is much more likely to have a second and a third bad experience . . . and without immediate help and understanding, his sexual performance can slide very rapidly downhill from then on. Worry breeds anxiety, anxiety breeds panic, and nobody can go to bed and make hot, hard, and passionate love if they're in a state of panic.

Every time a man fails to achieve or keep his erection, his feeling of stress and anxiety and failure increases and makes it that much more difficult for him to achieve it the next time.

If *your* man suffers any kind of sexual problems, try your best to talk them over with him. If he refuses, suggest that he discuss them with your family doctor or a close friend. If he *still* refuses, then there's still a great deal that you can do on your own.

Don't get upset. However taciturn and aggressive his behavior, he will be feeling vulnerable, frustrated, and unmanly. If he perceives that his lack of sexual performance is making you feel anxious or unsure of him, he will feel even worse.

Don't blame him. Even if his lack of sexual potency has been self-inflicted by overwork or alcohol. He is blaming himself enough already. No sexual problem was ever solved by accusations.

Don't think the worst. The first reaction that many women have when their lover fails to achieve or keep his erection is 'I don't turn him on any more.' Then they start thinking 'He doesn't love me any more.' *Then* they start thinking 'If he isn't sexually interested in me any longer, who *is* he interested in?' Two failed hard-ons in a row can generate a hideous fantasy of mistrust and suspicion and phantom mistresses before you can say "Fatal Attraction."

You should try to talk about his sexual failure calmly and rationally and even amusingly. Try and find out what's wrong but if you can't do that, take a good look at what's *right*. Does he obviously still love you? Is he generally happy at home? Does he appear to be in reasonable health and not under too much pressure at work?

Don't show that you're frustrated. No matter how sexually pent-up you feel, don't show him that you're frustrated. This will only serve to lower his sexual self-esteem and make a normal love life even more difficult to reestablish. Make a point of masturbating before he comes home. Take your time over it and enjoy it. Use a dildo or a vibrator, but this is one time when a little secrecy is not only excusable but necessary . . . don't let him know that you're easing your erotic tension with a plastic penis. It will only make him feel even more inadequate.

Break the cycle of sexual failure. This is the key part of your whole therapy. Once you've shown him that you're calm and understanding about his sexual dysfunction, now you can start working on him to restore his potency. Masters and Johnson did some fascinating pioneering work in this field with their "pleasuring" therapy—women sitting between their partner's legs and massaging their penises into erection until at last they were confident enough to get erections quite normally. Masters and Johnson also used sex surrogates—specially trained women therapists who would show your partner in no uncertain terms that he *could,* after all, get an erection and keep it—but I think I am probably right in assuming that this is a course of treatment you would rather not adopt.

You can break the cycle of sexual failure by keeping up a high level of sexual interest in him. Show him that you still think he's sexy, even though his cock may be soft. You can do this with small but significant displays of affection like kisses and hand-holding and always treating him in the company of other people as if he's a real man. Surprisingly, very few guides to sexual therapy mention the importance of creating this day-to-day ambiance of affection and eroticism, but it is tremendously helpful and supportive to a man who feels sexually inadequate.

Touch him intimately and fondle him whenever you get the opportunity. If he starts to get a hard-on and then loses it, don't take your hand away, don't show that you're disappointed (even though you will be).

The best way to solve a man's sexual failure is to restore his confidence in his ability to satisfy you . . . and at the same time, to divert his attention away from himself, and onto *your* sexual pleasure.

In other words, make him appreciate that he can still satisfy you, still excite you, even if he's experiencing a little trouble.

Although his penis may not be stiffening, his tongue and his fingers will still be able to bring you to orgasm, and you should encourage him to do this as often as possible.

Masters and Johnson found that almost every man who sought their help for sexual dysfunction was capable of cure . . . in the same way that almost every woman who was unable to reach orgasm was capable of cure. If you ever get discouraged by your lover's continued failure to achieve an erection, think to yourself: he can get out of it, and comparatively quickly, provided you don't panic or get frustrated or accuse him of failure.

Whatever you can do to help him conquer his impotence, it's an investment in your future happiness. You're going to benefit, he's going to benefit. You'll both be fulfilled.

Masters and Johnson, at the Reproductive Biology Research Foundation at St. Louis, devised a program for women to help their impotent lovers to return to potency through gentle manipulation and (when their penises began to stiffen) a gradual return to penetrative intercourse. In other words, some gentle rubbing, followed by some gentle and undemanding fucking.

In 1970, I talked at length with Fred Belliveau, Masters and Johnson's editor at Little, Brown, and one of the co-authors of *Human Sexual Inadequacy,* and we agreed that "pleasuring" was a considerable step forward in encouraging women to deal with the responsive problems from which thousands of men suffer.

More than two decades later, the therapeutic work that Masters and Johnson originated is still relevant, even if it is dated. At least they recognized that many men *do* have a problem, and that very few women know how to deal with it—or even that they *can* deal with it, or *should* deal with it.

One of the most important advances is that, these days, women are much more prepared to consider sexual variations . . . they're better-educated, they're sexually wise. Two decades ago, asking a woman to suck her lover's penis back to potency would have been considered risque, if not outrageous. Fellatio was strictly for prostitutes and groupies. Maybe it would have turned some men and women on to think about it . . . but actually to *do* it??

But one of the gentlest (yet one of the most stimulating) ways to help a man with sexual difficulties is to take his softened penis into your mouth, all of it, and gently suck him. At the same time, you can fondle his balls, and tickle his perineum (that bridge of flesh between his balls and his anus) and his anus, too.

Rhythmically suck his glans against the roof of your mouth (not too hard!), and circle your tongue around and around his shaft. Take advantage of his softness, and see if you can cram one of his balls into your mouth, too. Make a meal of it. Make him feel that you want to eat him up, sexually, and be as dirty as you like.

Crouch over him in the classic "sixty-nine" position and continue to suck his cock. Not too hard—even if it's stiffening—and don't expect anything out of it, either. The most crushing psychological blow that you can deliver to him now is to stop sucking him in obvious dissatisfaction. *Aren't you* ever *going to get erect?*

Lift your bottom and your vulva in front of his face. You can reach between your legs with one hand and open your vaginal lips, encouraging him to touch you and lick you. The very sight of your open vagina will help to arouse him. Let him know (as he's licking and fingering) that he's turning you on.

After a while, reach back between your legs again and dip one or two fingers into your vagina, right in front of him, where he can see, and then quickly push those fingers into his anus, as far as they will go. Continue to suck his penis as you rotate your fingers inside his rectum, stretching his anus as wide as you can. Remember that his anus is crammed with erotic nerve-endings, and that (to coin a phrase) you will be giving him no end of stimulation.

Although many women are quite familiar with anal touching and anal caressing and the insertion of one or more fingers into their anus by their lovers during sex, very few of them return the compliment by stimulating their lovers in the same way. This is a pity: because a man's anal region, like a woman's, is highly sensitive to sexual stimulation (hence the use of anal intercourse by some homosexuals).

A woman who is trying to break a cycle of impotence in her partner will find anal stimulation extremely useful. Two or three fingers inserted deep into his rectum and moved with a regular "beckoning," churning motion will give him extremely arousing sensations right in the floor of his pelvis, and encourage erection.

Anal stimulation is the only way in which a woman can penetrate a man—and, as we have seen from many of the sexual fantasies which men express—men can be just as aroused by acting out a sexually submissive role as they can by acting out a sexually aggressive role. Even if you are experiencing no difficulties in your sexual relationship at all, you can use anal stimulation of your lover to devastatingly exciting effect, including the insertion of fingers, strings of beads (slowly dragged out at the moment of ejaculation), so-called "butt plugs" (which are nothing more than squat, pyramidal vibrators), full-sized or giant-sized dildos, or even your entire hand, well-lubricated, in a surgical glove, with which you can reach inside his rectum for what is known as "fisting."

As I have often mentioned to women who have expressed reservations about anal intercourse, the lower rectum is usually empty until the moment of defecation. But of course the rectum harbors many bacteria, and a great deal of care should be taken to keep the anal area clean and to wash hands after anal stimulation. On no account should you insert anything into your vagina after you have used it for anal stimulation (and that includes your lover's penis).

If you learn to stimulate your lover's penis orally while your fingers probe his rectum, you will be giving him remarkably effective arousal which will do a great deal toward reviving his natural ability to achieve an erection. The "beckoning, churning" motion with your fingers will apply consistent pressure to his prostate gland. In his pamphlet on the intensification of male and female climaxes, Felix Berger describes how a man can do this himself:

"Lie back on the bed, draw your knees up and put your feet flat on the bed, then draw your legs even further up. Now insert your thumb in your rectum and press against the front wall. Now rub downwards in the direction of the anus. Do you feel your prostate? It is a soft mass, a few centimetres inside the intestine on the front wall. Take it easy, because stimulation of the prostate will produce a feeling that is not exactly pleasant at first. Be gentle with yourself. Or ask your partner to do it—it will certainly be much more pleasant. Many men report that when this was done they had a wonderful and hitherto unknown feeling, quite different from what they knew through loving fondling of the end of the penis. Do you notice how you are aroused when it is not your penis, but your prostate, which is rubbed? And you will find another surprising thing—you have an ejaculation. The semen flows out of your penis, it is not forced out."

This flow of semen (which is produced by direct manual stimulation of the prostate gland, rather than "normal" methods of arousal) can give your partner a very erotic and satisfying feeling. What's more, he doesn't necessarily have to have an erection in order to climax. If you *can* give him one of these flowing orgasms by anal and oral stimulation, then you will have taken a first important step toward rebuilding his confidence in his virility—and something else, too, which many therapy manuals forget. You will release a great deal of his underlying sexual tension. Even men who can't have erections feel sexually frustrated.

Make a point of emphasizing his ejaculation, even though his sperm will pour out rather than spurt out. Massage it over his penis and his balls and over your breasts, too, and then suck and lick it if you have a taste for it.

At the same time, you should be doing everything you can to encourage him to stimulate *you*—so that he thinks less about his own problems and more about being what both of you want him to be—which is your lover.

Sit on his face so that he has to lick and kiss and tongue your vulva. Encourage him to lick your anus and push his fingers into your rectum. Moan and sigh and show him that he's turning you on. He will give you plenty of genuinely arousing stimulation, and later on he will be able to make love to you in the usual way—proud, virile and hard. And he will have *you* to thank for his sexual success.

When it comes to trying penetration again, don't rush him and don't expect too much. Some men lose their erections as soon as they insert their penises, while others lose them during the sexual act itself. There are always mechanical, less exciting moments during intercourse, and at times like that, they start worrying about keeping their hard-ons, and their anxiety leads almost immediately to a severe case of the flops.

You will be frustrated. You may even be angry. But if you are going to rescue your sexual relationship, this is the most critical time of all. You will have to take a deep breath, kiss him, and then *gently* go down on him and give him a slow, lascivious, and nonurgent cocksucking. Don't expect anything out of it. He may not manage another erection, in which case you can gradually ease off the oral stimulation, hold him in your arms and tell him you love him.

On the other hand, your continuing sexual interest in him may produce another erection, in which case you may be able to try intercourse for a second time.

I'm not going to pretend for a moment that it's easy, restoring a man's sexual confidence and helping him to overcome the problem of impotence. You will probably find it helpful to talk to your doctor about it. At least you won't feel alone.

But even if you can't talk to your doctor, always remember that your lover *does* love you, and he *does* want you, and that you *do* turn him on—even when he can't manage to raise an erection. Always bear that in mind, and you should be able to find the strength and the patience to help him.

Helping your lover to overcome sexual problems can

be a long, slow business . . . but the rewards are infinite pleasure and complete satisfaction.

Coming Too Quickly

Another very common sexual problem from which men suffer is *premature ejaculation*. This means that they ejaculate far sooner than they want to—sometimes as soon as they insert their penis into your vagina. Because of that, every act of intercourse lasts only a few seconds, with the result that both of you wind up very frustrated.

Some women whose lovers suffer from premature ejaculation have told me that they are barely aroused before their lovemaking is all over.

During the course of their research, Masters and Johnson found many common elements in the sexual history of men who suffer from premature ejaculation. All of their early sexual experiences were hurried—what you might call "quickies"—either with prostitutes or with girlfriends in situations where they were likely to be discovered. It takes only two or three formative sexual incidents in which rapid ejaculation is considered to be a desirable accomplishment for the pattern to be imprinted forever.

Sometimes, the results of this imprinting can be disastrous and can cause sexual problems for years and years to come.

Premature ejaculation shouldn't be defined in terms of time. Nobody can say how long the ideal act of intercourse is supposed to last. As long as both of you are satisfied, it could be anything from fifteen seconds to fifteen hours. The clinical definition of a man suffering from a premature ejaculation is a man who is unable to prevent himself from ejaculating before his partner reaches an orgasm more than fifty percent of the times they make love.

Many men simply don't worry about premature ejaculation. Even today, in this age of sexual enlightenment, I am sorry to say that many men regard their partners as little more than sexual receptacles who are not supposed to have erotic feelings of their own. So if they ejaculate quickly and their partners remain unsatisfied they remain completely unconcerned.

In more sophisticated relationships, where the man *does* worry about his problem, there is still a danger of persistent and long-term problems. To begin with, a couple may console themselves that the man's premature ejaculation is caused by nothing more than sexual overexcitement and that the condition will eventually correct itself. Sometimes this happens, and the man does manage to assert control over his ejaculation. But in most cases it takes more than time.

In cases where premature ejaculation persists, the woman begins to feel more and more that she is being used for her partner's sexual satisfaction, and that he has no understanding of *her* needs and *her* frustration.

The man tries all kinds of self-help methods to delay his ejaculation, such as counting backwards or thinking about problems at work, but these are rarely effective and they take a great deal of the joy and spontaneity out of intercourse. Sometimes they have the reverse effect and cause the man to lose his erection altogether, which may bring on a case of impotence.

All of this conflict has the effect of taking the pleasure and passion out of a couple's sex life, and premature ejaculation can be a direct cause of couples losing sexual interest in each other and drifting apart.

Many men who suffer from premature ejaculation refuse to accept that the problem is theirs, and blame their partners instead for "not being sexy enough." In his analysis of Masters and Johnson's work, Fred Belliveau remarked "these men can hardly be blamed . . . the idea that women are entitled to sexual pleasure is a relatively recent one in our culture."

He wrote that in 1970. Sadly, I would say from the letters I receive that the situation hasn't changed all that much. When pressed, quite a high percentage of men will admit that women have a right to sexual satisfaction, but few of them know how to translate words into actions, and it is my view that sexual ignorance among men is just as serious a social problem now as it was in 1970. Satisfying a woman takes thought, care, skill and practice—and not enough men are prepared to learn how to do it. The result is a high level of sexual dissatisfaction, a high level of separation and divorce—and a great many good relationships unnecessarily broken up.

Men are notoriously bad at working out their own sexual problems, since they are usually so closely associated with problems of stress or problems of early imprinting. But an understanding and imaginative woman can usually work wonders.

If, for instance, the man in your life suffers from premature ejaculation, there *is* something you can do about it yourself. Before Masters and Johnson, most doctors and sex therapists recommended that the woman should avoid touching the man's penis during foreplay, as this would overstimulate it, and lead to an early climax. In fact this "no touch" idea didn't work at all, and often created more sexual tension, and even prompter ejaculation. Masters and Johnson took an idea first introduced in the *Southern Medical Journal* in 1956 and put it into practical use in St. Louis, with excellent results.

What they called "the direct genital approach" is still just as effective today, and you can use it to delay your man's ejaculation and actually train him to hold off his climax—if you're lucky, for hours on end.

If your man lies naked on his back, you can sit between his legs and massage his penis into erection. In this therapy, you will be doing the exact opposite of what I suggested in the chapter on handling your man's penis. You will be placing your thumb on his frenum, and two fingers on the opposite side of the thumb—one on each side of the ridge that separates the glans from the shaft. You can massage his penis into erection, but then you should squeeze your thumb and your two fingers together—quite hard, for three or four seconds at a time. This pressure will make your lover lose his urge to ejaculate—although, twenty-odd years after Masters and Johnson first tried it in their therapy center, nobody quite knows why.

Why it happens isn't especially important, except for research biologists. For an ordinary couple who are trying to save their sexual relationship, the only important part about it is that it *does* happen—and that you can stimulate your lover's penis for fifteen to twenty minutes without him ejaculating, provided you keep on squeezing him every time he looks or feels like he's nearing a climax.

This technique works so quickly and so well that a couple soon have their sexual happiness and their sexual confidence restored—and should be ready to try intercourse again.

When you do begin intercourse again, you should sit on top while your lover lies on his back. Guide his penis into your vagina and sit perfectly still, allowing him to become accustomed to the feeling of being inside you. Then gradually move yourself up and down. If he feels that he's close to ejaculation, you should take his penis out of you and apply the same "squeeze" technique that you applied before, until his urge to climax subsides. Then you can guide it back into your vagina, and start again.

Gradually, your lover will become accustomed to holding back his climax when he makes love, and will develop strong ejaculatory control. I should emphasize, though, that this "squeeze" technique only works with couples, and that a man on his own cannot train himself by squeezing his penis whenever he feels like ejaculating. It is something that he will have to do with you . . . a therapy which requires your active participation.

You should remember, though, that premature ejaculation is one of the easiest sexual problems to sort out, and that Masters and Johnson reported a success rate of well over ninety percent.

Many women find that a lack of sexual communication is one of the biggest problems in their relationships. Their lovers will make love to them in silence—never discussing any sexual fantasies or sexual preferences—and even though they may be competent and considerate, they always leave their women with a feeling of doubt and uncertainty. Did he really enjoy it? Was he really satisfied? Or has he turned over and gone to sleep, dreaming of some sexual act that I could never dream of?

The easiest way to deal with a problem of sexual communication is to pose your own sexual questions, and see what response you get. By "sexual questions," I mean that you should try out several different ways of turning your man on, and try to assess his response.

For instance, try dressing up sexily for him, in a short skirt or a clinging latex dress. Try being more sexually forward, and encouraging him to go to bed with you— even if it's lunchtime! Try touching him and manipulating him more. Try going down on him, and giving him a long, lascivious session of cocksucking. Try turning him over into different positions in bed. Try stripping for him at bedtime. Try shaving off your pubic hair. Try being hard-to-get. Try being whorish.

These are all sexual questions. See which question (or questions—some men have more than one sexual preference) provokes the most dynamite reaction.

This is all part of finding out what makes him sexually excited—all part of getting to know him better. And the better you know him, the easier it will be for you to turn him on.

Do-It-Yourself

Here's Katie, a thirty-one-year-old staff supervisor at a large hotel in Detroit, Michigan: "For about six to eight months, my husband and I didn't seem to be hitting it off in bed. I don't know . . . all the sparkle seemed to have gone out of it. I had the feeling that I didn't turn him on any longer. He still got hard, he still fucked me, but it all seemed so routine . . . like he was only doing it to get rid of some physical tension, and because fucking is what husbands and wives are supposed to do.

"He always used to be so sensitive, so creative, always finding something different to do, always finding someplace different to fuck. Our sex life was always warm and exciting . . . something to look forward to. Then it just kind of died away . . . like flat Coca-Cola. Still tastes the same, but no more fizz.

"First of all, I looked to him to blame. I thought to myself: you're working too hard, you're too worried about the next promotion, you're too worried what might happen if business gets bad and you're out of a job. You're too worried about your *pride,* man!

"But then I thought—of course he's worried about his job, of course he's worried about his promotion. Of course he's worried about his pride. Those are things that a man worries about, and he worries about them even more when he gets older. You know what I mean—his options start to close in.

"A whole lot of what was happening to us was *his* fault for sure. But then you said that when two people have sexual problems, it's their relationship that's the patient, not either of them. Blaming your partner doesn't get you anywhere. You have to think what you can do to revive the patient, no matter what your partner's doing about it. You have to *give* in order to *get.*

"I looked at myself in the mirror. Maybe he was working too hard, getting too stressed. But I was getting into a rut. I went out and had my hair done. I painted my nails. I went to a store and had a facial. I bought myself some new underwear—some white satin panties and a black nylon G-string and an oyster-colored teddy. I bathed myself and I pampered myself and when my husband came home, I greeted him wearing my teddy and nothing more.

"I spoiled him that evening. I did everything for him. He wanted to wash the dishes but I wouldn't let him. I said, 'Forget the dishes, take me to bed the way you always used to take me to bed,' and for once we went to bed without being tired, and I undressed him, and before he could say anything, I took hold of his big black stiff cock and I clamped my mouth around it and he lay back on that bed while I sucked him and ran my tongue-tip all the way down to his balls and way back up again.

"Then I climbed on top of him and I fucked him. I swung my breasts from side to side so that my nipples brushed his chest, and then I leaned forward and kissed him and nibbled his ears and told him how much I loved him, and that maybe I'd forgotten how much I loved him, but this was a way of saying, 'let's be lovers again.'

"His cock was huge, like a shiny black tree-trunk, and it slid in and out of me, all the way down to his balls. I could reach behind me and feel his tight slippery balls snug up against my bottom, and fondle them.

"We fucked real slow, for a very long time, don't ask me how long. But then our fucking got a little faster, and a little faster, and soon we were all sweat-shiny and fucking like crazy people. I had an orgasm, I couldn't help it, it hit me like a truck from behind, and I shook so much that his cock came out of me, and then *he* had a climax too, and his come spurted out all over my breasts and my stomach and slid down between my legs. It was like warm rain.

"I rubbed his come around and around my stomach, and then I touched his lips with it, so that he could taste it, too. He laughed and he kissed me. I'll never forget it. That was the night when we started to fall in love all over again. I gave and I got. There's no point in having too much pride when it comes to love. Love is all about loving, and loving means understanding, and caring, and whatever they said in that movie, loving means knowing when to say you're sorry, and *meaning* it."

However upset you may be feeling about your lover's failure to achieve erection or to satisfy you properly, the future of your sex life and maybe your whole relationship depends on you *not* being resentful, and giving yourself wholeheartedly to your partner. Think of it as an investment. An investment which—given time—will pay you back everything you put into it, with a very generous amount of interest.

One of the most interesting examples of self-help sexual therapy was described to me by twenty-seven-year-old Lara, a beautician from Santa Fe, New Mexico, who wrote and told me that her husband had been worried about his work and had turned to drinking and overeating as a way of consoling himself.

He had put on more than thirty pounds, and his interest in sex had—in her words—"taken a nosedive."

Stress is one of the most common causes of sexual problems. Stress about money, stress about career achievement, stress about health or family problems. It can cause both men and women to withdraw into themselves. Not only that, it can change their personality and make them seem unapproachable and strange, even to their lovers.

When your lover is stressed, he may be moody, argumentative, and difficult to get along with. You may not feel like being sexy and affectionate toward him. But this is the time when he needs your sexiness and your affection more than ever. Lovemaking is a wonderful way of uncorking bottled-up tension, not only because it helps you to forget your day-to-day anxieties, but because it uses up adrenaline. An excess of adrenaline in the system brings on all kinds of unpleasant symptoms, such as heart palpitations and stomach cramps, and a generally "leaden" feeling.

Lara had several serious arguments with her husband Jeff before she decided to do something practical about his problems.

"The trouble was, when he had been drinking, *I* had often been drinking, too, and I would deliberately say things that provoked him. Of course he had no right to shout at me but at the same time I could have defused the situation by saying okay, okay, let's forget it, instead of getting on his case. You only have to hear another couple arguing to understand how men and women provoke each other. She will accuse him of being weak, something less than a man. He will accuse her of being a nag and a sexless bitch. You will hear them saying all of these things to each other, and the better they know each other, the more hurtful their remarks will be. And you think, this is crazy, these people love each other, I know they do. How can they say such things?

"For a while, Jeff and I went through a period of arguments like this. They were so upsetting. I thought our whole marriage was over. I thought I would have to leave, and then it would be lawyers and divorce courts. But then I took time out to think about everything really carefully, and I suddenly realized that our relationship didn't have to be this way. He and I were going down the same downhill road to destruction, and all I was doing was making us get there faster.

"I started being positive instead of negative. I took stock of my looks; I took stock of the way I dressed. Jeff had put on weight, but that was no excuse for *me* to look frowzy. I started to groom myself the way I always used to groom myself when we first dated. I went on a diet.

I started taking pride in myself, which is something I hadn't done in a long time."

Lara's first steps were very constructive. One of the problems about sexual relationships that are going downhill is that there is little incentive for either partner to make any effort to be charming or sexy or flirtatious. Both partners feel frustrated and angry, and so your inner voice says, "Why should I do anything for *him*? He never satisfies me, he's always aggressive, he won't even tell me what's wrong, and quite frankly I don't care any more."

But in order to save the relationship, somebody has to break out of the spiral. Somebody has to say, "Hey, what are we doing here? I love him, I don't want this to happen." Breaking out doesn't mean giving in. It doesn't mean that you're surrendering your pride or your dignity or your feminine integrity. It simply means that you want to save your relationship, for your own sake as much as his, and that you've recognized the best way of doing it.

Lara wrote, "It took a little time for Jeff to understand that I wasn't playing the same game any more. I began to make sure that I always looked good when he came home. I also made sure that our apartment was always welcoming, so that it began to feel like a shared home again, instead of a battleground.

"To begin with, the hardest part was refusing to get involved in the fights and the arguments. He would start going on about the same old things, but instead of lashing back at him, I always—*always*—kept my cool. After a few weeks, the arguments died a natural death. I wouldn't feed them, so they died of starvation.

"There was a whole new friendly atmosphere between us. I listened to Jeff's problems and in return he started listening to mine. He found it difficult to give up drinking. One too many glasses of wine had started to become quite a habit. But it helped him a lot if I never drank. The only thing worse than being drunk when your partner's stone-cold sober is being stone-cold sober when your partner's drunk.

"When he saw how slim and trim I was getting, that really gave him a strong incentive to give up boozing and eating too much. He started to do exercises to firm up his stomach muscles, and to take out his bicycle instead of his car.

"All the same, it wasn't easy. It was a complete rehabilitation job. And the last thing that came back was the sex. We would hold each other at night, and cuddle, and most times he would get an erection, but it never seemed to last for more than a few moments.

"Then one evening I came into the bedroom and saw him doing his exercises. He was lying naked on his back on the floor with his feet up on a chair. He had his hands clasped behind the back of his head, and he was lifting his head up and down as far as he could, to firm up his stomach.

"I said, 'I bet you can't lick your own cock.' And so *he* said, 'I bet I can.' But of course he couldn't, even though he really strained his head and his neck, and he stuck out his tongue as far as it would go. I did notice, though, that his cock started to rise, and it stayed hard for quite a long time.

"The next night I found him naked on the bed. He had his shoulders on the pillows and his back up against the headboard and his legs doubled over. His cock was only about an inch away from his mouth, and he was trying to lick it. He had a huge hard-on, which helped, but he couldn't quite reach it.

"I laughed, but he said, 'You bet me I couldn't do it. I bet you I can.'

"Anyway, I sat down beside him on the bed, and put my hand on his bottom, and pushed downwards. He lifted his head as far as he could, but still he couldn't reach it. He said 'Again,' and so I pushed again, and this time he just managed to flick the top of his glans with the tip of his tongue.

"After that, he rolled over, and caught hold of me, and pushed me back onto the bed. He didn't say anything, but he kissed me, and pulled up my skirt, and tugged my panties to one side. I hadn't realized it, but my cunt was already wet. His cock slid into me like a candle into butter. He made love to me slowly, without any panic, and he kept his hard-on right to the very end. I didn't climax myself; I think I was too excited about what was happening. But I felt him climax, and when he took himself out of me I felt sperm sliding down between my legs, and that was just as satisfying as a climax, after everything we'd been through.

"He kept up his exercises, partly for fun, partly because they worked. Over a period of nine-ten weeks he became so much fitter and trimmer, just like he was when I first met him. One evening, after I'd finished my shower, I found him doubled-up on the bed again, but this time he said, 'Look at this.' He opened his mouth, lifted his head up, and I saw the whole of his cock-head disappearing into his mouth. He had actually managed to suck his own cock.

"You'll be deep-throating yourself soon"

"I thought it was incredible. I said, 'You'll be deep-throating yourself next.' But he said, 'Come and help me.' I knelt on the bed beside him, and helped him to fuck his own mouth by pushing down on his bottom with rhythmical strokes. Of course the cheeks of his bottom were wide apart and I wet my middle finger with saliva and pushed into his anus, to give him more sensation. His balls were totally vulnerable, too, and I played with them and tickled them while he sucked his cock.

"Suddenly I felt his asshole tighten. He went totally tense, and his cock swelled, and a huge gush of white sperm poured out of his cock over his lips and into his open mouth. I was so turned on that I pushed my finger even harder into his ass, and bit and licked him just behind the balls. He turned over, and I climbed on top of him and kissed him, and we shared his sperm, a whole sticky mouthful of it.

"He rolled me over and opened up my legs and he licked and sucked my cunt until I climaxed, too, which didn't take long. Then he fucked me. He couldn't climax; he'd shot out too much already and I guess his cock must have been pretty sore. But he kept his hard-on long enough for us to enjoy it.

"These days, he doesn't give himself self-administered blowjobs very often. I guess the novelty's worn off, although it's pretty hard on the back, too. But our sex life is hot, hot, hot. And we're much better friends, too. In fact we love each other better than we ever did.

"It's easy to forget how hard it was, or how much effort I had to put into it. But it sure paid off in the end. The very hardest thing was learning to keep my mouth shut and being cool whenever a row started. The second hardest thing was remembering why we were together. I think far too many couples look at each other across the breakfast table and don't even know what they're doing there. You're together to be friends. You're together to make each other feel good. You're together to be happy."

12

Video Love

One of the most interesting and exciting aids to sexual communication is the video camcorder. Of course many couples who own a camcorder make home videos of themselves making love, which they can later watch as an erotic stimulant. But you can also use a camcorder to express some of your most intimate sexual desires to your partner . . . without the difficulty of having to put them into words.

Few of us are brought up to talk about sex without coyness or embarrassment. What kind of words are you supposed to use when discussing your sexual feelings with the man or the woman you love? Most sex words are either ridiculously clinical (let's face it, "I love it when you tickle my *corposum spongiosum*" is hardly a romantic thing to say) or else they're hopelessly euphemistic ("manhood" or "downstairs") or else they're Anglo-Saxon and coarse ("cunt" and "asshole").

Dolores, a thirty-two-year-old travel agent from Denver, Colorado, has been married for seven years and considers her sexual relationship with her husband Mike to be "really close, really terrific." Yet she still finds it difficult to discuss sex with him. "I don't know what words to use without sounding stupid. My mother always used to call her private parts 'my Mary-Sue,' and I was fourteen years old before I discovered that nobody else did. There doesn't seem to be any way of telling Mike what I enjoy most . . . not without using words that really embarrass me.

" 'Caress my vagina' sounds so formal, do you know what I mean? Yet I can't bring myself to say the other thing. I just can't."

Even if one or both of you find it difficult to talk about sex, it's always worth making the effort to put your erotic feelings into words. If some words genuinely upset you, or make you feel as if you're swearing rather than making love, then you could try devising some new, inoffensive words of your own. I've encountered dozens of different pet names over the years. One woman called her vagina her "candy cave." Other names for the female parts include "muppet," "fluff," "purse," "pinky," and "cookie." Similarly, many women give their lovers' penises names like "rod" or "johnny" or "trunk."

It doesn't matter what names you use, provided you try to talk about your needs and feelings as clearly and as affectionately as possible. Explaining your sexual desires to your lover is the first step toward total fulfillment. In a really successful sexual relationship, there are no secrets whatsoever—no hidden desires. Neither of you should feel shy about discussing *everything* you feel and fantasize about. You'll be surprised how liberating and also how *erotic* it can be to reveal to your lover all of those sexual thoughts that you've always kept to yourself.

Sharing your sexual secrets, however, means listening to your partner's sexual secrets, too. And no matter how extreme they are—no matter how much they may surprise you—you must do your best to respond with interest, understanding and excitement. Don't show shock or disgust, even if shock or disgust are your initial reactions. Simply by sharing his or her most intimate thoughts, your partner is showing you how much he or she trusts you and loves you and wants to confide in you.

"My husband David and I were talking about sex one evening," explained twenty-six-year-old Selena, a homemaker from Los Angeles, California. "I told him that I had always had a fantasy about a man coming on my breasts, and then massaging the come around and around, which was something that he had never done. Well, that was fine . . . we were both turned on by that idea. But then I asked him what his most secret fantasy was, and when he told me I couldn't believe my ears. I remember going cold all over and thinking '*my* David wants me to do that?' He said he had once seen a picture in a porno magazine in which a girl had her complete hand up a man's bottom, right up to the wrist, while she was masturbating his cock with the other hand. I didn't know what to say and I didn't know what to do. I loved the idea of him coming on my breasts, but what was I supposed to do? Push my whole hand up his ass? I didn't even think it was physically possible. It turned me off so much I couldn't sleep all night and I couldn't make love to him for days. I kept wondering if he was a masochist or if he was gay."

Of course, he was neither of these things. The majority of women are unaware that men can derive a considerable amount of erotic pleasure from anal penetration. "Fisting"—which is the slang phrase for the insertion of the entire hand into the anus—is not particularly common, although it can be done if the man is sufficiently compliant and relaxed and if he is used to anal penetration. If you want to try it, I recommend the wearing of a surgical glove for the sake of hygiene and also to prevent your nails from scratching the delicate lining of your lover's rectum. I also recommend a generous application of KY lubricant jelly!

Less extreme ways of giving your lover anal pleasure are simply to insert one or two fingers, massaging and stretching his anus and his rectum. If you make sure that you apply strong, rhythmic pressure to the front wall of the rectum, you will be stimulating his prostate gland, which produces his seminal fluid. After some practice, many women find that they can make their lovers climax by anal massage alone, without touching his penis at all. An anally induced climax tends to be less violent than a climax induced by intercourse or masturbation, and usually produces a warm, satisfying, and very copious flow of sperm.

There are also dozens of different sex-aids specifically designed for anal stimulation, both for men and women, from vibrating "butt plugs" to slender vibrators to "love wands" which can probe almost anywhere. I describe these more fully in the next chapter.

Gayle, a twenty-eight-year-old radiologist from Houston, Texas, considered herself to be "very liberated" when it came to sex. But when she discovered a leather penis restraint in her husband Dean's sock drawer, she said, "I was horrified. I began to think that I'd married a pervert."

There are many varieties of penis restraint, and they are part of the paraphernalia of sexual bondage. They are usually made out of leather or rubber, with chains or buckles or rings which the dominant mistress can use to apply as much pressure as she wants on her "slave's" penis and testicles, or to pull him around with, like an obedient dog. Different restraints have names like "Punk Cock" and "Peter Choker" and "Cock Corsette."

It was obvious that Gayle's husband had a mild fantasy about bondage. Gayle didn't know what made her feel worse—"the fact that he was interested in bondage and that he was obviously strapping himself into this thing and masturbating, the fact that he didn't find our day-to-day sex to be satisfying enough for him, or the fact that he hadn't been able to pluck up the courage to tell me that bondage turned him on."

Her anger and her sense of having been betrayed came from all of these feelings combined. Her first reaction was to confront him and express her anger. Then she thought that it would be better if she tried to forget that she had ever found his penis restraint, and tried to put his interest in bondage completely out of her mind. But my advice was that an outburst of anger would do nothing but humiliate her husband and damage her relationship, while at the same time it would be impossible for her to forget about what she had found, and that trying to put it out of her mind would simply poison her attitude toward her husband and eventually lead to a partial or total breakdown of their marriage.

I suggested to Gayle that she should tell her husband that she had discovered his penis restraint, and that she should ask him about it and why it turned him on. She should show an interest, and an eagerness to understand, and *not* allow herself to be frightened or repelled by what—after all—is a very common fantasy.

Gayle said, "It wasn't an easy conversation. My husband didn't really want to discuss it. We didn't have a shouting match, but after a whole evening of trying to talk to him, the whole thing was kind of left up in the air, unresolved. At first I was depressed about it. But then I told myself that at least I'd made a start. At least I'd managed to tell him that I knew about it. I also think that I'd managed to show him that I wasn't hostile or disgusted or anything like that."

We'll see later how Gayle managed to resolve this particular problem. But the lesson to be learned from her experience is that there is *no* kind of erotic desire which should shock or disgust you. Remember: you are under no obligation to fulfill your lover's fantasies for real, especially if you really don't find them arousing. In fact, many of the more extreme forms of stimulation are much more exciting to think about and talk about than they are to do. But don't think any the less of your lover if he or she has fantasies that you yourself don't like. Everybody's sexual makeup is different. Everybody is excited by different sexual ideas. Just remember that a sexual relationship cannot expand and develop and improve unless both of you are prepared at the very least to listen to each other's needs.

I can't pretend that discussing sex with your partner will always be easy—especially when it comes to those very extreme fantasies which may need some very extreme language to describe. But do *try* . . . and if necessary show this chapter to your partner so that he or she will understand the importance of being candid about your sexual feelings, and the benefits of *not* keeping any of your desires concealed. You have only one life: why live it feeling sexually dissatisfied?

Make Your Own Sex Movie

However, if you're really lost for words, using a camcorder can be a very direct, simple and arousing way of communicating your needs to your partner—and also of showing them how much you want to stimulate them sexually. In only a few minutes of videotape, you can overcome much of your shyness, and explain to your partner just how you feel about him in bed.

Out of dozens of letters from women who had told me that they found great difficulty in talking to their husbands or lovers about sex, I selected five. Then, as an experiment, I asked each of them to use a camcorder to see if they found it easier to "explain" what they felt about their partners and what they wanted out of their sex lives if they did it visually.

I suggested to each of them that they make a five-minute "minimovie," starring themselves, and that they did it completely privately, in their own homes, and then showed it to their lovers when they next met them, or when they came back from work.

The results were fascinating. Let's look first at Laura, a twenty-five-year-old brunette from St. Louis, Missouri, who had been feeling discontented with her sex life for six or seven months. She felt that her husband, Jim, had been putting far too much energy into his work as an architect and that their sexual relationship had stagnated. "He always made love to me like he had half a mind on load-bearing pillars and architraves and prestressed concrete." Intercourse occurred only three or four times every month, and when it did, it seemed absentminded, perfunctory, and it almost always left Laura feeling dissatisfied.

"The problem is, I don't find it easy to talk about sex. I was brought up in a very straitlaced, God-fearing family, and my mother never discussed such things. She gave me a book about childbirth but that was as far as it went. I want to tell Jim that I need more sex, but every time I try to, I become completely tongue-tied. Also, I'm worried that he might take it as a personal criticism and feel hurt and angry."

Laura made a home video that was designed to be flirtatious and to catch Jim's attention. "I wanted to show him what he was missing, right there, right in front of his nose, right in his own home."

She did this by presenting "A Day in the Life of Laura." "I started by pretending to be asleep in bed. I always sleep in the nude, so I arranged the covers so that my breasts were bare. I just lay there with my eyes closed for a while, then I stirred and stretched and pretended to wake up.

"I climbed out of bed and walked across to the bathroom in the nude. Then I moved the camera into the bathroom so that I could film myself taking a shower. I left the shower stall open, and I didn't run the water too hot in case the lens steamed up! I soaped myself all over, especially my breasts, and let the soapy water run down between my legs.

"When I was through showering, I dried myself and went back to the bedroom. I stood nude in front of the mirror, admiring myself and pinching some color into my cheeks and tweaking my nipples, too. Then I dressed in a sleeveless pink top and my shortest white miniskirt. I put on my lipstick with one leg raised on a chair, so that the camera could look up my skirt and show that I wasn't wearing panties. I sat on the bed to put on my shoes, lifting one leg at a time so that the camera could see right between my legs.

"I did a housework sequence, kind of tidying up and vacuum cleaning and stuff like that. I made sure that I kept bending over and hunkering down so that I was showing myself all the time. There's one shot where I'm hunkered down, sorting through a stack of magazines and newspapers, and I positioned the camera real close, right underneath my skirt, so you can see my vagina open wide.

"Then I took the camera into the living room, and I sat on the couch, looking at a photograph of Jim. I kissed the photograph, and then I started to squeeze and fondle my breasts through my top. I pulled the top to one side so that one of my breasts was bare, and I did a close-up of tweaking and tugging my nipples, which is something I really like Jim to do. I pulled the top right down to my waist, and then I pinched both of my nipples and lifted my breasts right up, just by the nipples.

"I kissed the photograph again, then I raised my skirt and started to massage my clitoris.

"Jim occasionally used to touch me down there, but he never knew exactly how I liked it. So I set up the camera on the coffee table directly in front of me, and opened my legs wide, and took a long, long sequence of touching my clitoris with my fingertips, and stroking the lips of my vagina, and of sliding two fingers inside. Then I stretched my vaginal lips wide apart, as wide as I could, so that my hole was wide open, too, and the camera could look right inside.

"I found this incredibly exciting, and I started to rub my clitoris quicker and quicker. I reached underneath my bottom with my other hand, so that I could slide my middle finger into myself, and also keep pulling on my vaginal lips. I've always found that very sexy, too, having my vaginal lips tugged and played with when I'm having sex. At last I had an orgasm and you can hear me screaming. For a while, you can't see anything much but a pink blur. Then you can hear me panting, and see a long close-up sequence of me gently touching and stroking my wet vaginal lips and sliding two fingers in and out."

What was Jim's reaction to Laura's videotape? "I was worried about showing it to him, because I thought he might be annoyed. He's one of these men who's pretty sensitive about his masculinity. I didn't want him to think that I masturbated regularly, when he was away at work, although I have to admit that I usually *do* masturbate once or twice a month, if I'm feeling very frustrated.

"I explained to him that I missed him during the day, and was always thinking about him, and that I had made him a video to show him how much. I brought him a glass of wine and we sat down together on the couch and watched it.

"He made love to me on the couch"

"I needn't have worried. He loved it! He thought it was the best video that he'd ever seen. And it turned him on, too. While we watched it, I kissed him and played with him, and it didn't take long before he was so hard that I had to take him out of his pants, and rub him. He made love to me on the couch, right then and there, and it was one of the best times we'd had together for months.

"We've watched it two or three times, and now he keeps asking me to make another one. But it worked like a charm. I was able to show him what I wanted in bed without having to say a single word . . . except that I loved him.''

Melissa, a very beautiful black twenty-two-year-old secretary from Sacramento, California, wanted to show her live-in lover Paul that their lovemaking could be much more varied . . . if only he was more imaginative in bed. Her complaint? "He makes love only one way, him on top and me underneath, and he never tries anything different, such as oral sex.

"I'm not very experienced. I've only had two lovers before Paul. But even though I love him, I'm beginning to find his lovemaking very predictable and dull, and I'm worried that I'm going to lose interest in him altogether.''

Melissa communicated her need to Paul by making an erotic videotape at a friend's home at Mill Valley, just north of San Francisco, where she was house-sitting for the weekend. "The beautiful part about this house is that it has a completely private yard, full of flowers, where you can sunbathe nude without anybody overlooking you.''

She began the videotape with a dance sequence. "I put on one of Paul's favorite Prince records, and you see me dancing in the living room, naked, but only from the back. Then right at the end of the record I turn around, with one arm covering my breasts and my other hand covering my pussy, and I come up close to the camera and I say in this really sexy voice, 'You can have me, Paul . . . so many different ways.'

"Next, the camera's outside in the yard, but I'm still inside the house. The patio door is open, and I'm standing behind this white net drape. I wrap it all around me so that you can see the shape of my bare body through the net, with my nipples sticking up and everything. I reach down between my legs and push my fingers into my pussy, so that the net is tucked right up into it. I think that's a real sexy scene . . . all you can see is this white wrapped-up woman's body, with her nipples protruding and the net vanishing into her crack.

"Then I come outside into the yard. I walk around smelling the flowers and looking pretty! Then I sit on the sun lounger and start rubbing sun oil into myself. I do it real slow and sensual, massaging my breasts and rubbing it down my stomach and between my thighs. I love that

sun oil scene. In the end it shows me with my thighs
wide apart, pouring this thin stream of sun oil into my
pussy so that it all drips down between my legs. My
pussy's completely shaved so you can see everything. I
massage and fondle my breasts and my pussy for a while,
then I say to the camera, 'You really can do it every
which way.'

"I bring out this black glass pastry pin which I borrowed from my friend's kitchen. It's like a huge black
cock, with a knob on the end, except that it's bigger than
a cock. I take it in my mouth and start sucking it and
licking it, and I say, 'You can use your tongue if you
want to.'

"Then I put it between my breasts and slide it up and
down. Every time it slides up, I stick my tongue out and
give the end of it a quick lick. I say, 'You can even use
your breasts if you want to.'

"After a while I roll it down my stomach. Then I lie
back on the sun lounger, and I open my legs wide, and
I hold my pussy open with one hand while I slide the
pastry pin right inside me with the other. I can still remember what that felt like, sliding up inside me, so cool
and shiny. Then I do a close-up, so that you can see that
shiny black pin sliding in and out, and the inside of my
pussy bright pink.

"I say, 'You can do it on your back' . . . then I turn
around and kneel on the sun lounger, and position the
pastry pin in between my legs, and slowly slide down on
it, until it's up inside my pussy as far as it will go. I put
my hands behind my head, and slowly circle my hips with
this huge pastry pin sticking out of my pussy like a massive
black cock. I say, 'You can do it any way you care to.'

"In the end I'm kneeling on the sun lounger with my
head against the pillow and my bottom up in the air.
This looks real sexy when you see it on the videotape,
but I almost didn't manage to do it, because it hurt. I
open the cheeks of my bottom with my left hand, and
push the pastry pin into my ass with the other hand. I
really have to push it and push it, and work it around
and around, but at last I managed to force it inside. It
didn't hurt so much, once it was in, and I managed to
push it halfway inside my ass. But it was only when I

saw the video myself that I realized how wide it had stretched me.

"You see me slowly pulling the pastry pin out, all big and greasy and black, and my ass is clinging around it like it doesn't want to let it go.

"After that, the video cuts to another dance sequence, much slower, and at the very end I come close to the camera again, and I say, 'I love you, honey . . . this is for you.' "

Paul's reaction? "He saw it the same evening, when he drove down to Mill Valley to collect me. He wasn't too pleased at first. Or leastways he *pretended* he wasn't too pleased. In actual fact I think he found it pretty exciting. The only trouble was, he had to go through his macho bit and say what the hell was wrong with his love-making, and what was I trying to do, belittle his virility or something? But we watched the video together, and after a while he said he liked it, it was good. When we made love that night, and I climbed on top of him, instead of the other way round, he didn't argue about it. Then, in the middle of the night, I was woken up by the feeling of something sliding up my ass. It was Paul's cock, and it felt bigger and harder than I'd ever felt it before. . . . It went right inside me, right up to the balls, but because my ass had been stretched open so wide that morning and was much more relaxed I could take him right in without any difficulty at all. He fucked me very hard and very fast, until both of us were gasping, and then he came in my ass, which was the first time ever. We kissed and cuddled for a while, and then he fell asleep, but I lay awake for a long time, gently touching my ass with my fingertips, and feeling his sperm dripping out of it, drip by drip."

No Sexual Stimulation Is "Perverted," Unless . . .

An interesting side effect of the camcorder experiment was that once the women involved had agreed to make

a videotape and show it to the men in their lives, it
seemed to make it much easier for them to talk about
sex much more frankly. Melissa said afterward that she
would never have considered discussing her love life with
anybody else before, nor would she have revealed such
intimate physical details. "I wouldn't have told you what
size T-shirt I took, let alone the fact that I shave my
pussy or that I pushed a pastry pin up myself." She could
hardly believe her own liberation and her own new ability to
be able to talk about sex and her own sexual pleasures.
"I think the difference is that I'm proud of myself, and
I'm proud of my skill as a lover. People talk about the
pleasure they get from food, or exercise, or sport, or
wine. Why *shouldn't* we talk about the pleasure we get
from making love?"

That, of course, is a social and moral question that
we're not trying to answer in this book. But there is no
doubt at all that those couples who have taken the trouble to widen their sexual knowledge and who have made
a serious effort to share their sexual desires with each
other have relationships that are far more fulfilling and
stable than couples who—for one reason or another—
are afraid of the subject of sex.

There is no sexual stimulation that is "wrong" or
"dirty" or "perverted," unless it is likely to cause physical injury, or unless it is inflicted on somebody against
their will. The greatest sexual problem in the world today
is ignorance—ignorance of fundamental physical facts, ignorance of sexual technique, ignorance of contraception,
ignorance of sexually transmitted diseases, ignorance of
sexual problems and how to cope with them.

Tessa, a thirty-five-year-old social worker from Boston, Massachusetts, went through two failed marriages
before she met Bill, a dentist six years her junior. On
the whole, their sexual relationship was quite good, but
unhappy experiences with her first two husbands had left
Tessa with a strong dislike of oral sex—both fellatio and
cunnilingus.

"I found it impossible to discuss my problem with Bill.
He didn't like to hear about my first two husbands, because it made him jealous. He made no secret of his
possessiveness. It was actually one of the reasons I fell

in love with him in the first place. Neither Ron nor Gordon were ever possessive. Because I was shy and quiet and I didn't stand up to them, they both treated me as if I were something they owned. I had never had oral sex with a man before I married Ron. I was only nineteen and on our wedding night he sat astride me and tried to force his erect penis into my mouth. I didn't like it, but he was so insistent that I assumed it was one of the things that married women were supposed to do, so I opened my mouth and let him put it in. I didn't even know what I was meant to do next. I think he had just been to see *Deep Throat* or something like that, because he pushed his penis completely into my mouth until I gagged. He was so angry, I was terrified. He kept saying, 'Don't gag, don't gag, I'm fucking your throat.' He was right over my face, literally raping my mouth. Fortunately it didn't last very long. He shot sperm right down my throat, and then smeared his penis all over my face. I managed to push him off, but I was absolutely devastated. This was my wedding night, remember!

"After that, he insisted on having oral sex at least twice a week. Sometimes he used to wake me up in the night by pushing his penis into my mouth. Other times he wouldn't even bother to wake me up: he would just masturbate all over my face and in the morning my face would be covered in dried sperm. I had nightmares about suffocating. I couldn't eat and I couldn't sleep and I was really ill. Ron said that I was being a bad wife and I believed him. In the end my doctor noticed that there was something wrong with me, and I told her. She couldn't believe it. I divorced him and that was a blessed relief.

"The trouble was, I married Gordon on the rebound and if anything Gordon was worse. He was really charming, and nobody believed that he was so sadistic. He was fine at first: loving and gentle and considerate. But then he started to hurt me whenever we made love. He liked to bite my nipples until I screamed, and twist my pubic hair around his fingers. Sometimes he used to go down on me, and take the whole of my vagina in his mouth and bite me. He liked to push things up me, too: anything he could think of. He would roll up newspapers and magazines and force them up me. Once he pushed a lighted flashlight into my vagina and the vacuum cleaner hose into my anus.

"I suppose you think I was completely stupid and weak for putting up with that kind of behavior. But Gordon was very threatening, and I knew that he would hurt me if I ever made him angry. Apart from that, I didn't know anything about sex before I was married. I wasn't a virgin, but I was totally innocent, and I don't think that either Ron or Gordon really knew anything about sex, either. They were ignorant and brutal and that was all.

"I know now that sexual variations can be really exciting and lots of fun. But like everything else, you have to know what you're doing. You have to have limits, and you have to respect the person you're doing them with. You need patience, too. At least, *I* do. The only trouble is, Bill thinks I'm inhibited because I don't like him going down on me, and I can't take his cock into my mouth. I'm really worried that he's going to grow tired of me and leave me for somebody else."

I suggested to Tessa that she make a videotape which not only showed Bill that she was interested in oral sex and other variations; but which helped her to overcome her own sexual phobias. I expected a fairly straightforward videotape full of oral images. But what she produced was extraordinary. It certainly galvanized her relationship with Bill, and if she were ever to release it as a commercial videotape, it would probably be regarded as an erotic classic.

She showed it to me, and this is the way that she described it as we watched it: "This is me going to the mailbox and collecting a parcel that the letter carrier has left for me. Okay . . . I'm coming up the path now and I look pleased, because I know what it is. I'm wearing nothing but one of the outsize T-shirts that I usually sleep in. I close the door . . . I take the box into the bedroom. Now you can see me opening it up. Do you like the music in the background? That's Grieg. I really adore it. During all of the worst times with Gordon I used to play it, and it really helped me to keep my head together.

"You suggested that I use the video to overcome my phobia about oral sex. I thought about that for a long

time, and in the end I decided that I would have to have
some kind of a penis substitute . . . do you see what I'm
trying to say? I would have to get used to the idea of
kissing a penis and taking a penis into my mouth . . .
but I needed to be fully in control of it, at least to start
with. That's why—here, you can see it now, I'm opening
the box and taking out the dildo I've ordered.

"My friend Ann organizes those parties where you can
buy sexy underwear and vibrators and things like that.
I've never been to one, but she lent me the catalog. This
dildo was supposed to be the most lifelike dildo of all,
so I ordered it. There—I'm taking it out of the box and
holding it up. It really is lifelike, except that it's slightly
bigger than life-size . . . well, it's slightly bigger than Bill,
let's put it that way! It feels exactly like real skin, and
look, it has balls and everything . . . the only thing that's
missing is the rest of the man.

"I'm taking off my T-shirt now and I'm naked . . . I
never knew my breasts were so big until I saw this video.
I've switched on the dildo, you can just hear it buzzing.
Now I'm rolling it around my breasts, and tickling my
nipples with it. You can see how stiff my nipples are
growing.

"I was a little frightened of the dildo at first. It reminded me of those terrible nights with Gordon. But
then I told myself, there's nobody else here, *I'm* in
charge of this particular object, and it won't be forced
into my mouth or up into my vagina in the way that Ron
and Gordon used to force themselves into me.

"Now you can see I'm running the dildo down my arms
and around my stomach. Now I lie back on the bed. I
thought of Bill when I did this. I closed my eyes and
tried to imagine that it was him. I was really gentle with
myself, the way that Bill always is. There, I'm lifting up
my knees and opening my legs, and I'm pressing the head
of the dildo up against my cunt, so that I can feel the
vibrations in my clitoris. You may not believe it, but that
was the very first time I ever used a dildo, or even *saw*
one. It wasn't nearly as threatening or as horrible as I
thought it was going to be . . . in fact there was something kind of friendly and obedient about it . . . unlike
a man! And it felt so good, that insistent buzzing, it made

me feel warm and very aroused and it didn't stop or
change pace or slow down or scratch me . . . you know,
the way that real men do.

"I'm doing it faster now, in and out"

"There . . . you can see me sliding it inside now. It
felt good, I have to admit. If only you could get a real
penis to vibrate like that. I'm slowly sliding it in and out,
and you can see by the look on my face that the feeling
was fantastic. There, you can see that I start rubbing
myself as well, with my other hand. . . .

"That was the first time I willingly took anything up
inside me . . . apart from Bill, that is, and the first boyfriend I ever slept with, whose name was Alan, and he
was sweet. I'm doing it faster now, in and out, and I'm
getting very close to an orgasm.

"This is when I take it out—that's it. It's all shiny with
juice, so that it looks almost like a real penis. I lift it up,
there—and hold it over my face. Then I reach up with
the tip of my tongue and I lick the very end of it. I lick
it very gently, around and around the glans, and then I
give it butterfly kisses with my eyelashes. Then real
kisses, with my lips . . . but I don't take it into my
mouth, I just gently rub it from side to side, and against
my cheeks.

"While I was doing that, I kept thinking of Ron, and
the way he used to say that he was going to fuck my
throat whether I liked it or not. But now I could open
my mouth and gently suck my dildo as much or as little
as I wanted . . . *I* was in control—and I think that if men
want their women to give them oral sex, they should
make sure that their women do feel as if they're in control . . . in other words, making love to a woman's mouth
isn't at all the same thing as making love to her cunt.
The woman should be able to feel that she can take as
much in her mouth as she wants to . . . or as little as
she wants to, or none at all.

"Anyway, look—I'm sucking just half of the glans. My
eyes are closed . . . and when my eyes were closed I

could hardly believe that I wasn't sucking a real penis,
except that I wasn't having it rammed down my throat.
Now I've taken it out . . . and this is where I squeeze
the balls, because the balls have cream in them, and the
cream squirts out all over my lips, and drips down my
chin.

"That last scene was only acting—but it turned Bill
on!"

So what did Bill think of her videotape? "At first, he
said he couldn't understand why I'd done it. I don't think
he knew whether he ought to be angry or not. But by
showing him the video, I found it easier to explain to
him that I loved him, that I was still happy to try some
interesting things in bed, provided I didn't feel that he
was pushing me, the way that Ron and Gordon had
pushed me. I said that he couldn't be jealous of a dildo,
surely! And I think that broke the ice, for both of us.

"We made love that evening and I did for Bill exactly
what I'd done for that dildo. I wasn't afraid any more
and Bill didn't try to force me, and it was really
beautiful. . . . I hadn't realized that oral sex can actually
be wonderful . . . gentle, subtle, slow, and really seductive. Bill lay on his back and I slowly licked and sucked
and rubbed his penis . . . for what seemed like *hours,*
but I never once felt as if I was under pressure, as if I
was being forced.

"We still haven't gotten around to Bill going down on
me. . . . I'm still cautious about it, after the way that
Gordon hurt me. But I know it's going to happen, sooner
or later, and when it does, I'm sure that it's going to be
great."

One of the greatest failures of modern sex education
is that young men and women are very rarely brought
together to discuss their sexual feelings. Teachers are
often too shy; school boards are often too concerned
about complaints. The result is that even when young
people have a reasonably clear understanding of the
physical side of sex, they hardly ever have an insight into
the needs and desires of their partners or their partners-
to-be.

Ask any young man whether women generally feel
like intercourse (a) less frequently, or (b) more often

than men. Ask any young woman if a man would prefer her (a) to take the sexual initiative, or (b) behave submissively. More often than not, the answer is that they simply don't know. The result is confusion and misunderstanding—and relationships that break down simply because the man and the woman are playing two different games. The man's playing pro football while the woman's playing mah-jongg.

That's one of the reasons why I launched my videotape experiments. They're still in their early days, but already they're beginning to prove themselves as a very graphic and intimate way in which men and women can talk to their partners about sex. Now they can not only say what they mean, but also *show* what they mean, too.

In contrast to Gayle's oral sex video, which dealt with the way in which she was trying to overcome a particular sexual hangup, Jane's video was a way in which she was trying to express her whole personality, both sexual and emotional.

Jane is a twenty-one-year-old art student from Fremont, Nebraska. She has ambitions to be a leading fashion designer. At the age of eighteen, however—in an effort to break free from her family, and in particular from her domineering father—she married her high school sweetheart Carl, a twenty-three-year-old salesman of heavy agricultural machinery.

"I love Carl," she wrote, "no doubt about it. He's handsome, kind, and dutiful, and he loves me too. It's very difficult for me to put my problem into words. We make love quite regularly, three or four times a week, and I'm happy and satisfied with his lovemaking as far as it goes. But sometimes I look to the future and I see the same lovemaking stretching ahead of me as far as the eye can discern, dutiful and kind but scarcely what you might call exciting. I've tried to talk to Carl about sex on numerable [sic] occasions, but he won't speak about it. He asks me if I'm happy and if I say yes, which is true, and which I always do, then all he says is 'well, then,' and there's an end to the conversation."

In order to show Carl how she felt, Jane borrowed a camcorder and went out one warm afternoon into the woods close to their home with her two Labrador dogs.

Jane's video was probably the best-planned and filmed of all the five videos, and took her over three-and-a-half hours to shoot just eight minutes.

It opens with her walking up a rocky slope in the woods, in dappled sunlight, accompanied by her two dogs, who are running and playing all around her. She's wearing a pale blue checkered blouse and blue jeans sawn off at the knee, and she's carrying a backpack. She's a small girl, about five feet, four inches, with blonde hair tied back in a pony tail. She looks three or four years younger than twenty-one.

Next we see her in a clearing. There are close-ups of butterflies and sunlit flowers. Then, through a screen of sunlit leaves, we see her undressing. It's difficult to believe that she's managed to make this video all by herself—adjusting the camcorder every time she wanted a different angle or a new shot.

Now she's walking through the woods completely naked. We see her on the crest of a hill, overlooking a stream, and she's shaking her hair loose—shaking off the last restrictions of orthodoxy. She clambers down to the stream, and next she's up to her thighs in the rushing water. She splashes herself, caressing and massaging her breasts. Then we see her lighting a campfire and sitting beside it in the smoke and the sunlight. The two dogs come up to her and she strokes them and kisses them and roughs up their hair.

We see her playing on the grass with the dogs, tumbling over and over, naked. Then she's lying on the grass beside the campfire, and she's fondling her breasts with both hands, squeezing them together and playing with her nipples. Eventually one hand strays down between her thighs and she starts flicking her clitoris with her middle finger, while stroking her labia with the other fingers. After a while, she comes into extreme close-up, so that we can see her caressing her clitoris and her labia in detail, with bright sunlight instead of a spotlight, and grasses gently nodding and waving against her bare thighs.

Next we see her with her hips raised, supported by her back pack. Her thighs are wide apart and she's masturbating with both hands—one hand stretching open her labia and the other hand quickly rubbing her clitoris. Her vulva is glistening with juices. Every now and then she quickly dips a fingertip into her anus, and each time lets out a little birdlike cry.

It Gives Her Very Deep Sensations

Now she inserts two fingers into her open vagina, then three, then she gradually twists her whole hand into herself, up to her wrist. She's gasping now, because (as she explained later) she is massaging her cervix, the neck of her womb, which gives her very deep internal sensations of pleasure.

What she is doing, in fact, is a self-applied version of the stimulatory technique I mentioned earlier in this chapter, "fisting." It isn't easy to do it to yourself, unless you're very supple, but Jane regularly swam and danced and worked out—apart from which, she had masturbated since childhood by inserting three or more fingers into her vagina. The porno movie star Dolly Buster includes self-fisting in many of her movies as a specialty.

As the video comes to its climax, Jane starts to cry out. Her two dogs watch her as she plunges her hand deeper and deeper into her vagina. At last she shakes with orgasm, and lies on her back on the grass, her cheeks flushed, her skin shiny with perspiration.

She described the video as a way of showing Carl that she was a "free, wild, adventurous kind of person." The outdoor setting was a metaphor for her need to explore sex without any inhibitions.

Carl's response to Jane's video? "I think he was upset, to begin with. He knew that I wanted more exciting sex, he'd been listening to me, but he hadn't really heard me. I don't think he wanted to. He never had much confidence in himself, sexually, and he didn't know very much about it. I think he stuck to the same old position and the same old technique because he was afraid of making a fool of himself. But, to me, that's the whole point about making love. You may try a different position and end up falling over and laughing, but that only makes it more fun. I think too many people are too *serious* about sex. It's supposed to be fun. It's supposed to be a pleasure. Why should anybody be *grim* about it?''

Eventually, however—when she had explained to Carl what the message of her video really was—Jane found that he became more adventurous and more sexually responsive. His first suggestion was that they visit the same location in the woods where she had made the video, so that they could make love in the open air. This they did—and it was then, too, that Carl asked her whether she would do "that thing with your hand" for him—in other words, fist herself.

"I did it for him after he had climaxed inside me, so that my pussy was very slippery. He stood over me and watched, and he had another hard-on almost at once, which I've never seen him do before. He rubbed his cock while he was watching me, and when I had an orgasm, he had another climax, too, and he shot his sperm all over my arm and my bottom."

So—for Jane—very much more stimulating and varied lovemaking. But lastly, let's take a look at Gayle, whose problem we discussed at the beginning of this chapter. Gayle, you will remember, found a penis restraint hidden in her husband's drawer and received a very negative response from him when she told him about it.

"Dean gave me the feeling that he didn't want to discuss it, ever again, and that made me feel terrible. I didn't know whether he was going to go on using it, without telling me, or whether he would stop using it altogether—in which case, was he going to feel sexually frustrated and then start blaming me for it?"

I decided that it would be a good idea for Gayle to take part in the video experiment. Since her attempts at discussing Dean's interest in bondage had come to an impasse, perhaps she could *show* him that she wasn't disgusted or angry or sexually turned-off by what she had discovered.

"The trouble was, he was ashamed of it—that's why he kept it secret. And so of course he must have felt desperately embarrassed when I found out about it."

At her own request, I gave Gayle a catalog of bondage clothing and equipment. She looked through it, and ordered several items—which, when they arrived, she used to make a video in her own home.

"I bought a tight black leather waspy corset that left my breasts completely bare, although it had a studded strap that went around my neck and two studded straps that buckled tightly between my legs, either side of my pussy.

"I also bought a leather cat o' nine tails with what they describe in the catalog as a 'G spot peni-handle.' It was so outrageous that I just had to have it! It had nine leather thongs, all knotted at the end, and a huge black handle in the shape of a curved penis.

"I was amazed how much all of this stuff cost—the waspy corset was over $150 and the cat o' nine tails was nearly $90. I guess you have to be pretty wealthy to be a fetishist!

"I covered the living room floor and the couch with black vinyl sheeting. It was really shiny and crinkly; Dean had been given a huge roll of it by our builders, after they finished laying a new floor in the kitchen. Then I set up the video camera and made my movie!

"I was nervous at first, I kept laughing, and that meant I had to rewind the camera and start again. But then I had the idea of putting on some music, a Tina Turner album, and that calmed me down.

"The video starts with me walking into the living room, dressed in an ordinary cotton-print dress. The waspy corset is hanging on a clothes stand next to me. I look at it, and then I look at the camera, and I'm obviously thinking hmmm . . . this looks interesting. I turn my back to the camera and unzip my dress, and gradually shrug my way out of it, until it's lying on the floor. Then I reach behind me and unhook my bra, although I still don't turn around. I'm wearing nothing but small white panties, which I ease down real slow. Then at last I turn around.

"There are two chrome rings through my nipples. At least, it *looks* like there are two chrome rings through my nipples, but in fact they're just key rings, which I pried apart and then pinched into my nipples, so that they look as if they're pierced. My pussy is completely smooth and bare, no hair at all; I don't usually have very much anyway, because of wearing swimsuits and dance clothes and stuff. One side of my pussy is decorated with a tattoo of a cobra . . . which isn't a real tattoo, but felt-tipped pens work just as well! I look pretty kinky, even if I say so myself!

"I pick up the whip"

"I take the waspy corset off the clothes stand, and I put it around me and lace up the laces until I can hardly breathe, and then I buckle up the buckles, real tight, so that my breasts bulge out and my pussy bulges out, too. You can see me admiring myself in the mirror, turning this way and that. The strange part about it was that dressing up this way really excited me. I never thought it would. But to see myself all strapped up in leather really had me panting. You can see it in the video; my cheeks are all flushed and my eyes are bright.

"I turn to the camera and say, very sternly, 'What are you looking at? Don't you know that your mistress forbids you to spy on her? For that, you will have to be punished.'

"I pick up the whip and fondle the handle and run the braids through my fingers a few times. Then I snap it at the camera as if I'm whipping whoever's watching me—in this case, of course, it's Dean. It actually looks pretty effective, like I'm really whipping somebody.

"I pick up his penis restraint and say, 'You'll have to put this on, now,' and I approach the camera with it and pretend to buckle it on. Then I say, 'I'm going to allow you to watch me now, but you mustn't touch.'

"I kneel on the bed, and I start to play with the whip. I draw the braids across my bare breasts, and then I slide the handle up and down my cleavage. All the time I'm making these moaning noises, and believe me, after a while I was making them for real. It was fantastically exciting, making my own sex video like that, especially nobody was watching me and I could do what I liked . . . and if I decided when I'd finished it that I didn't want Dean to see it, all I had to do was erase it.

"I start pulling the braids of the whip between my legs, dragging them tightly between the lips of my pussy. I'm rubbing myself with my fingers, too, and you can see that my fingers are all juicy. I'm really turned on by now! At last you can see me opening my legs wide, and slowly pushing this big black leather whip handle up into my pussy, right up, as far as it will go, so that all the braids of the whip are dangling down.

"After that, I didn't care too much about the camera. You can see me propping myself up with one hand, lifting up my left leg, and ramming that whip handle in and out of me faster and faster. In the end I turn over onto my back, and furiously diddle my clitoris, too. You can't see very much because I was too excited and I forgot to make sure that the camera was pointing directly at me. You can *hear* me, though, especially when I'm coming!

"At the very end of the video, I come up close to the camera, and hold up the whip handle, which is still juicy, and I say 'You shouldn't have watched! You've disobeyed me! Now you're going to get the whip where it hurts! Bend over!' I pretend to push the handle into my imaginary 'slave' and that's the end of the video."

How did Dean react to Gayle's homemade leather fetish video? "I thought to begin with that I might have made a terrible mistake. He sat and watched it all the way through and didn't say a word. I was frightened that he was going to think that I was mocking him. But when it was all over, he simply said, 'Have you still got that outfit?' and I said, 'Yes, I have,' and then he said, 'The whip, too?' and I said 'Yes.' There was a long pause and I was literally shaking! But then he said, 'Come on then, let's act it out for real.'

"So we did . . . exactly the way I'd made it, and we had some of the most exciting and satisfying lovemaking that we'd enjoyed for years. Right at the end, I had to say all that stuff about 'now you're going to get the whip where it hurts!' Dean bent over, and I forced that huge whip handle right up his ass and tugged at his cock at the same time. He climaxed at once, and he pumped out so much sperm I couldn't believe it. It was running all down my arm and dripping down my leg.

"Afterward we had a long talk about what we both

needed from sex, and what we both liked, and in a way that was even more exciting and satisfying than the love-making. We're both very, very close now. We don't do the leather stuff very often . . . but occasionally we both enjoy playing 'mistress and slave' and there's certainly no harm in it. In fact there's a whole lot of good."

Gayle's video enabled her to explain something pictori-ally which she found almost impossible to explain in words. She was able to show Dean that she didn't find his mild interest in bondage and fetishism to be dis-gusting; and that (to a limited extent) she would be pre-pared to share his interest, particularly since it would help to enhance their sexual satisfaction and their emo-tional intimacy.

Any demonstrations of your interest in lovemaking and your affection for your partner are always worthwhile. Making an erotic video for him must be one of the most vivid.

13

Sex Toys-R-Us

Even a happy and healthy sexual relationship can benefit from novelty and surprise. In the past three or four years, there has been a remarkable boom in the development of new sex aids—ranging from sexy clothing to highly advanced artificial penises and vaginas.

Sex aids are widely available through mail-order and can no longer be regarded as weird or perverted. Thousands of people buy them and use them—either as aids to masturbation or aids to more exciting intercourse.

It's significant that sex-aid catalogs are no longer coy about describing their products as "aids to masturbation." When I first started writing sexual "how-to" books in the mid-1970s, vibrators were advertised as "soothing and relaxing . . . an indispensable aid for tired muscles," and the accompanying photographs would show a girl using a vibrator to massage her shoulders, her calves, and even her cheeks. Heaven forbid that she would actually think of inserting it into her vagina!

Masturbation has lost its stigma. Socially, we recognize that self-stimulation is not only completely harmless but beneficial, too. Nobody ever went blind or mad from masturbation, or grew hairs on the palms of their hands. In times of stress or loneliness, masturbation can be a considerable comfort both to men and to women, and it gives us all a chance to know our own bodies and explore our own capacity for sexual pleasure.

If you examine the way that you masturbate, you can show your lover exactly what kind of stimulation you enjoy the most . . . and then you can encourage him to do it for you. Not only will you find his manipulation more exciting, you will make him feel happier and more confident, too.

Gina, twenty-three, a post-graduate sociology student from Phoenix, Arizona, said: "I always used to masturbate by stretching open the upper part of my vaginal lips wide open with my thumb and my index finger and stretching open the lower part with my other fingers. Then I would diddle my middle finger across my clitoris, very fast and very light. Now . . . how could my boyfriend have learned to do that unless I showed him?"

We've seen how you can use your sexuality to sort out any problems in your love life. Now let's look at what games you can play to make a good sex life even more exciting.

First of all, there are dressing-up games, and these days we're not just talking Frederick's of Hollywood, but every imaginable type of sexy clothing. I gave catalogs of erotic clothing to over a hundred men to look at—and then the same catalogs to their partners. I was interested to discover what a sample of men found the most erotic compared with what women found the most appealing . . . and see if there was any appreciable difference in their sexual tastes.

As far as outerwear was concerned, women were attracted by a slim 1950s-style pencil-skirt, to be worn topless with a pair of elbow-length red vinyl gloves. They also liked a lambada outfit, which consisted of a clinging nylon body stocking with a back cut so high that it left the buttocks completely exposed. There was a choice of two kinds of miniskirt to be worn over this body stocking—one in shimmer fabric, the other transparent. Both would fly up during "dirty dancing" to reveal the woman's bare bottom.

Women gave high marks to an elegant black minidress in crushed velvet. It was so short that it would barely cover the cheeks of the wearer's bottom, and it had a deeply plunging neckline, but it was made of soft and stretchy fabric, and it was extremely flattering to any kind of figure. Another popular choice was a breathtakingly short minidress with long sleeves and a high neck. It was made of poly-cire, so that it clung and shimmered, and felt like "a second skin." It could be worn without any underwear because its stretchiness gave quite a high degree of figure control.

Another dress that women liked was a long-sleeved minidress made of black see-through lace—and, again, intended to be worn without any underwear. Several women said that they would actually like to try wearing it to parties, just to see people wondering "Is she . . . or isn't she?"

They showed a considerable interest in a long black evening dress made of shiny latex rubber, and a black rubber Madonna-style corselette with black rubber stockings, but that was about as fetishistic as they wanted to get. What they liked most of all were soft, short, clingy garments that showed off their legs. Almost eighty percent said that they considered their legs to be their best feature, and so any clothing that displayed their legs to their advantage would be their first choice.

Men tended to prefer very short skirts rather than dresses, and very tight short-shorts. They were also much more interested in erotic outerwear that showed off a woman's breasts. For instance, one of the most popular choices was a very short minidress in tightly clinging elastic nylon, very deeply cut at the front with the thinnest of shoulder straps. They particularly liked it in white, because the darkness of the woman's nipples showed through.

Men also went for a silky one-piece pants suit. It was soft and flowing and very feminine, and it showed off every bounce and movement of the wearer's breasts.

But they were also aroused by more space-age outfits, such as a playsuit in black stretch nylon which covered a woman in front, but left her back completely bare.

Remember, of course, that this clothing was all specialty garments . . . very little of it meant for wearing out to parties or out on the street. Not without causing some kind of riot, anyway.

When it came to underwear, I asked six women to select an item of erotic underwear from one of the larger catalogs, wear them with their partners, and then tell me what kind of response they had received. You can take your own pick of the underwear that you think would turn your man on the most.

Suzanna, twenty-four, a fashion model from Denver, Colorado: "I chose the Love Briefs, because they looked so pretty. The Love Briefs are a pair of white satin panties with a thin lacy strap around the back and two shell-shaped lace and satin panels in the front. These two panels meet in the middle but they divide again down between your legs so that your vagina is completely exposed. When I first put them on I realized that I would have to shave myself, because here were these beautiful satin panties with a plume of dark brown pubic hair sticking out of them. And they're supposed to look very pretty and young and innocent. So I completely shaved and depilated myself, and the result was real pretty—just these two shell-shaped panels with the little pink slit of my vagina peeping out. I put them on before my boyfriend Tom came home that evening, with nothing but a blouse on top. When he saw them, he looked like somebody had hit him on the head with a hammer, he was so knocked out. He couldn't stop kissing me and touching me and telling me how adorable and pretty I was. We didn't even make it to the bedroom. We made love on the rug right in front of the TV, and of course the beauty of the Love Briefs is that you don't even have to take them off."

"I chose the topless basque"

Fay, thirty-three, a schoolteacher from Lansing, Michigan: "I chose the topless red satin basque with the garters and stockings. I have quite big breasts (36DD) which means that I don't look very good in teddies or playsuits or anything like that. Also my waistline needs a little discipline! Apart from that, I've always fancied myself as one of those good-time girls in the Wild West, and that's exactly what I looked like when I put on this basque. I felt very turn-of-the-century and very feminine. I could have done with some ostrich feathers but maybe that would have been gilding the lily. I wore the basque underneath my dress when my husband John and I went to the theater. When we came back we were both in a mellow, affectionate mood. I undressed right in the middle of the bedroom. John was sitting on the end of the bed unfastening his cufflinks. He just stared at me and said, 'You've been wearing that *all evening*?' So I said 'Yes.' He said, 'You've been wearing that all evening and *I didn't know*?" He reached out for me and I came over and straddled his lap. He looked down between my legs and saw that I wasn't wearing any panties, either. He fondled my breasts and kissed my nipples. He was so ardent I think he could have eaten my breasts, right there and then. I opened his pants and wrestled his cock out. It was hot and hard. I rubbed it up against my pubic hair and my open lips until it was good and slippery. Then I eased myself down on him, and his cock went right up inside me. I rode his lap for a while, and then I pushed him back onto the bed and fucked him until he shouted out. It was terrific. I was a whore, I was a queen. I was anything I wanted to be."

Jeannette, twenty-nine, a nurse from San Diego, California: "I was always turned on by the idea of those peephole bras, so in the end I chose a lacy black and gold bodice with holes in the front that left my nipples exposed, and what *looked* like a very modest pair of black panties with a matching frill. When I put them on, I realized that the panties were actually divided in the front—and that every time I bent over they would open up and expose my pussy. Rick had been away for a week in LA, and he didn't come home until the middle of Tuesday afternoon. He was pretty bushed, too, so I didn't try on my underwear until it was bedtime. By nine o'clock Rick was yawning and ready for sleep, so I took a shower and came out wearing my bodice and my naughty panties. You never saw anybody wake up so fast! He couldn't get enough of me. I thought he had seven pairs of hands, the way he kept touching my breasts through the holes in my bodice. I said, 'Let's go to bed, let's make love,' and while he was undressing I deliberately bent over to pick up his shirt. That turned him on so much he almost exploded on the spot. He came up behind me and slipped his hand between my thighs and touched and caressed me between my legs. . . . Then he said 'Bend forward' and I bent over so that my hands were resting on the arms of the bedroom chair. He pulled down his shorts and then he opened up my panties at the back and he thrust himself straight into me. As he fucked me, he reached around and kept on playing with my nipples, which was something he didn't normally do very much. He didn't climax; he was actually too tired, but I woke him up in the middle of the night and we did it again. I've worn my underwear quite a few times now, and Rick still seems to find it exciting. I'm crazy for anal intercourse, and Rick adores the idea of fucking me up the ass while I'm still wearing panties."

Lucinda, twenty-one, an art gallery salesperson from New York City, said: "Kevin my boyfriend isn't much of an underwear kind of guy. He prefers nudity, you know. That's what really turns him on. But I chose a white lace teddy with a very deep V-neck that's slashed right down to the navel and beyond. It looks quite demure from the front, it doesn't actually show anything at all, but it leaves my bottom completely bare at the back. I found it quite comfortable to wear, and I thought it was perfect for lounging around the house in the morning or maybe for after a bath on a warm night. Kevin didn't really go for it much and wanted me to take it off, but all the same it made *me* feel sexy. One Saturday I wore it all day, and posed in front of the mirror a lot. I also wore it one night when Kevin was away in Chicago. I piled my hair up and pretended I was a great French courtesan."

Amy, twenty-five, is an aerobics instructor from Seattle, Washington. She said: "I've never been a girl for frillies. I guess that's a reaction against the way my mom used to dress me when I was little. All my panties had frills and all my dresses had frills. I chose a kinky leather strap suit, which is nothing more than a kind of body harness made up of black leather straps, all joined together with chrome metal rings and buckles. Actually, when I was wearing it I was still completely nude, because it has two circular straps that go around your breasts and a strap that goes around your waist and a strap that goes right between your legs, and that's all. I found it a little complicated to get into, to tell you the truth, but it was okay once I'd adjusted all the buckles.

The strap between my legs was really tight and cut into my cunt so that it bulged out on either side. I looked very erotic and it *felt* very erotic, but after about an hour it began to get a little sore, so I wouldn't recommend the strap suit for daily wear! I took the liberty of ordering a pair of men's black leather training briefs for Dennis. All they are is a strap which fits around his waist, with a chrome ring that he has to push his cock and his balls through. He's completely naked, too, when he wears it, and it forces his balls up really high, so I love it! We played quite a few sexy games when we first tried this underwear. First I was Dennis's slave. I had to kneel on the floor in front of him and get as much of his cock into my mouth as I could. Then he was my slave, and I clipped his cock-ring to a dog-leash and pulled him around the bedroom. Then I pulled him on top of me, and he had to fuck me, still wearing this cold metal ring around his cock, and if I thought he wasn't fucking me hard enough, I tugged on the dog-chain. We had fun!"

Christie, nineteen, a medical student from Los Angeles, California, said: "I picked out a classic baby-doll nightie. It was white, see-through, with a little pair of white G-string briefs to go with it. My boyfriend is more than twelve years older than me, and he loves me in stuff like that—anything to make me look girlish. I wore it to bed and he really flipped. He really liked it. But what he enjoys most of all is watching me wear it around his apartment, without the briefs underneath. I sit at the breakfast counter with my legs apart, so that he can sit in his chair and look up my nightie. Or else I sit in the window seat clutching my knees, so that my pussy's exposed. He loves things like that. He says it's all so unconscious and innocent. Anybody would think that I'm a kid!"

The moral of these reports is that a little erotic underwear can go a very long way. In fact, the smaller the better! *Where* and *when* you dress in erotic clothing is also a critical factor in turning your lover on. On the beach, the tiniest of bikinis looks like nothing. But if you wear nothing but your lover's shirt while you're tidying the house, or nothing but a pair of lacy panties while you're working on your company's annual accounts, or nothing at all while you're practicing the piano, then you have created a contrast between your dress and your surroundings which can be highly erotic.

Erotic underwear isn't meant for daily wear although a great many ordinary women wear thongs these days, to eliminate the dreaded "panty-line," and many women wear soft or quarter-cup bras to give their blouses or sweaters a little nipple-emphasis. Marlene Dietrich used to overcome the nipple-emphasis problem by having two prominent pearls sewn into the bodice of her evening gowns.

Erotic underwear is intended to surprise, to excite—to turn men on because of the contrast of skin and lace, leather and satin. It is clothing that is designed to expose and to emphasize, not to cover.

A few erotic items in your closet can add novelty and spice to your love life, and arouse his passion all over again.

I have only one warning about erotic underwear. A very few men have a hypocritically puritanical streak in them. They're often the kind of men who regard their wives as their own property, and whose sexual attentions are selfish and occasionally violent. They are frequently ignorant about sex and sexual matters—which makes them very defensive and aggressive when they are confronted with anything that is openly erotic. Men with this kind of personality may not react well to your wearing erotic underwear. "No wife of mine is going to dress like a common harlot, etcetera, etcetera."

I doubt very much that you are unlucky enough to be living with a man like this, but before you try erotic underwear, do think carefully about your man's probable response. It's for your own protection as well as your own pleasure.

On a lighter note, let's turn now to the extraordinary range of new sex toys that have been flooding the mail-order market in recent years. The introduction of lifelike plastics and much more sophisticated molding machinery has meant that some sex toys feel quite remarkably real. I am frequently asked to recommend the best, so let's take a look at some of the newest and most exciting.

Best of the newer toys are the Fantasy Plus and the

Fantasy Plus Dong. The Fantasy Plus is technically described as a "penis extension—masturbator." In actual fact it is an eleven-inch penis made of flexible plastic which a man can slip over his own penis and use as a masturbating device. "Just imagine slipping on your incredibly lifelike Fantasy Plus, stroking it up and down your cock as the silky smooth throat sucks and clings to your shaft while you watch your huge eleven-inch Fantasy Plus swaying heavily backward and forward just inches from your chin.

"Each unique Fantasy Plus is individually manufactured of a revolutionary new material which reproduces every wrinkle and pore of a living penis, and is then handpainted to show the veins, head, and foreskin in perfect detail. Especially made to satisfy a man's needs or for moments when those extra inches count."

There is also a Fantasy Plus Dong for women—"so real and so lifelike she'll never know the difference"— except, presumably, that it doesn't have a man attached. "The exquisitely detailed look and feel of an erect penis will make her pussy or ass quiver in delight." The Fantasy Plus Dong comes in eight-inch regular solid, or ten-inch super with moving balls, ejaculation feature and in-built vibrator. The cost of the super version is about $100.

Another handy gadget for both men and women is the Vagi-Penis—"for enjoyment alone or together." It is a thick penis made of flesh-colored latex with a vulva at its base, so that a man alone can insert his own cock into it and use it as a simulated vagina, or a woman alone can use it as a simulated penis. It's also possible for the man to insert his penis into it and then make love to his partner with it gripping his erection. "Suddenly—your penis is 25 cm long with a diameter of 6 cm!"

Akin to the Vagi-Penis are several quite useful sex aids for men who are having erection difficulty. There's a Penis Corsette which is a tight plastic sleeve which grips the shaft of the penis very tightly, leaving the glans exposed, and which helps in maintaining stiffness throughout intercourse. Then there's the Ripple Penis, which is a ripple-textured sleeve which fits entirely over the man's penis and allows him to make love to his partner even when he is unable to achieve an erection.

Although aids like these are no substitute for the kind of self-help therapy that I mentioned in the previous chapter, they can still be quite useful in boosting a man's sexual confidence just when he needs it most.

There are scores of different dildos, from the tiny Pocket Pal, a multispeed vibrator with highly exaggerated glans and veins which you can slip into your purse for use wherever you go, to the Real Feel Penis, allegedly molded from the actual ten-inch penis of sex superstud Buck Bronson, whose penis, when flaccid, swings down between his knees. The Real Feel Penis "was produced by taking a plaster cast of the real thing and then manufactured from the most realistic fleshy material which even sweats like a real penis on a boner—with real feel testicles."

Completely unrealistic in appearance but highly stimulating is the so-called Vibrator with Ears. This is a bright pink vibrator made of a fleshlike plastic which both twists and vibrates. It also contains a bulge halfway down its shaft, filled with brightly colored plastic pearls, which pulsate when the vibrator is switched on, and massage the inner walls of your vagina. At the base of this vibrator is an extra protrusion with two soft jellyish "ears" which also vibrate and flick at your clitoris. It is also possible to turn the vibrator around and insert this extra protrusion into your anus, so that the "ears" tickle the inside of your rectum.

The inventions go on and on . . . but I have heard excellent reports of the Butterfly Vibrator, which is a soft butterfly- or heart-shaped cushion of vibrating plastic which you can actually strap to your clitoral area, so that the pleasure goes on and on. Many women have reported using various different versions of the Butterfly Vibrator, and say that they have experienced multiple orgasms which have rippled through them all afternoon.

Then there are the new Orgasm Briefs . . . a pair of plain panties with a 17 cm vibrating penis inside the gusset. "On the bus, in the office, or when you're out shopping—now you can experience erotic ecstasy all day long."

Not so new, but still well-recommended is the Double Dong, which is nothing more than two multispeed dildos joined together, so that you can stimulate your vagina and your rectum at the same time. The anal dildo is slightly narrower in diameter than the vaginal dildo, but they are both 21 cm long.

I have been shown scores of new anal stimulation devices. Ten years ago, it was possible to mention anal stimulation only in the discreetest of terms, and apart from the regular vibrator, the only other sex toy which you could use for anal stimulation was a string of pearls. You could push the pearls into your rectum, leaving two or three dangling from your anus, and then slowly but surely pull them out at the moment of orgasm.

These days, however, vibrating anal plugs and anal vibration kits are offered openly, and illustrated in glowing color. There is the Anal Deranger—a slender vibrator with rows of ridges around it—"imagine something so soft and bendy and yet so perfectly shaped to maximize the sensation of anal stimulation to the ultimate limits of endurance." And what you might call the executive version is the Anal Vibro Kit, with six different heads for "brand new anal sensations." There's "The Long Hot Finger," the "Anal Explorer," and "Anal Anemone," and "Anal Cactus," the "Ultra-Deep Anal Probe," and the shattering screw-thread vibrator.

One of the simplest anal stimulators, however, is a solid latex dildo which your lover attaches to his own penis (simply by inserting his erect cock through the plastic ring in the base). He can then make love to you vaginally and anally at the same time. It has a built-in vibrator so that "she will drown in pleasure."

These are only a few of scores of new sex toys which are being invented and marketed every month. They're not dramatically expensive, and if you show your man that you're interested in trying some of them out, you may be surprised at how enthusiastic his reaction is. Send off for some catalogs and see what you can buy. Even if you don't buy, it can be amusing and exciting just to browse through the pages and fantasize about what you *might* buy.

The sexual world has changed dramatically in recent

years—sociologically, medically, and technologically. It's more than worth any woman's while to keep in touch with what's happening in sex, because so many of the new ideas and so many of the new devices could help you to drive your man wilder than ever.

Now it's your turn . . . go out and enjoy yourself, safely, passionately and wholeheartedly. And—as the title of this book promises—here are One Hundred Ways in which to do it.

14

100 Ways
to Drive Your Man Wild

1. Wake him in the morning by fondling his penis.
2. Wake him in the middle of the night by sucking his penis.
3. Open his pants and masturbate him while he's watching TV (make sure it's the World Series, or his favorite comedy).
4. Surprise him in the shower by stepping in naked . . . and washing his cock for him.
5. Bring him an early morning cup of coffee in the nude . . .
6. . . . and then *stay* nude while you serve him breakfast.
7. Masturbate him with a handful of marmalade, jelly or honey . . . all over his cock and all over his balls, and then suck him clean.
8. Ask him to wear your soiled panties to work, under his business suit.
9. Phone him up during the day and tell him that you'd love to pull down those soiled panties and suck his cock.
10. Phone him up again and tell him that you can't wait for him to come home, and that you're massaging your breasts and playing with your nipples.
11. Phone him up again and tell him that you're playing with your clitoris, and that you're totally turned on.
12. Phone him up yet again and tell him that you're sliding a huge vibrator in and out of your vagina. Tell him how slippery it is. Tell him how it feels.

13. Don't phone him for a while . . . then phone and tell him that you haven't been able to reach orgasm yet, and what you need is a real live cock.

14. When he comes home, greet him at the door naked, except for an apron.

15. Serve him dinner, dressed in nothing but your apron (and don't worry about this being sexist . . . you can insist that he serve *you* dinner dressed in just the same way).

16. After dinner, take off your apron and reveal that you've shaved off all your pubic hair.

17. Make sure you have your video camera ready. Tell him you're going to give him a cabaret, and that he can film it for future excitement. Then put on some of your favorite music and give him a slow, erotic dance.

18. From the dinner table, take an empty wine bottle and slowly push the neck of it inside your vagina (tell him to film every detail).

19. Then take one of the candles from the dinner table, bend over, and push it into your anus (make sure you keep a grip on the end). Wiggle it vigorously from side to side and round and round, so that he can film every detail.

20. Undress him and take him to bed. Make sure that you set up the video camera on a shelf or nightstand or tripod, so that you can record every detail. Insist that he isn't allowed to touch you until you say so. Then lick him all over, finally arriving at his cock.

21. Suck his cock like you never sucked it before. Forget all your prejudices, forget all your reservations. Take it into your mouth and make a meal of it. Give him passion and pleasure.

22. Turn yourself around and open your legs and lower yourself over his face. Rotate your hips so that you smear his face with your sexual juices. Don't be hesitant. Don't be shy. Make him lick and suck and swallow.

23. Turn around again and mount him. Yes—you on top, this is your party. Make love to him slowly

and rhythmically, like you're riding on the most beautiful palomino there ever was.

24. The following night, rerun the video of what you did *last* night, and make love all over again.

25. Buy yourself one item of erotic clothing and wear it for him tonight. Quarter-cup bra, G-string, anything . . . so long as you're sure that it's going to turn him on.

26. Dress in a way that you know will excite him. Like going topless (or bottomless).

27. Insist that he undress you. Make him take off everything, including bra and panties.

28. Insist that he draw a bath for you, and washes you all over (especially the intimate bits).

29. Insist that he lather and shave off your pubic hair (if you still have any).

30. Ask him to climb into the bath with you. Soap and wash him all over.

31. Lather and shave off all of *his* pubic hair, so that his cock is completely bare.

32. Ask him to show you how he masturbates . . . then try to imitate him.

33. Lie back, open your legs, and show him how *you* masturbate.

34. Lie next to him and closely examine and caress his penis. Take your time. Get to know every vein.

35. Lie back and invite him to explore you. Tell him to take as long as he likes . . . to go as deep as he likes, with finger or tongue. Remember that men are always very aroused by the visual side of sex.

36. Turn over, with your bottom lifted, and invite him to explore your anus with his tongue and finger. Don't tense up too much . . . remember that your anal sphincter is relaxed by pushing *against* an intruding object.

37. Ask him to lie back and lift his legs . . . then explore his anus with your finger. Don't be frightened, and if the pressure of his muscles gets too strong for you, tell him to relax. Push your finger inside as far as you can, then see if you

can locate the spongy-feeling mass of his prostate. You can steadily massage this organ and produce a flow of semen from his cock.

38. Watch a pornographic video together. Have him lie behind you with his cock inside you ("spoons") and make love v - e - r - y slowly while you're watching it.

39. Buy yourself a vibrator . . . the bigger and gaudier the better. As you've seen from Chapter Thirteen, they come in all sizes and all colors. How about a huge blue one or a veiny black one? Ask your lover to try it out on you.

40. When he's on top of you, making love to you, have that vibrator ready, slicked with plenty of lubricating jelly, and push it (fully vibrating) up your lover's ass.

41. . . . and just to add a little more excitement, have another one ready, slicked with plenty of lubricating jelly, and push it (fully vibrating) up your own ass.

42. Winter, spring, summer or fall . . . venture naked out of your back door and make love in your backyard. Do it on the grass. Do it up against a tree. Do it in the flowerbeds. Do it anyplace at all.

43. On a warm night, lie naked in the great outdoors (even if the great outdoors is only a balcony or a patio), and hold each other in your arms and fondle each other and *be romantic.*

44. On that same warm night, lift your legs into the air and spread them wide and ask your lover to place his hand over your open vulva with his fingers spread. Then pee without shame or restriction.

45. Ask him to take off all of his clothes and masturbate for you—while you video-film it in close-up.

46. Dress up like a dominatrix in black leather or black rubber. Handcuff his wrists and ankles (soft leather restraints are easily available mail-order). Then do whatever you want to do . . . tickle or lick or gently bite his cock. Take one

of his balls into your mouth and threaten to bite it off. Squeeze his cock (not too hard) in a pair of nutcrackers. Force vibrators into his anus. He's yours, you can do what you want.

47. Book a table at a romantic restaurant and take *him* out to dinner. When they're harassed or busy, many men forget to be seductive. In the middle of dinner, tell him that you're wearing black stockings and a garter belt, but no panties.

48. Buy some scented massage oil and massage his tensions away . . . both of you naked, both of you calm. Don't think about lovemaking, don't rush . . . just gently soothe away your problems.

49. Ask him to massage you in return, paying particular attention to your breasts and nipples.

50. Teach him how to masturbate you the way you like best. While he's caressing you, tell him exactly what each stroke of his fingers feels like . . . up, down, harder, softer, so that he knows how to please you. Even the best lover in the world isn't psychic.

51. Ask him to describe in detail a sexual fantasy that he's always been embarrassed to tell you before.

52. Describe to him in detail a sexual fantasy that you've always been embarrassed to tell him.

53. Pick him up in your car after work, totally naked except for shoes, hold-up stockings, and a raincoat.

54. Open his pants when he's driving long-distance and massage his cock. (But be careful of the traffic conditions. I'd rather have you frustrated and alive than satisfied and dead.)

55. Arrange a Sex Weekend when you and he are going to be alone together and do nothing but fuck and drink and eat and fuck and watch TV and fuck. Send the kids to your mother . . . your mother will understand.

56. Go through a sex-toy catalog together and each pick out a toy that you would like to use on the

other. Whatever you choose—whether it's a foot-long replica penis or an inflatable boy-doll with a vibrating penis and an accommodating anus, you *have* to use it, that's the deal.

57. Buy a stack of pornographic magazines and go through them together. If you see any sexual act that takes your fancy or any sexual position that you fancy, then try it.

58. If you've been cautious about oral sex, try it more often, even if you only suck the head of his penis for a while.

59. Try the taste of sperm by masturbating him into a champagne glass. Lick a little, see what you think about it. There's never any obligation, but many women who try it a little at a time find that they like it . . . and end up drinking the entire glassful, and wanting more.

60. Join him in the shower, and ask him to piss so that you can watch and feel his urine as it comes gushing out, and masturbate him at the same time.

61. In the middle of the night, while he's asleep, sit astride his face and "kiss" his lips with your vulva, until he wakes up. Then see what he does.

62. In the middle of the night, while he's asleep, lubricate your finger and work it up his anus and caress his prostate gland. Reach around and gently stroke his cock, too. Be very gentle. See if you can make him have a wet dream.

63. Arrange to meet him under an assumed name in a town where neither of you have ever been before. Assume a very whorish identity—black underwear, false eyelashes, you name it. Book a motel room and behave like a whore.

64. Have an evening of erotic consequence, in which you describe yourselves as two lovers who are stranded in a mythical land where sexual pleasure is everything. Take turns in telling the story, and do everything you can to turn each other on. "Slowly she lowered herself

onto the huge bronze phallus of the bronze mi-
notaur . . ." and so on.

65. While your lover is relaxed naked on the bed,
pleasure him anally. Slowly masturbate him—and
at the same time, with plenty of water-soluble
lubricant, see how many fingers you can wriggle
into his anus. One? Two? Three? If you fold
your fingers close together, and your lover is
willing, you should be able to insert your whole
hand into his rectum, at the same time masturbating him faster and faster.

66. Buy one of those books which show you "Fifty-
Nine Sexual Positions" and (even though most
of them will be quite impractical) try all of
them.

67. Have him insert his penis into your vagina and
then hold it quite still. You have a ring of muscle
around the entrance to your vagina—the pubo-
coccygeus or PC muscle—which you can flex,
and hold him tighter. Keep him there as long as
you can, squeezing your "love muscle" from time
to time to stimulate yourself and to keep him
erect. But don't let him move.

68. If that last experiment wasn't too successful, your
PC muscle needs some training. Take time out
every day to exercise your PC muscle by flexing
it around a narrow object such as a thin (clean)
carrot or a ballpen, until your muscle is toned
up enough to grip it quite tightly.

69. What can I suggest for sixty-nine? Try sucking
your lover's penis while he licks your vulva.
"Soixante-neuf" rarely leads to simultaneous orgasm, but it is still highly pleasurable.

70. Sponge him between the legs with a hot face
cloth and then with an ice-cold face cloth. The
sensation is very erotic, but it is also beneficial
to the prostate gland, because it stimulates con-
traction of the prostate muscle and helps to clear
out excess fluid. So you'll be looking after his
health, as well as turning him on.

71. Massage his penis in unaccustomed parts of
your body—between the soles of your feet, be-

tween your thighs, under your arms, in your cleavage.

72. Wrap his penis in your hair and masturbate him with your hand, using your hair to give him an extra-stimulating sensation.

73. Encourage him to have anal intercourse with you (if you want to) . . . but do it gently with the maximum of preparation and foreplay and lubricant. Remember that pushing your anal muscles *against* his penis will make it easier for him to enter you deeply. See if you can take his cock into your anus right up to his balls. Then hold it there and discipline yourself gently to squeeze it, the same as you did with your PC muscle. Don't squeeze too hard, or you will squeeze him right out. (Don't have anal intercourse with strangers or with men whom you know or suspect to be promiscuous or bisexual or users of intravenously injected drugs. Don't have anal intercourse without a condom unless you are 100 percent certain that both you and he are HIV-negative. There are absolutely no exceptions to these rules.)

74. Pose for nude Polaroids for him. Or—if you dare—send them to a magazine which prints pictures of "reader's wives."

75. When he goes away on a business trip, make sure that he discovers a long and very erotic letter in his briefcase (preferably with illustrative sketches).

76. When he goes away on a short business trip, make sure that he finds a pretty pink or lilac envelope in his briefcase, addressed to him and marked private. Inside that envelope, make sure that he discovers the tiny lacy G-string which you have been wearing for the past two days, and which you were wearing when you masturbated and thought of him . . .

77. Wear black stockings and a garter belt and high-heeled shoes when you go to bed.

78. Wear thigh-length boots and full-length gloves when you go to bed.

79. Make him wear your filmiest panties to work, under his business suit.

80. Make him wear your stockings and your garter belt in bed.

81. Insist that he lie still while you lick him all over—leaving the best bit till last!

82. Try having sex in the pool (it helps if he smears his penis with Vaseline or any other petroleum jelly).

83. Make love naked in the back seat of your car (while it's still parked in the garage).

84. Encourage him to fondle you intimately even when you're not interested in making love . . . when you're reading or watching TV or listening to music.

85. Encourage him to caress you with his mouth more often; it feels good and it's good practice. Lift up your skirt in the kitchen and let him kneel between your legs and lick you and suck you for a while. Get used to the idea of having more sex, more often, in more different places.

86. . . . and while you're in the kitchen, peel a banana, push it into your vagina so that only the end is sticking out, sit on a chair with your legs apart and ask him to eat it out of you. The process can be deliciously slow. . . .

87. Masturbate him more often . . . it won't hurt your lovemaking. It's certainly no worse than eating between meals. Let him ejaculate onto your breasts, and massage the sperm into your nipples. Or let him ejaculate onto your forehead, and give you a sperm facial. One woman wrote and told me that she loved her husband ejaculating on the soles of her feet.

88. Exercise together, every day, using a proper exercise regimen. You will both feel better and make love better. Make it more arousing, however, by exercising together in the nude.

89. Play a game of sexual forfeits. Ask each other Trivial Pursuit questions. Every incorrect answer merits one small sexual act which the loser has

to perform on the other . . . from baring your breasts to kissing his penis.

90. Try to find a place by the ocean or in the wilds where you can take off all of your clothes and make love naked under the sky. Al fresco sex is always memorable and romantic . . . but take some bug repellent.

91. Change yourself, in some subtle but sexual way. Wear a gold chain around your ankle. Dye your pubic hair blond. Apply a washable tattoo to your left breast.

92. Call him at work and masturbate with the telephone. Some of the slimmer handsets can slide right into your vagina, but the best sound effects are achieved by pressing the mouthpiece flat against your vulva.

93. Make it obvious over and over that you like sex . . . that he turns you on and you want to turn him on. Do one sexy thing every single day . . . even if it's just to squeeze his cock through his pants while he's washing the dishes for you.

94. Next time you shave your pubic hair, let him do it.

95. Buy him some erotic underwear . . . some of it leather, some of it latex, some of it mock-leopard. The funniest one is the elephant G-string with ears and eyes in which his cock fits into the poor animal's trunk. There are even some frontless briefs for men which support his balls while leaving his penis bare.

96. Go on a gentle long-term diet. Watch those calories! As you grow older, you will find it harder to keep your figure, and if you start losing confidence in your attractiveness, you won't give off so much sexual sparkle.

97. Never be afraid to tell him what a good lover he is. Do it often.

98. Leave this book around the bedroom so that he'll read it. Maybe he'll pick up some pointers.

99. Have confidence in your own sexuality. You're an attractive woman who can please any man. Just remember that—in marriages and long-term sex-

ual relationships—there will always come times when you have to give in order to get.

100. Make love to him *tonight*. Don't be too tired. Don't have a headache. Don't put it off. A happier sex life is yours for the taking.

The Facts about AIDS

AIDS is surrounded by so much myth and superstition and unwarranted fear that many people tend to forget that you can protect yourself from the risk of infection by following a very few simple dos and don'ts.

AIDS is caused by a virus called HIV (Human Immunodeficiency Virus). This can damage the body's natural defense system so that it cannot fight off certain infections.

HIV is not passed on through everyday social contact. But it *is* transmitted in three main ways:

1. Through unprotected sexual intercourse, both vaginal and anal.
2. By injecting-drug users sharing equipment, including syringes and needles.
3. From an infected mother to her unborn child.

HIV—the virus that can cause AIDS—is found in the fluids exchanged during sexual intercourse (men's semen and women's vaginal fluids).

You can protect yourself by trying to make safe sex a part of your life. The more people with whom you have unprotected intercourse the more likely you are to meet somebody with HIV and become infected yourself. The same applies for your partners. You are also likely to become infected with other sexually transmitted diseases like gonorrhea, herpes, chlamydia, and hepatitis B and to pass them on to someone else.

Some methods of sex carry a higher risk than others.

1. Unprotected anal intercourse. This is when the penis enters the anus or back passage. It carries a particularly high risk.

2. Unprotected vaginal intercourse. This carries a risk. The virus can be passed by both men and women to their sexual partners through men's semen and women's vaginal fluids.

3. Oral sex. When one partner stimulates the other's genitals with the mouth or tongue there is theoretically some risk. The virus could pass through semen and women's vaginal fluids into the other person's body, particularly if they have cuts or sores in their mouth. However, this is extremely unlikely to occur.

4. Sharing sex toys. Sharing sexual aids like vibrators could carry a risk as the infection could be passed from one person to another.

It is extremely unlikely that the HIV virus could be passed on through kissing—even deep French kissing. There have been no proven cases of this happening.

Using a condom can help stop the HIV virus—and other sexually transmitted diseases. To be effective, however, a condom must be used properly.

Only use a condom after the penis becomes erect and before it makes contact with your partner's genital area. If you use a lubricant with a condom, make sure it is a water-based one (such as KY). Oil-based lubricants weaken the rubber and can cause it to break.

Gently squeeze the last centimeter of the closed end of the condom between finger and thumb to expel the trapped air and make space for the semen. Keeping this space "air free," hold the condom at the tip of the erect penis and roll it carefully over the penis. After climaxing—but before erection is completely lost—hold the condom rim firmly around the penis and withdraw the penis from your partner so that the condom does not slip off.

Dispose of condoms carefully. Wrapped in tissues, they should flush away. Never re-use a condom.

HIV and skin piercing. Any device that punctures the skin, including tattooing and acupuncture needles and equipment for ear-piercing or removing hair by electrolysis, may be contaminated with blood and could, in theory, pass on the HIV virus.

Reliable practitioners will sterilize their equipment, as will barbers their razors. If you are unsure that equipment is sterilized, don't be afraid to ask. Although the risks are extremely small, avoid sharing toothbrushes and razors.

How HIV is not passed on. Everyday contact with someone who has HIV or AIDS is perfectly safe. The virus cannot be passed on through touching, shaking hands or hugging.

1. You cannot be infected with HIV by touch or by sharing objects used by an infected person: cups, cutlery, glasses, food, clothes, towels, door knobs, or toilet seats (whether they're still warm or not).
2. HIV cannot be passed on by coughing or sneezing.
3. Swimming pools are safe, too.
4. HIV is not known to be passed on by tears or sweat.
5. You cannot be infected with HIV by mosquitoes or other insects.

Most people who have been infected with the virus HIV can remain healthy for a long time, sometimes for years. In fact many of them may not know that they *are* infected, which potentially makes them a greater risk to others. Some people may have less severe illnesses while others may be seriously sick. From what we know about AIDS to date, most people infected with HIV will eventually develop AIDS.

Some people with HIV and AIDS have been treated badly and discriminated against. Don't break up a friendship because someone you know has AIDS or HIV—there's no need. Friendship and support are the two most important things you have to offer.

I am indebted to the Surgeon General and to the British Health Education Authority for their guidance and information.